JOURNALISM TODAY

Trends, Ethics & Laws

JOURNALISM TODAY

Trends, Ethics & Laws

Edited by

K. Vishnu Datta

AKANSHA PUBLISHING HOUSE

NEW DELHI - 110 002 (INDIA)

AKANSHA PUBLISHING HOUSE
4649/21-B, Ansari Road,
Daryaganj, New Delhi - 110 002
Phones: 23263193, 9811582579
E-mail: ektabooks@yahoo.com

Journalism Today: Trends, Ethics & Laws

First Published, 2006

ISBN 81-8370-036-5

PRINTED IN INDIA

Published by M.P. Misra for Akansha Publishing House, New Delhi - 110 002 and Printed at Tarun Offset Press, Delhi

Contents

Contents

Preface

Journalism or the 'Press' which is termed the fourth estate in modern democracies, is considered the real custodian of public opinion—when the first three organs (legislature, executive and judiciary) fail to uphold the righteousness. The overall quality of news coverage — including issues ranging from decreased accuracy to increased sensationalism — remains the most important problem area in journalism today, according to the press. But its relative seriousness has plummeted compared to the loss of credibility with the public.

"People don't trust us the way they used to, and they have good reason not to, a lot of stuff now is slanted toward sensationalism."

"Journalists are down among used car salesmen in credibility."

"I'm concerned about the blurring of the lines between the kind of fact-based journalism that I grew up with — and which I hope to continue to practice — and the proliferation of celebrity pundits who are constantly barraging the public with views that aren't fact-based."

"Journalists feel the need to entertain people as opposed to the need to inform them."

"Anything is fair game for the media today."

The above statement indicate to recent trends in journalism. Overall, journalists and news media executives see plenty of room for improvement in the press.

The news media are also concerned that pressure to attract audiences is pushing their industry too far in the direction of 'infotainment'. In the USA two-thirds of those in national, local and Internet news say that efforts to attract readers or viewers take them too far in this direction. This criticism is especially strong among news staff members.

A narrow majority of journalists and news media executives now believe that by covering the personal and ethical behavior of public figures, news organizations often drive controversies rather than simply report the news. In spite of this widespread self-criticism, journalists and media executives still strongly adhere Media's to the value of the watchdog role. Nearly 90% admit that criticism of political leaders is worth it because it keeps those leaders from doing things that should not be done. Less than 10% think that such criticism keeps political leaders from doing their job. This holds true across markets and mediums.

This book, as is obvious from the name of title, covers the recent trends, ethics and laws in the field of journalism.

The major themes covered herein are: Journalism Today: An Introduction; The News and The New Media; Errors of Modern Journalism; Printing for the Journalist; Journalism: Education & Training; The Elements of Journalism; Journalism: Views on Performance; Journalism: Case Study Curriculum; News and Sales; Professional Values and Motivations; Journalism & Right to Information; The Codes of Ethics for Journalism; Towards Future of Indian Journalism; The Journalism Law; Setting Professional Standards; A Responsible Press; The Press Under Pressure and The Full Dimensions of the News etc. An exhaustive Bibliography and Glossary of Terms further add to utility. The original text of Press Council Act, 1978 and other laws appended to the book will prove of utmost use.

Since the entire book is designed and devised on the opinions, research findings and works of leading journalists from the country and abroad, I owe a deep sense of gratitude to them all for taking liberty on subscribing them. Friends, colleagues and well wishers deserve my thankfulness for their moral support and inspiration.

Finally, Mr. M.P. Misra, my publisher deserve all appreciation for lending enthusiastic attitude toward the project and shouldering the responsibility to bring the book. I am solely responsible for presentation of every shortcoming(s) in reading materials. But the credit for information contained herein ought go the original contributors, my professional fraternity.

—Editor

1

Journalism Today: An Introduction

Honest differences of views and honest debate are not disunity. They are the vital process of policy-making among free men.

—Herbert Hoover

Restless and discontent are the first necessities of progress.

—Thomas A. Edison

Journalists increasingly agree with public criticism of their profession and the quality of their work. Overwhelmingly, news media professionals say the lines have blurred between commentary and reporting and between entertainment and news. A growing number of reporters, editors and news executives also say that news reports are full of factual errors and sloppy reporting.

Across all mediums — print, television, radio and the Internet — the news media share public misgivings about their watchdog role. More of the news media today than just a few years ago say the press drives controversies rather than just reports the news in the way it covers the personal and ethical behavior of public figures. Clear majorities in the national and local press, for example, agree with the public that the Clinton-Lewinsky scandal was overcovered.

The impact of these shortcomings is not lost on the

press. Lack of credibility is the single issue most often cited by the news media as the most important problem facing journalism today. Alarm about faltering credibility is far more prevalent in the current survey than in a comparable 1989 Center survey. Moreover, the press itself says that the loss of public trust is a leading cause of declining news audiences.

To reporters and editors, the reasons for journalism's problems are just as clear — growing financial and business pressures. At both the local and national levels, majorities of working journalists say that increased bottom-line pressure is hurting the quality of coverage. This view is more common than it was just four years ago, although it is less often shared by media executives.

For all these changes and troubles, the news media continue to value traditional, high standards for accuracy, sourcing and objectivity. Across mediums, markets and generations, there is near unanimous agreement on the core principles that define journalism — getting the facts right, covering both sides and refusing to publish rumors. Moreover, most members of the press agree that journalism is distinguished because of its contributions to society, providing people with information they need.

These are the principal findings of a new Pew Research Center (USA) survey of 552 top executives, mid-level editors and producers, and working reporters and editors from both the national and local news media. In addition to print, radio, and broadcast and cable television, a sample of those working in Internet news was also included. Unless otherwise noted, references to public opinion are from a February 18-21, 1999 poll, which can be found immediately following the results of the press survey.

Business Pressures

Increased concern about financial pressure is evident

in both the print and television press, although it has grown more among those in television and radio, particularly national television. In this group, a 53%-to-38% majority of journalists and news executives say that pressure to make a profit is hurting the quality of coverage rather than just changing the way things are done. Opinion has reversed since 1995, when the national television media split 37%-to-46% on this question.

There are other indications that those working in television news find financial pressure particularly troublesome. They are more likely than their counterparts in print to cite quality issues as journalism's top problem and to say that in order to attract new audiences, the news media crosses the line between entertainment and news.

While almost all news media respondents think that ownership of news organizations by diversified corporations has had a negative effect on their profession, most add that corporate owners have little influence on what is covered or emphasized. Similarly, few in the press report that advertising concerns play much of a role in news decisions.

Difference on Financial Pressure

The survey found that news executives and their staffs agree about the problems facing journalism, but executives are more defensive about the impact of financial pressures. At both the national and local levels, for example, fewer news organization chiefs than those in the newsroom ranks say the line is being crossed between entertainment and news.

Top executives are even more adamant about the general effects of the changed economic climate. Unlike their subordinates, clear majorities of news executives think that financial pressures are just changing the way things are done rather than reducing quality. Most mid-level editors and news staff disagree, especially in national news organizations.

Despite these important differences in opinion, most working journalists rate their leadership as excellent or good. Print journalists in national news organizations stand out for their positive views of their leadership: 47% say their bosses share their values a great deal, compared to 29% of national television journalists and roughly one-quarter of local news people.

Press and Public

Most members of the news media concede that they are out of touch with the public, and they blame themselves more than the public for declining audiences. News media executives and journalists view the public not as uninterested or uninformed, but as feeling overloaded by news and information.

> But Americans do not share this view. Two-thirds of the public says they like having so many information sources available; only 28% say they feel overloaded.

The press also points to its loss of credibility with the public as a major reason for losing readers, viewers and listeners. About half of news media executives and journalists rank lack of credibility with the public as a major reason for declining audiences. This represents a significant jump since 1989, when only one-third of the press said this.

> Americans' evaluations of the news media's credibility have declined since the mid-1980s. Network news believability is down an average of 11 percentage points; local television news has dropped 12 points and daily newspapers have tumbled 17 points since 1985.

More people in local news organizations (46%) than national (31%) think that what the public is interested in should be given a great deal of consideration in news coverage decisions. While older members of the news media on both the local and national levels are more reluctant to take public interests into account, the public rewards the consideration given them by the local media.

Local television news tops the list of Americans' favorite news sources — 64% of the public watches their local news regularly. Only 38% of the public regularly watches national network news.

Press vs. Public on Watchdog Role

The press continues to value its watchdog role much more than the public does. Less than 10% of the news media — compared to nearly one-third of the public — believe press criticism of political leaders keeps those leaders from doing their jobs. The vast majority (more than 85%) think such criticism is worthwhile, because it keeps politicians from doing things that should not be done.

"As journalists, we are not just communicators, but watchdogs," says a national cable news correspondent. "We are a very important part of this society's system of checks and balances."

The press and the public are more in sync in their criticism of how the media carries out its watchdog role. About half of journalists and media executives say that in reporting on the personal and ethical behavior of public figures, news organizations often drive the controversies rather than merely report the facts. Fully 72% of Americans say such reporting perpetuates scandal.

Conclusions

- Most journalists and news executives agree that they are overly focused on internal dynamics, too often competing with each other and writing more for colleagues than consumers.
- The press gives itself only lukewarm grades for striking the right balance between what audiences

want to know and what is important for them to know. This criticism is especially strong in the national television news: Only 38% of those working in this arena say an appropriate balance is struck today, compared to 60% of the national print press and more than half of the local news media in both mediums.

- Two-thirds of those in national and local news say that news organizations' attempts to attract readers or viewers has pushed them toward infotainment instead of news.
- Internet journalists share many values with those in the mainstream national news media, but there are some differences. While three-quarters of the national media say remaining neutral is a core principle of journalism, just 52% of those who work in Internet news agree.
- Journalists under the age of 35 are the least likely to know of official ethics programs within their news organizations and the most likely to want more of an organized effort.

Though the above-mentioned information pertains to journalism scenario in the USA, in the present age when the world is considered as a global village, the findings can be generalised, thus applicable to entire globe on more or less similar lines.

2

The News and The New Media

Waste is worse than loss. The time is coming when every person who lays claim to ability will keep the question of waste before him constantly. The scope of thrift is limitless.

—*Thomas A. Edison*

While the news media appreciate the utility of new technologies in their work, they are mixed in their views of the way journalism is practiced in these new mediums. The advent of online-only news sites and the proliferation of cable channels are given only lukewarm endorsements by the news media today, particularly among older members of the press and those in local news.

The most striking difference between the men and women working for Internet news outlets and those in mainstream news is the Internet media's equivocation about neutrality. The ambivalence can be explained in part by the different news gathering techniques endorsed by the Internet news media. Journalists and executives in Internet news are divided 52%-to-48% over the importance of remaining neutral, but three-quarters of those in national and local news declare it to be a journalistic cornerstone.

"There's an ever-growing tendency toward pack journalism as the Internet breaks down editorial barriers," says a network television executive. "Traditional journalists will have to be much better editors, identifying news values and being discerning about those values."

The Internet news media are also slightly more likely than are the national and local press to say that providing an interpretation to news is a core principle of their profession. Finally, only one-quarter of those in Internet news say that always avoiding the first person is a core principle of journalism, while 40% of the national news and 46% of the local news media agree.

Net As a Tool

For the most part, the press feels good about the way new technologies have changed their profession. Roughly half of the news media say the emergence of the Internet has made journalism better. Not surprisingly, those in Internet news are even more positive about the impact of their medium on journalism.

The national and local news media alike have positive views of the Internet as a resource. Fifty-four percent of the national press say the emergence of the Internet has made journalism better; only 12% say it has made journalism worse. Among the local press, 47% say the Internet has made things better, 8% say worse. The local news media are also more likely than their national counterparts to say the Internet hasn't made much of a difference (42% and 26%, respectively). Local news executives are among the least enthusiastic about the Internet — only 25% think it has made journalism better.

Use of the Internet is far more commonplace in newsrooms than living rooms: Over 90% of the press have direct access to the Internet at work; just half of the public goes online.

Younger journalists and those who work in online news have much more positive views of the Internet than do older members of the news media. Fully 70% of those between 18 and 34 think the Internet has made journalism better, compared to 53% of those 35-54 and 40% of those 55 and older. Over 80% of the online press say the Internet has improved journalism.

Online News

The ability of newspapers and TV networks to establish their own websites is viewed as a positive development by 78% of national journalists and executives, 74% of the local news media and 89% of those in Internet news. Executives, news managers and staff are in agreement on this point.

This consensus, however, does not extend to online-only publications. The national and local news media are modestly positive about the emergence of online-only newspages and magazines: 61% and 51%, respectively say such developments have had a positive effect on journalism. Not surprisingly, the Internet press unanimously applauds the emergence of their field: 93% say it has had a positive effect.

The online and mainstream press also differ on the value of the public's direct access to news via the Internet. Three-quarters of those in online news say that the public's ability to bypass the news media and go directly to information sources is a good thing — only half of the national press and less than one-third of the local press express similar enthusiasm. The local print press is among the least likely to see the merit in eliminating the middle man — only 23% say this has been a good thing; 47% think it has been detrimental.

News Magazines

Journalists and media executives are somewhat ambivalent about the value of network TV news magazines. Among the national news media, 35% say these news magazines have had a positive effect on journalism; 41% say they have a negative effect. Those who work in local news are slightly more positive — 46% say TV news magazines are a plus, 30% say they are negative. Local television news folks stand out: 60% see news magazines as positive.

Americans think of these television magazines as news — not entertainment. Fully 81% of the public says 60 Minutes is news and 71% say the same of Dateline NBC. And, the public likes these programs. As many Americans watch television news magazines regularly (37%) as watch the national nightly network news (38%).

Virtually all news media executives and journalists agree that tabloid television programs have hurt their profession. Roughly 85% of the national and local news media say shows like "Hard Copy" and "Inside Edition" have had a negative effect on journalism. Only 3%-4% say the effect has been positive. This sentiment is shared by the print and television news media. Interestingly, national news media executives are much more critical of tabloid TV than are their local counterparts. Fully 91% of national executives say tabloid shows have had a negative impact, compared to 72% of those in local markets.

Evaluations of tabloid TV are harsher today than they were 10 years ago. In 1989, 61% of the press thought these programs were having a negative effect, 15% said their effect was positive and 19% said they weren't having much of an impact either way.

> The public's view of tabloid TV is more critical than it was in the past, as well. In 1989, by a ratio of 39%-to-28% Americans considered A Current Affair to be news, not entertainment. Now, most (56%) see it as entertainment; only one-in-four consider it news.

Growth of Cable

Most in the media say the increasing number of cable news outlets has had a positive effect on the profession. Those in national news are slightly more upbeat about this trend than those in local: 60% of the national press says the proliferation of cable outlets has been a good thing, 52% of locals agree.

When asked about the competition spawned by the increased number of cable outlets, the press is somewhat less positive. Roughly four-in-ten say competition and the increased number of cable news outlets has made journalism better, while one-third say this trend has made journalism worse.

At both the national and local levels, those in television news have a more positive view of this trend. More than half of national television journalists think this competition has made journalism better, compared to only 36% of national print journalists. Similarly, 45% of those who work in local television news say this has made things better; 35% of the local print press agree.

Among those who think competition and the increased number of cable outlets has hurt journalism, many say the need to compete has lowered journalistic standards. Those in the national media also think competition has fostered an interest in getting the story first rather than getting the story right. Many in local television news complain that, as a result of increased competition, ratings now take precedence over quality.

REFERENCES

1. "Fewer Favor Media Scrutiny of Political Leaders," The Pew Research Center for The People & The Press," March 1997.
2. "Internet News Takes Off," The Pew Research Center for The People & The Press," June 1998.

3

Errors of Modern Journalism

> Be unselfish. That is the first and final commandment for those who would be useful, and happy in their usefulness. If you think of yourself only, you cannot develop because you are chocking the sources of development, which spiritual expansion through though for others.
>
> —*Dr. Charles W. Eliot*

Inspite of all the rhetoric from Thomas Jefferson down to the latest self-important musings of journalists about journalism's being the first, best hope for a healthy polity, your newspaper is lying to you. While assuring you that it provides precise information about public policy issues, in many cases it is only pushing speculation and rumor in the guise of fact. Most of the time you have no independent way to confirm its claims, so how can you tell when a newspaper is lying?

Here's a hint: watch out for the numbers. Newspapers are filled with contextless reports of the latest things government officials have said or decided. But newspapers do like to throw in a number now and then to add verisimilitude to the tales they tell.

Knowledge of the media's inability to get it straight, especially when dealing with numbers and statistics, has become widespread enough to inspire a widely reviewed book entitled—Tainted Truth: The Manipulation of Fact in America by Cynthia Crossen. It has also given rise to a new magazine, the quarterly Forbes MediaCritic, the latest addition to the Forbes family of publications.

While ideologues of all persuasions like to blame media inaccuracies on political biases, the causes of journalism's troubles are, unfortunately, inherent in the way daily newspapers, those first drafts of history, are written: hurriedly and by generalists who, even if they are unfailingly scrupulous (which can't always be assumed), are often ignorant of the topics on which they write and depend blindly on what others tell them—and what others tell them is very often biased. Unfortunately, those first drafts of history are all most laypersons read.

Our intellectual culture is drunk on numbers, addicted to them: we need them in every situation, we feel utterly dependent on them. As sociologist Richard Gelles aptly put it in a July 25, 1994, Newsweek story on the media's problems with numbers, "Reporters don't ask, `How do you know it?' They're on deadline. They just want the figures so they can go back to their word processors." The culture of the poll dominates: the foolish notion that not only every fact but every thought, whim, and emotion of the populace can be stated in scientifically valid and valuable numbers.

The lust for numbers can, at its best, lead people to do hard research and dig up interesting and useful information. More often, however, it leads to dignifying guesses with misleadingly precise numbers. For example, it wasn't enough to know that people were dying in Somalia; as Michael Maren reports in the Fall 1994 Forbes MediaCritic, reporters felt it necessary to latch onto some relief workers' guesses and repeat them over and over, only occasionally letting slip honest acknowledgments that no one really knew how many people were actually dying and that no one was taking the trouble to attempt accurate counts.

The obsession with numbers leads to particularly egregious errors in reports on economic figures and aggregates and the federal budget. Those errors include calling spending that doesn't equal what had been planned a "cut" in spending, even if more is being spent than the year before; relying on static economic analysis, especially when calculating the effects of tax increases and their concomitant revenues (because they assume that people do not change their behavior when their taxes are raised, members of Congress and reporters make grievously wrong predictions about expected revenues); and relying uncritically on numerical tools such as the Consumer Price Index.

Especially during the 1992 election, "quintile" analysis of the effects of the Reagan-Bush years on income and tax-burden equality abounded, with hardly any explanation of the complications of such analyses. Those complications include the fact that when people in lower income quintiles become richer, they often move into a higher quintile rather than buoy the average of the lower one. Yet income added to the highest quintile can do nothing but increase that quintile's average income. That creates a misleading picture of the rich getting much richer while the poor stagnate.

Quintile analysis is also static, but income mobility is common in America, so it's not always the same people who languish in lower quintiles or whoop it up at the top. And quintile analysis often relies on households, not individuals— the top quintile can have more than 20 percent of Americans, the bottom less than 20 percent. But all of those complications are overlooked in the media's craving for numbers to toss around.

The media even ignore the fact that "counts" of macroeconomic variables can change retroactively—1993 data on 1992 quantities can be different from 1994 data.

As an example, in 1993 the Bureau of Labor Statistics listed Arkansas as the state with the highest percentage rise (3 percent) in nonfarm employment from July 1991 to July 1992. Candidate Clinton touted that percentage in campaign ads. But by March 1994 the facts had changed. Although Arkansas was then thought to have had a 3.7 percent rise in employment during the 1991-92 period, it ranked behind Montana's 4.22 percent and Idaho's 4.21.

Macroeconomic aggregates, such as gross national product, on which the media often rely for numerical ballast, are often riddled with conceptual problems, such as that of counting as additions to our national product any cash transactions, including the classic example of neighbors' paying each other to mow each other's lawns, and ignoring any noncash transaction that adds to economic well- being. Other economic numbers bandied about by the media, such as unemployment rates, job growth, and the "cost" of various tax increases or cuts, are often derived from random samplings, self- reported information, and guesswork. Economics is a study of human action, not of numbers; the press's over dependence on frequently dubious aggregates helps disguise the problem and muddles readers' understanding of what economics—and prosperity—is really about.

There are many ways to mislead while allegedly presenting accurate counts or measures to the public. The most sinister is to simply make up numbers or make completely bald-faced guesses. That happens more often than you might think. The demand for information has far outstripped the supply. Coming up with reliable numbers to support all the things that journalists want to say and the public wants to know is often prohibitively expensive, in money or effort, or both. But the misuse and misunderstanding of numbers lead to erroneous reporting.

The total number of breast cancer victims has become

a matter of much concern since the National Cancer Institute and the American Cancer Society frightened the world with the declaration that American women face a one-in-eight chance of contracting breast cancer. That scary figure, however, applies only to women who have already managed to live to age 95; one out of eight of them will most likely contract breast cancer. According to the NCI's own figures, a 25-year-old woman runs only a 1-in-19,608 risk.

Those very precise figures are themselves based on a phony notion: that we know how many people have breast or any other cancer. As two journalists concerned about cancer admitted in the Nation (September 26, 1994), "Not only is there no central national agency to report cancer cases to . . . but there is no uniform way that cases are reported, no one specialist responsible for reporting the case." So any discussion of cancer rates in the United States is based on guesswork, and one can only hope that the guesswork is based on some attempt to be true to the facts as they are known.

In the case of other health threats, such as AIDS, we know that isn't the case. In The Myth of Heterosexual AIDS, journalist Michael Fumento documented the discrepancy between the rhetoric about the plague like threat of AIDS to the nongay and non-drug-using populace and official statistics on the actual prevalence of the syndrome, which indicated that no more than 0.02 percent of people who tested HIV positive were not in those risk groups. (And even such heterosexual AIDS cases as are recorded run into a self-reporting problem: many people may not want to admit to anyone that they have had gay sex or used drugs.) As Fumento explained, projections of the future growth of the AIDS epidemic (even ones that were not hysterical pure guesses tossed out by interest groups) were often based on straight extrapolations of earlier doubling times for the epidemic (which inevitably—for any disease—lead to the absurd result of everyone on the planet and then some dying of the disease) or cobbled together from guess piled on guess. Even when the Centers for Disease Control would lower earlier estimates on the basis of new information, or make clearly unofficial speculations about higher numbers, journalists would continue to report the higher and more alarming numbers.

In the case of figures about AIDS in Africa, even the most basic numbers are not to be trusted. Journalist Celia Farber documented in Spin magazine how African health officials inflate the number of deaths from the complications of AIDS, both because AIDS cases attract foreign aid money, whereas traditional African disease and death do not, and because there is no accurate method of counting.

One relief worker told Farber that counts of children orphaned by AIDS in an African village "were virtually meaningless, I made them up myself... then, to my amazement, they were published as official figures in the World Health Organization (WHO)... book on African AIDS.... The figure has more than doubled, based on I don't know what evidence, since these people have never been here.... If people die of malaria, it is called AIDS, if they die of herpes it is called AIDS. I've even seen people die in accidents and it's been attributed to AIDS. The AIDS figures out of Africa are pure lies."

Anthony Burgess in his autobiography gives further insight into the generation of "official" figures. He tells of creating completely fraudulent records of the classes he supposedly taught fellow soldiers while stationed in Gibraltar during World War II. His bogus "statistics were sent to the War Office. These, presumably, got into official records which nobody read." For the sake of accuracy, we can only hope so. But if a journalist got hold of those numbers, he'd be apt to repeat them.

Similarly farcical figures are taken completely seriously by journalists. For example, activist Mitch Snyder's assertion that the United States suffered the presence of 3 million homeless people became common wisdom for the bulk of the 1980s. Snyder's figure was made up; he simply assumed that 1 percent of Americans were homeless to get an initial number of 2.2 million in 1980, then arbitrarily decided that since he knew the problem was getting worse, the number would hit 3 million by 1983. He claimed to be working from extrapolations based on reports from fellow homeless activists around the country, but there was no counting, no surveying, no extrapolation behind his assertion. And yet most major American newspapers reported the number; it became part of our received cultural wisdom.

In her recent book, *Who Stole Feminism? How Women Have Betrayed Women*, Christina Hoff Sommers actually tried to track to their sources numbers spread by feminist activists. One of the much- reported stories she debunked was that 150,000 women a year die of anorexia, which an outraged Gloria Steinem reported in her popular book Revolution from Within. Steinem cited another popular feminist tome by Naomi Wolf as her source; Wolf cited a book about anorexia written by a women's studies academic, which cited the American Anorexia and Bulimia Center. Sommers actually checked with that group and discovered that all they'd said was that many women are anorexic. Oops.

Another feminist canard is that domestic violence is responsible for more birth defects than all other causes combined. Time and many newspapers had ascribed that finding to a March of Dimes report. Sommers tracked the assertion back through three sources, beginning with the Time reporter, and discovered that it was the result of a misunderstanding of something that had been said in the introduction of a speaker at a 1989 conference—no such March of Dimes report existed. Still, the errors of Time and the Boston Globe and the Dallas Morning News are in more clip files and data banks than is Sommers's debunking.

The march of that particular error will doubtless continue.

A third famous feminist factoid is that Super Bowl Sunday sees a 40 percent rise in cases of wife beating. That claim, said to be supported by a university study, was made in an activist press conference. (The story was also spread by a group ironically named Fairness and Accuracy in Reporting.) Similar claims began coming from other sources. Ken Ringle of the Washington Post took the time to double-check them and found that the university study's authors denied that their study said any such thing and that the other sources that claimed to have independent confirmation of the "fact" refused to disclose their data. When a concerned activist makes up a number, few bother to be skeptical, and credulous reporting tends to drown out the few debunkers.

Unfortunately, erroneous numbers in journalism are not always the result of sincere attempts to quantify the relevant data. If you can't imagine someone's making the effort to really count something, and if you can imagine any reason for the source's having an ulterior motive, best take the number with a large grain of salt. This is not a call for ad hominem attacks; it is merely a warning about when to look especially askance at numbers. Even when one is following what seems on its face to be defensible standards of sample and extrapolation, ludicrous results can ensue. For example, Robert Rector of the Heritage Foundation wrote that 22,000 Americans below the poverty line had hot tubs, and many conservative publications uncritically trumpeted the figure. But Rector's figure was "extrapolated" from one case in a survey sample. It's disingenuous to claim that because one poor family in a sample of 10,000 has a hot tub, 22,000 poor families have hot tubs.

One more example of numbers being attached to the uncounted, and probably uncountable, is the debate over species extinctions. Economist Julian Simon has explained that the conventionally accepted figures on the number of species disappearing yearly are based on no counts and no extrapolations from past knowledge; they are based on guesses about the current rate of extinction, and that rate is arbitrarily increased to produce the frightening number of 40,000 per year. Norman Myers, one of the leading promulgators of that figure, admits that "we have no way of knowing the actual current rate of extinction in tropical forest, nor can we even make an accurate guess." Yet he is willing to make guesses about future rates.

To cite a much-touted scare figure, on workplace violence, was recently debunked in the pages of the Wall Street Journal. Erik Larson found that reports and statistics on the prevalence of workplace violence were shoddy or misleading in various respects. One report, which concluded that workers have a one-in-four chance of being attacked or threatened at work, was based on the replies of only 600 workers, who represented only 29 percent of the people whom the survey had tried to reach, which made the groups largely self- selected within the original sample. Statisticians frown, with reason, on self-selected samples, which are very likely to be biased.

Larson also found that a Bureau of Labor Statistics report, which said that homicide is the second most frequent cause of death in the workplace, far from referring to coworkers or disgruntled ex- coworkers blasting away at their comrades, showed that three- quarters of the deaths occurred during robberies, and that many others involved police or security guards, whose jobs obviously are dangerous. But the media, and an industry of self-serving workplace violence consultants, inspired by half-understood studies and vivid memories of crazed postal workers, created an aura of offices as the Wild, Wild West that caught the imagination of many. In this case, data were not so much bogus or warped as wildly misinterpreted.

Checking the Checkers

It might seem paradoxical to condemn journalists for incessantly parroting errors when it is journalists themselves who occasionally expose errors. After all, who else would? The problem is, they don't do it nearly enough, and no one else ever does. Even though Larson's story appeared in the October 13, 1994, Wall Street Journal, it's a given that many other writers and TV reporters will have missed it and sometime in the future will again parrot false suppositions about the danger of mortal violence in the workplace.

The culture of journalism is based on the principle of the citation or quote: if someone else said it, or wrote it, it's okay to repeat it. Almost any editor or writer would scoff at that brash formulation. After all, journalists pride themselves on their withering skepticism, their credo of "if your mother says she loves you, check it out." But the reader would be terribly naive to believe that journalists, under the crush of daily deadlines, under the pressure of maintaining long-term relationships with sources, and occasionally under the spell of ideology, always meet that standard. In the future, you can count on it, someone will go back to some story about workplace violence, or the homeless, or wife beating, written before the debunking was done, and come to an incorrect conclusion. Dogged checking of sources is rare indeed.

You'd think that constant checking and rechecking of the sources of claims would be the rule in journalism. Unfortunately, it is not. Nor, apparently, is it in science. In Betrayers of the Truth, William Broad and Nicholas Wade reported on fraud and deceit—and acceptance of the same—in the scientific establishment. They found that, like journalism's conceit about checking on whether your mother loves you, science's conceit of being built on an elaborate system of cross checking and confirming the results of others is mostly a myth. Hardly anyone ever checks what other people claim to have found or done.

All too often readers assume that everyone is doing his work scrupulously and well, but unfortunately, that's not always the case, as Broad and Wade, Sommers, Fumento, Larson, Farber, and others have shown. Readers should be much more skeptical than they are.

Total skepticism is probably impossible. But greater awareness of the sorts of errors journalists tend to make can only help. Watch out for macroeconomic aggregates; try to figure out where huge counts are coming from and how they are being made; try to check the methodology and phrasing of polls; check on the self-interest of the groups that promulgate scary numbers; and remember that scary stories make great copy and should be mistrusted all the more for that reason.

If journalism were merely entertainment, this wouldn't be so important. But despite how bad they are at it, journalists' conceit about their key role in public policy is, unfortunately, true. Bad information can only lead to bad policy. The first step in an intelligent approach to public policy is to get the facts as straight as we can, even when we don't have precise numbers.

4

Printing for the Journalist

Two things, well considered, would prevent many quarrels: first, to have it well ascertained whether we are not disputing about terms rather than things and, second, to examine whether that on which we differ is worth contending about.

—*Charles C. Colton*

As is natural, the production of journals in India has run closely parallel to that of their contemporaries in the West. The first large efforts in print came from the West, mostly in the successful attempts by missionaries to found presses. Private and official presses sprang up and, in the case of the former, often died a natural death, or, in the case of the latter, stayed to give service to officialdom. As English was the language used in the early stages of journalism in India, there was another strong bond with the West, and the debt owed thereto is freely and gladly acknowledged.

In the late eighteenth century and for some time later, there was no real attempt at display of printed matter in journalism, the capitals of the text type, set at the head of the column, being the first heading. The development of display was slow and still today the after-effects of the old ways are clearly discernible in journals which regard with suspicion any attempt at display beyond a certain size of type.

Since World War First, the renaissance of the beautiful old Continental type faces and the tremendous impact of the modernistic style of type and display have caused far-reaching changes. In the main this has been for the good of journalistic display, but sometimes to its detriment, such as when display goes to the head of the display man and he loses part of his sense of discretion.

A thorough examination of the press of India will show how closely it is allied in style to the West. Main news on the first page, leading articles on the left main inside page, sport at the end, small ads *on* the second page, and so on, are general, although, of course, there are variations depending on the wishes of those in charge and their desire to attract readership.

What is Printing?

Print in all its forms is the desire in tangible form to convey an idea or ideas from the one or the few to the many. It is duplication that cannot convey sound but can reproduce symbols of it, cannot convey the actual sight of a thing or event but can reproduce in illustration and description a reasonable method of making permanent a memorial of it. It cannot paint or carve, but it can make possible to millions the sight of painting and carving that normally would never have been seen by them. Hence, print is the expression of ideas laid out in such a way as to attract readers, sometimes of a certain kind, often of any kind. There is an internationalism in print that makes good print in one country good print in another two. A well-laid out newspaper is a well-laid out newspaper in any language. So there is no such thing as a borderline that divides countries in the standards of print. Scripts may differ—and do, to an amazing extent—one from another, but the reproduction of those scripts has standards that are international.

Add to this the following facts. Machinery in print production differs only in the manner it is designed. Type composition is done mechanically in practically every country in the world by the same kinds of machines. Paper is universally used. There also are such minor matters as headings being in larger type than the main body. Thus India and the rest of the world are one in their use of print to express their ideas.

The Production Routine

What is print itself— how is it produced ? Let us assume that you have had an article accepted, that it has been sub-edited and is ready for setting in type. Your article has two main parts, the heading, possibly sub-headings or an introduction added for you, and the main text, that which is your part of it. The layout man, who knows the style of the journal, whether magazine or newspaper, lays out, that is, draws the heading and marks on it the style and sizes of type to be used. Look at the next few magazines you pick up and you will see the tremendous variety of layout possible. Indeed, it is no exaggeration to say that, even with the limitations that are laid upon a layout man, no two men will produce exactly the same layout for your article's heading and style.

Notably, every journal has its own distinct style—or should have. If it has not, then the magazine is at the mercy of the printer and if he is not a trained man . . .

While the marking up of the heading type is being done and the compositor is setting the type, the text is being composed, with paragraph headings to add and maintain interest.

Eventually, the whole is in type and the first proofs are pulled. When everything is ready, your article is fitted in with the other features on the same page (unless you are fortunate enough to have a whole page) and if the journal is big enough, a stereo is made. This is a large plate, semi-circular, containing a page at a time, which, after trimming, is placed round the cylinder on the press. When all is ready, and the machines move, your article is there in print for you to enjoy, probably more than anyone else to begin with. Folding on the larger machines is done immediately after printing and the paper is ready to sell on the spot.

That, very briefly, is how an article reaches the reader from the manuscript through to the journal ready for the reader. Today the production of print is more and more a matter of mechanization. There still are Urdu newspapers drawn by hand and reproduced by the lithographical process, but the pen is giving way to the keyboard. In other languages, mechanical type-setting has been used increasingly since the first mechanical setting twenty years ago. A typical example is Hindi available on slug (solid lines) and in single-letter setting by machine. Mechanization has revolutionized the setting of journals by reducing the time taken in setting by as much as five times. If progress in earlier experiments was slow, in comparison today's changes are rapid. When the processes of designing adapting age-old scripts, with their tremendous varieties of characters, and making matrices from which the types are cast, are taken into consideration, it will be seen what a great work has been done by makers of type-setting machines—not always for financial advantage by any means.

It is a far different matter from designing 26 letters in a roman alphabet and its punctuation signs to designing an alphabet with 600 characters—not all on the same level. Add to this the number of languages in India, based on the Sanskrit and Arabic scripts, with all the variations of line and curve between say, Assamese and Tamil then, the task of making Indian journals independent of slow handsetting methods has been one of the greatest achievements in print the world has seen.

The years after World War I gave India the opportunity to modernize her plant. With the West eager to export and the East anxious to import, India was able to place herself in a strong position as regards her plant. Linotypes, Intertypes, and Monotypes, have increased her typesetting facilities. Rotaiy presses, printing from paper in the reel and not from the flat sheet, have been installed by the dozen—if not hundred, for these machines, masterly examples of the engineer's craft, are expensive. Stereo equipment, Ludlows and Elrods for headings, rules and borders, have reinforced the all-round ability of the other typesetting machines. In addition, all the other general machines, such as folders, stitchers and sewing machines, cutting machines, proof presses, and cameras and full equipment for block-making, have added to India's strength, these are the basic requirements in good journalistic production today. In America and Great Britain there have been experiments in such advanced methods as electronics, photo-composing machines, improvements in telecommunication, plastics (blocks made in this material are common today) and mobile transmitters.

How to Attract the Reader?

Let us leave mechanism and return to the business of attracting the reader. This is the work of the layout man once he has been given the material in the way of "copy". It is his job to translate "copy" into a heading or display to call attention to what follows. (Of-course, if the prospective reader is bewildered by the erudition of your subject or it is not within his scope of interest, then, unless a trick heading is used, the chances are that he will not read your article anyway, like the attractive magazine cover that drew one to open its pages to show a very conservative style of journal discussing a very obscure—to one—foreign bird.)

Every page of the text of a journal, of whatever publication period—daily with several editions or annual with one edition— is originally a blank sheet to be filled with print in a way to draw the attention of the reader. And the kind of page depends just as much on the kind of reader as the reverse applies. A printed page has space, headings, columns, advertisements, rules and borders, bold type, light type, italics, scripts, and pictures, hand-drawn lettering, footnotes and captions, and other ornaments and additions, not always at once of course and not all pages. Basically it has print, and paper beneath the print, forming a harmonious whole. If it does not form a harmonious whole, then somebody is at fault.

It is possible to recognize a journal by its style of presentation without seeing its name anywhere, simply by the way in which it is displayed.

The treatment of display depends to a large extent on the contents. The daily newspaper, made to be read and kept for a day (unless some great event or personal consideration calls for its preservation), obviously needs different treatment from the monthly, which is largely articles and reviews.

Sensational news calls for daring treatment—the banner headline across the page, the large type, the heavy sub-heading, the photographs, double-column headings, boxes (those little panels containing special news items that are out of the ordinary)—while a scientific treatise with its reasoned statements and arguments, backed by references and figures, asks for quietness and the atmosphere of study. Obviously, of course, there is much variety in the way newspapers handle different stories. The quieter style simply keeps to its headings and relies on its content to make the emphasis. The 'screamer' tries to catch the reader, and often distorts by its over-emphasis.

Certain magazines with temporary and contemporary appeal, vary their covers and presentation of contents with every issue. This is an eye-catching appeal that has more than a stunt for its basis. The magazine that changes its style reflects the trends of the day and is a mirror of the day. Architecture and the streamlining of cars and machines are part of the same growing trend.

Changes in every issue inevitably call for ingenuity and a high degree of skill in handling type. They also call for a wide range of type faces and added expense in blocks. The cost of producing such journals tends to place them in the luxury class, but the difference between them and the ordinary run makes the extra cost worthwhile.

Making up a newspaper calls for rapid thinking. Every page must be filled and filled correctly, with nothing overhanging and little over-running to other pages. Sub-editors on the spot decide values, but the display man should be there to give expression to the values. The day of the single column, top to bottom style of display is gone forever, but in India today there is still far too much unimaginative setting out of pages. It is not difficult to extend to double—and triple-column headings, but one would not think so if some efforts were regarded as the norm. The most stodgy page often is the editorial page, which should be, but is not, readily made attractive as any. Variety without sensationalism is easy to attain, but not in our daily papers as yet.

A factor in the make-up of any journal is the style and size of types decided upon. These may range from the hit-and-hit-hard style of certain Bombay journals to the peace-perfect-peace makeups of far too many dailies and weeklies. It is a simple and inexpensive matter today to have a range of heading types and useful borders. Amazingly few journals realize this.

Magazine Make-up

Magazines are much easier to make up than dailies, although a newspaper with a trained typographer could revolutionize itself without spoiling its character, that intangible factor that combines writing and editorial style with type display. Magazine headings can be set almost at leisure. The time factor is much less troublesome. Variations may be tried and the final results made really satisfactory and satisfying. The only way most dailies can approach this is by keeping strictly to a style and using good heading faces. The two *Times*—of New York and London—illustrate this, although some readers regard polish as being nearer a vice than a virtue when carried beyond certain limits.

Most of the smaller magazines rely on the old two-column setting. This gives the opportunity for variety, although the more columns the bigger the chance for display work. Even with a tiny single column journal, display can be varied surprisingly. By using capitals and lower case, italics and small caps, bold and light faces, even in one type size, a rich mixture can be obtained without trouble. The main word of a heading generally stands out, then come the intermediary and the minor. By emphasizing the first, using quieter type for the second, and the quietest of all for the third, the message can be given and the reader impressed by the heading as the layout man intends him to be. Setting type in the centre is not always necessary. Spaced in from the left or set with the main word over to the right and the following lines of the headings also set to the right, there can be change and novelty with no cheap striving after-effect. The main heading set centre, followed by the sub-heading immediately beneath and plenty of space round, and there you have a simple setting that is clear. Move the main line or word to the left and run the remainder from a point, say, half an inch in from the left, and you have a change. Put the author's name top left or right and space it out between letters and you can have emphasis without distortion.

In fact, all typesetting is a matter of rhythm. There is a certain "swing" about good setting that is difficult to define but easy to see when there. It is more than a matter of balance, for in the more modern settings balance would seem to be the last effect obtained. Yet the rhythm is there clearly, syncopated to a degree. Many text-books have been written about typesetting and layout; it is not difficult to obtain copies from any large bookshop, on order.

The word "heading" has become a misnomer. An article in *Indian Print & Paper* once stated, "There is no such thing as a heading" and proceeded to show this by having its heading at the foot of the text, a logical place and by no means incongruous, for in recent years many of the rules previously accepted as sacrosanct have been discarded and the consequences are a joy to the reader, whether he knows anything about typography or not.

The layout man has more choice when the magazine has two columns. Here he can begin to use an extended range of ideas.

Across the columns, along two and then one; one alone; heading along the top, sub-heading along the foot of the page; heading at the foot of the first column, and so on, with illustrations, which should not be made to "any" size but be accepted as an integral part of the design, helping to build up the ultimate effect, in the place where they serve best. A strong effect can be given by placing the photograph at the bead with the heading immediately below, or with it at the left Side and the heading to the right. There is simple variety within one page to convey a number of effects.

The larger the magazine the greater the scope, although some of the best display work is seen in the pocket-sized digests, where typesetting has been brought to a fine art. Three columns give room for really extending oneself. Many trade, journals, especially those connected with print, run to three columns, with two columns as a variation to prevent monotony. Two columns in a bigger journal give dignity, three columns stimulate interest. Four columns can be unwieldy if one article is concerned, but this can be offset by using bold headings and sound, emphatic illustrations.

The 'straight up-and-down' style is gone. Cut across columns with different matter, with a rule or border above to separate from the main article, add a column in different type to prevent too large a desert of plain text type, place an interesting paragraph or a series of paragraphs' within a 'box' or border, and the reader's interest is not allowed to flag.

Type

Before passing on to the modern style of setting, where earlier rules are being broken again and again, let us consider the material we have mentioned so much : type. Here we have a subject that occupies volumes and never ceases to fascinate and instruct. Briefly, type may be divided into two styles—old and new, And the interpretation if the words "old" and "new" may be divided again into old-style methods of type design and new-style type design. For our purpose, let us discard the first interpretation, which refers to the serifs, those little continuations of the main strokes of letters, and consider the differences between the actual type designs.

The designs, of thirty years ago were, broadly, of the kind that held sway for fifty years before. Then came a change, so sweeping is to discard good taste and established ideas, but refreshing enough to make type users think very hard and revise their techniques to an extent scarcely conceived. The change began on the continent of Europe and once the first shock had passed, after World War I, the old "everything in the middle and all the lines level" style was left temporarily on one side for the new eccentric "anything for a change" technique. Slowly the equilibrium adjusted itself and it was realized that the two styles could live perfectly amicably side by side.

To mark the change, and part of it, new type designs came. They caused raised eyebrows and much dolorous shaking of heads, but there was no withstanding the change and it has become part of print today, enriching and strengthening it immensely.

A "rash" of new styles followed. The years have sorted these out. Much that was too outlandish died a natural death. But the influence remained and, although the reader may not know it, almost every journal today, without exception, has some example of the new style of type and setting.

Which leads us to the asymmetrical style of layout. This seems to leave aside all pre-conceived ideas and rely on eccentricity for its appeal. This is not so, in actuality. Provided a layout man keeps in mind the subject he is translating into print, stunt for its own sake is superfluous. As has been said, print is ideas translated into a record. But it is a record with the emphasis on the subject.

Where do you find the leading examples of change—as regards layout ? In the journal selling on appeal to the eye, in several ways, although the daily press is changing more rapidly than it was. There is a difference between a woman's popular magazine and an art journal, but both rely on presentation of ideas. Fashion journals, light reading in periodicals—the sort of publication you buy to read on a railway journey or to while away a spare hour or so. Among art journals must be listed printing and publicity technical journals, for the printer and publicity man must produce a publication that will satisfy the keenest critics—printers and publicity men. In the art journal gone are the straight columns and the sedate headings. Fancy is free.

Blocks are allowed to dominate, headings vary and switch around, text is fitted in almost as an afterthought, although careful examination shows that free and easy setting is often the result of the most meticulous attention to detail. This kind of layout demands the greatest attention of type and block and message as one integrated whole. It is more than one plus one plus one making three. It must be a one, a whole expressing itself that the reader may follow what is said and meant without interference by type or block, so that the whole is accepted as a single entity almost unconsciously by the reader.

The reader will have noticed that there is a style that allows the block printing to run off the edge of the paper. The technical term for this is "bleed-off". When first seen, it swept through the World of print, giving a needed freshness. The cost of "bleed-off" is heavier than normal printing, as the block prints beyond the normal edge of the paper. If the block impression went continuously on to the printing cylinder at the edge of the paper, disaster would follow quickly, so the paper for printing is a larger size and is trimmed on the cutting machine to the right size before publication.

Many journals in India follow this style, which is easily recognizable. Where there is no paper visible at the edge of a sheet, there is bleed-off, which gives the effect of running the picture into infinity beyond the paper.

Recent developments in magazine layout have included the use of larger type in introductions, more use of sans serif in the 'square' and expanded faces and still more freedom of layout. Space between lines of headings—using type as though it had no 'beard' at the foot—has also been prominent. Thick plain rules for emphasis and outlined letters have become popular.

Two new type faces have improved the appearance of

dailies : Linotype's Jubilee and Intertype's Royal. An innovation has been Linotype's Caledonia Bold and Bold Italic for headings, a refreshing change, and one Western daily has used the classical Garamond Italic with striking effect. Magazine sections of Sunday papers are being revolutionized and any student of newspaper layout would find inspiration in the study of these developments. That it is possible to be progressive is to be seen from the pages of a recent book on newspaper layout, which showed the sports pages of a London daily. By the time the book was selling well, the illustration was out-dated by changes in layout. Indeed, recent layout changes in the London daily press have been more pronounced than for many years. A newspaper or magazine *must* be contemporary if it is to reflect its era.

Imitation has been a retarding influence in the development of an Indian style of make-up, There are the house journals of big business firms, with the best that print in India can produce. For maintenance of prestige a house magazine can have a wide influence. There has been the same development in India as in the West, where house journals have been designed and produced through advertising agencies. The printer has lost his place in production of print of this kind, although here and there is to be seen the pleasant picture of customer and printer working harmoniously together to produce journals commendable by any standard. Lest it be thought that advertising agencies are to be condemned for commanding the house journal field, let me hasten to assure the reader that the printer has not fulfilled his obligation as craftsman and the artist has stepped in. Advertising agencies have helped print in many ways and have contributed generously to its improvement in India.

The prospects for the future of magazine production in India are probably greater than almost anywhere else in the world at present, both as regards numerical production and the presentation of the individual issue. The scope is tremendous, almost unbelievably so.

Earlier we stated that printing is international. This is a truism accepted everywhere where print is used. The proper use of paper, good inking and machining, sound binding, and so on, are good in any part of the world. This, however, does not mean that there is no difference between the print of one country and any other. Print in America is clearly different from print in England, France, Italy, or Germany, all considerations of language differences being excluded. No two countries have the same characteristics in print, as in other cultural respects. No one could mistake a sari for a tweed costume. The one is Eastern and the other Western, each admirable for its purpose and each is clothing. No one, however, can say that India has evolved her own special unmistakable brand of print. India has yet to express herself in print. She should now be making her own way, at least the first few steps. India has her own languages, all in script, most available on the keyboard for mechanical setting. She has her own climate and immense variety of scenery, custom, dress, trees, birds, animals, indigenous traditional designs, and her own self. But unless the artist draws those scenes and a block is made, she has no means of expressing herself in print.

There are few borders and type ornaments, purely Indian motifs and themes expressing that splendid inheritance that is her special contribution to the culture of the world. She has to rely mainly on the exhaustive array of the West, rich in itself—but not India. Where are the ornaments in type metal to augment the sturdiness of Hindi, the grace of Urdu, the circular sweep of Oriya, the strength of Tamil, and the varied characteristics of her other languages?

Bringing out new borders and ornament rules is expensive and the type foundries of India are not big concerns. India needs artists willing to produce the drawings, and type foundries equally willing to turn their art into type. There is a fortune awaiting the firm willing to venture as well as for men who will produce type faces in her own languages.

Concurrent with the need for craftsmen in production is the need for layout men, lovers of type and the beauty of its disciplined expression. The newspapers of India 'have failed lamentably so far by not employing layout men, those so-called luxuries. They have let their type-setting in advertisements reach the dregs in depth, and often illustrations remotely resembling a photograph are accepted as good enough. Smaller newspapers and journals with weak resources are not the biggest offenders by any means. The big circulation journals are the most blameworthy. Instead of leading they have complacently ambled along their easy way and allowed themselves to become slothful. Few newspapers in India are innocent of the charge of the failure to accept their responsibilities in typography. No consideration is given to the choice of type faces and the splendid array of faces allying beauty with utility is left to show its splendour in less accessible publications. Until the big men show the way, the smaller ones can hardly be expected to follow. What are the prospects in journalistic print ? Immeasurable. As with her culture, so with her readership resources. For literacy becomes more general, there is the biggest field for journals in the world. So far we have few all-India magazines. The daily press confines itself to certain areas, and no newspaper has more than three places of publication. What is to stop the daily newspaper from publication on the lines of the digests and their multi-language issues ? The same applies to the weekly and the monthly. There are hundreds of millions of prospective readers and will continue to be. Circulations could reach fantastic figures, for once the people of India can read they will clamour for reading material.

Coming changes will give Indian journalism the greatest opportunity in its history, but a new depth and range of vision is needed to meet the change. There must be a preparedness for an unparalleled situation by men able to finance print and men able to produce it well and extensively enough to cover the whole country and many thousands of Indians living beyond her borders.

Though use of new technology in printing and use of computers in composing the text has brought revolution in production of journals in India as elsewhere, the foregoing information is very important for a budding journalist which reveals the journey of printing technology upto now.

Now, computers have made every process very easy and instant. Most of the newspapers and magazines are produced elegantly in multicolour that too with comparative lower costs. You can design and devise your journals as per your will without much efforts in fascinating way.

5

Journalism: Education & Training

The bee is more honored than other animals, not because she labours, but because she labour for others.

—*St. John Chrysostom*

If I can stop one heart from breaking.
    I shall not live in vain.
If I can ease one life the aching.
    Or cool one pain.
Or help one fainting robin
    Unto his nest again,
I shall not live in vain.

—*Emily Dickinson*

As journalism is a much sought after career at present the need of training and education have increased manifold. Besides Delhi-based Institute of Mass Media and Communication, journalism as a discipline is being taught at many institutes and university departments. With the emergence of electronic media and internet, training in journalism has gone tremendous changes. Now we have many institutions, training our journalists with latest techniques. Here in this article we have tried to delineate the history of journalism education in India.

The interest in journalism education, is related to the great need for education of all kinds. The yen for schooling in more orthodox subjects has spread even to the relatively new area of journalism.

But it is an interest that hardly is novel, for there has been a University Department of Journalism in India since 1941 and three other recognized institutions of higher learning have had courses since 1947 or 1950. Several more had offered instruction from time to time earlier but they failed.

Journalistic education has not developed in India much beyond the stage it reached in pioneering countries a half century ago. Then in the U. S. A. particularly a few universities offered courses whose merits were debated, with journalists generally sceptical. Now in India similar scepticism exists but the point of argument is not so much whether training is valuable as what form it shall take. Indian journalists have been influenced by British journalism to be uncertain about a plan that integrates journalistic education with standard college study. When the system is explained, opponents shift to the position that while it no doubt is effective and even necessary in a country like the U.S.A., in India it can be neither of these because of language difficulties, a smaller press, a generally lower economic level that makes journalism a less desirable occupation than it has become in the states, and a high illiteracy rate.

Instruction Development

In modern sense, India's first journalistic instruction at the modern university level probably was that offered in 1938 at Aligarh Muslim University, a diploma course. The class was begun that year by the late Sir Shah Muhammad Sulaiman, judge of the Federal Court of India.

Rahm Ali Alhashmi was in charge of the class, who brought experience in both English and Urdu journalism as his background for the post he held as lecturer. He arranged for professionals to lecture on various phases of journalism and took students on visits to newspaper offices. After the death in 1940 of Sir Shah Sulaiman, the teacher in charge resigned "on account of some differences with the authorities." and the course was abolished.

The country's first continuing professional journalism instruction was established in 1941 at the University of the Punjab at Lahore. A department was set up by a University of Missouri graduate in journalism, P.P. Singh, who had worked for International News Service and on *The Pioneer* and other Indian papers. About thirty students received diplomas in journalism each year until 1947, when partition divided the university and with it the department of journalism. Among the university staff which fled to the Indian side of the border was Professor Singh, who set up a new department in New Delhi. The original one continued in Pakistan, headed by a graduate.

The refugee institution, Panjab University, has continued to turn out from 30 to 70 graduates of its diploma course yearly. Under Professor Singh, while the department was at New Delhi and in spite of inadequate facilities, excellent relationships have been maintained with the New Delhi press, some of whose staff members have served on the faculty as lecturers. The Punjab graduates have found places on the papers and magazines of New Delhi and other areas, although as with all other journalism education institutions in India, some have not entered journalism at all.

The Punjab department, moved in 1962 to the university's new site in Chandigarh, offers courses in reporting, sub-editing, editorial writing, article writing, make-up and typography, law, sports, and advertising. Open only to college graduates, the course uses laboratory, discussion, and lecture methods of instruction. A well-printed and illustrated tabloid-size experimental laboratory paper, *Puja Chronicle,* is issued at intervals, Professor Singh directing the student staff.

The Madras Course

The University of Madras opened its course in 1947. It consists chiefly of a series of lectures by Madras journalists. Together they teach as examination subjects an omnibus course called "journalism", which embraces reporting, copy-editing, magazine features, and editorial methods and techniques, as well as separate classes in history of freedom of the press, ethics of journalism, composition, precis writing, and proof correction. Radio news editing and broadcasting is a non-examination subject. Also given are special lectures in shorthand and typing. The lecture method is the principal means of instruction. A diploma is granted; twelve students are accepted annually, and three or four complete the work each year.

The Calcutta Course

In 1950, the University of Calcutta opened the only two-year course to date: a diploma programme offering not only practical journalistic instruction but also insisting upon further study of such background subjects as Constitutional Law and political, sociological, and economic developments. Optional is study of literature and art and scientific and cultural trends. Strictly journalistic subjects are principles and history of journalism, the making of a journal, business and journalism, commercial journalism, sports, stage and screen, art of advertisement and layout, editing of monthlies and periodicals, press and production, and an internship in which the important Calcutta press co-operates. Local newsmen handle the subjects, which are administered by a standing committee. Fifty-five students were in the first class, which was reduced to about 25 by the end of the first full course.

Because it insists upon proper backgrounding in certain non-journalistic subjects, the Calcutta course in one respect is the soundest of all. Applicants for studies in journalism come from various Indian universities and bring differing amounts of study, if any, in such subjects as Constitutional Law, Sociology, Politics, Literature, and Art. The men in charge of the Calcutta programme, who include some of the leading editors of the past and present, anticipated this uneven background in studies all journalists require, and have required two years of work for the diploma, daring which deficiencies are met. This policy was adopted in face of certain knowledge that the mortality in enrolment would be great as a result, which it was.

Another way in which the Calcutta plan is superior to all others is the insistence that every person earning the diploma first have assurance of a position in journalism. This plan is a defence against the wasted training which occurs so often unless there is implementation of the sort. Calcutta insists upon an internship period, which the students must arrange for themselves.

Admission regulations are somewhat more liberal than might be expected considering the other requirements. The prospectus declares:

> Graduates of the Calcutta University or of any recognized University and those who have passed the Intermediate Examination of the Calcutta University or of any recognized University and have at least one year's experience in a Newspaper, Periodical or News Agency office will be eligible for admission to the course.

The Mysore Course

In 1951 the University of Mysore, through Maharajah's College in Mysore City, introduced three journalism subjects in its Bachelor of Arts programme: history and survey of journalism, journalistic practice, and newspaper administration. This plan, although now altered, was such a variation from those at other universities, since it was in the undergraduate programme, that it is worth special attention.

"Our aim," Dr. B.L. Manjunath, the Vice-Chancellor, explained when the programme was under reconsideration, "is to teach Journalism as a subject of general studies as one of the three subjects required for the B.A. degree. The objective has been more to introduce students to journalism than to train them as professional journalists."

An English teacher, a teacher of history, and a professional journalist combined their efforts to develop this plan, which at first was headed by Prof. O.K. Nambiar, of the Mysore English department. In 1953 instruction was turned over to a professional journalist, N. Krishna Murthy, who like Professor Singh of the Punjab University department received his journalistic education at the University of Missouri in the U.S.A. Enrolment was set at about twenty ; a small collection of journalism books was obtained and a practice paper issued. For a time interest in the programme lapsed but in 1959 it was strengthened and by 1962 a 3-year plan was in operation, the only degree course available in India.

The Hislop Programme

A diploma-certificate programme in journalism for Hislop College, a 1,100-student liberal arts institution affiliated with Nagpur University, was requested by a university committee in 1946 but did not materialize until 1952. It differs in several ways from the programmes at other universities. For the present it is a one-year diploma programme also offering a certificate to experienced journalists without college education. Diploma candidates must have completed their undergraduate study creditably and certificate seekers must have demonstrated journalistic ability.

This liberal admission attitude is one innovation. Another is the reliance not only on internship, lectures, and laboratory but also on project methods and greater class participation. A third is the offering, in addition to the standard courses—news writing and reporting, radio journalism, editing, article and feature writing, an internship, introduction to journalism, fundamentals of writing, business and law of journalism, seminar in journalism research— with current events and shorthand and typing as extras—of one never before available in India and probably nowhere else. It is study of and practice in the preparation of written materials for use in social education work.

The Hislop students, about twenty a year, work on the Nagpur newspapers for practice and also produce their own printed fortnightly newspaper, a tabloid-sized publication for the whole college called *The Hislop Herald.* In recent years the department also has published an annual, *The Hislop Journalist,* with general articles on journalism in India. In addition the students go on a tour of the major main communication centres and visit leading publications and meet prominent Indian journalists and civic leaders. Hislop, as are several other institutions, contemplates a postgraduate programme that will lead to a master's degree in journalism.

OTHER COURSES

In 1954 a course was established at Osmania University, offering classes in journalistic practice somewhat like the programme at Hislop. This was under the direction of the late Dr. Deforest O'Dell, It has since undergone various changes, and in 1961 was put in the charge of an experienced Indian journalist.

Several other programmes, not related to educational institutions, have been available. Some have been correspondence courses, others private institutions, such as the Horniman School of Journalism in Bombay, and more recently the Bombay College of Journalism.

This latter college has received more professional support

than such private institutions usually command and even more than some of the academically sanctioned programmes. Begun in 1960, its sponsor is the Hyderabad (Sind) National Collegiate Board, which conducts arts colleges, a science college, a law, and a commerce college, all affiliated to Bombay University. The College of Journalism had not received such affiliation by 1962.

Open to college graduates only, it accepts about sixty students, all non-professionals, and offers a diploma. The teachers are mainly people experienced in various aspects of journalism, supplemented by lecturers from advertising agencies and public information offices, and publication executives. Three months practical training is provided for each student. Because of the close relationship to the Bombay publishing industry its graduates find places of employment with no more difficulty than those who attend university classes.

Another Bombay institution, the College of Journalism, Advertising and Printing, was established in 1961, Sponsored by, the Bharatiya Vidya Bhavan, it offers three separate series of courses each two years long, in journalism, advertising, sales promotion and public relations, and printing.

National Organisation

Journalism education in India received national impetus from the encouragement of the Press Commission. Although it had been suggested earlier by some of the professors, formal organization of a national association of teachers of the subject was speeded by the attention to training from the Commission. The Indian Association of Education in Journalism was founded in Calcutta in 1956. The pioneers in its establishment were Professor Singh, the first president ; Dr. D.N. Sen of Calcutta University ; Prof. Everton Conger, then department head at Hislop, and Dr. O' Dell.

The association's aim is to develop co-operation between departments and the profession and to maintain high standards in journalism education. It has served as a means to generate government interest in training fur journalism and as a forum for exchange of ideas and discussion of mutual problems. It has sent delegates to both national and international journalism and journalism education meetings.

A South and East Asia Association of Journalism Educators was formed in 1961 during a UNESCO sponsored seminar on journalism training methods held in the Philippines.

Press Commission on Training

The Press Commission, in its report made in 1954, noted that, "There is no well-defined system of recruitment to the editorial staff of newspapers," and said that the recruiting is done "in a haphazard fashion." The report went on to observe that whereas there is much human material available to meet the needs of the profession of journalism, "it has to be educated and trained along proper lines. At present, the educational standard and intellectual equipment of some of the journalists who have entered the profession has been woefully unsatisfactory."

Higher standards should be maintained in the schools and colleges, the report said. "It should be possible for our school and University authorities to have a course in world affairs, essay-writing and precis-writing not merely as a special qualification for those who want to enter journalism, but as an integral part of a sound and liberal education."

The report then discussed journalism education directly. "It is too early at present to insist that the new entrants to journalism should be persons who have obtained a journalistic qualification either by way of a degree or a diploma," its authors said. They then examined the university courses available.

"On the whole," they wrote, "it seems to us that the list of subjects laid down for study in most of the Universities is generally satisfactory but the time allotted for the study of these subjects is quite insufficient."

Recommended was a diploma or degree course at the postgraduate level, of 2-years' duration ; there was objection to journalism being taught at the under-graduate level. Urged was practical training in newspaper offices as an internship and the publication by the journalism students of campus newspapers "as is done in the American universities".

A further recommendation was the setting up, by the Press Council, of an Institute of Journalism "which can keep a watch on the methods of training in the University and also conduct refresher courses." The Institute might also carry out research "into the problems of the profession and if necessary conduct institutions of its own for training in journalism."

In answer to the point sometimes made that journalism education would put too many persons on the market, the report lists some of the various places of employment and concludes: "We estimate that the output of such trained graduates should not normally exceed about 300 a year during the course of the next ten years, if we are to avoid the risk of unemployment and the consequent hardship to these graduates."

Except that they were encouraging to the universities already teaching journalism and to those considering such a programme, the Press Commission findings had not, eight years after the Report's publication, come to any concrete results. But the *Report* contains a brief outline of what might develop and gave support to the heads of departments at Punjab and Nagpur with their practice of directing students in the publication of experimental newspapers and the operation of internships, although these were in operation before the Press Commission's Report was written.

In 1959 a commission was set up by the Inter-University Board for Education in Journalism. Beginning in the early 1960'$, the University Grants Commission took interest in journalism education by promising support for new plans for the expansion of certain programmes.

While in some parts of India working journalists, especially those who have reached positions of influence without benefit of college training, provide some obstacles of a negative type, such as refusal to let students come into their office;; for practice work ; the academic world has set up barriers also.

In addition to the usual one of disbelief in the idea of professional training at the university level, which exists in some Indian academic circles, is insistence that journalism, like non-technical subjects, can be learned largely through memorizing prescribed textbooks and listening to lectures. An almost uncanny repetition of the early U.S. experience is the academic view that journalism needs little special equipment; in the few courses offered, therefore, only the minimum is provided.

Usually typewriters are not provided, nor typographic laboratories or other such necessities. The teachers must make do with the help of the local press and by inducing students to obtain their own writing machines, cameras, and other equipment, if possible. A university may induce wealthy industrialists to provide many lakhs of rupees for medical or science colleges but make no attempt to interest a newspaper proprietor in financing a first-rate journalistic plant. This is indicative of the requirements of the press as understood by the academic mind. There is little realization of the talent and skill needed to do a good journalistic job because good jobs are done often enough.

Textbooks

From the foregoing the textbook situation may be imagined. Not a half-dozen textbooks on journalistic practice in India have been published, in any language. The few that exist are usually little more than pamphlets, in the vernacular languages (and therefore not widely usable), and, moreover, generally are out of print. In fact, the total number of books dealing with Indian Journalism is under a hundred. These are either historical, autobiographical, reminiscent, or discussional. Their subjects more often than not, are freedom of the press or the press and political affairs.

British and American texts are respected and used if any can be. But in most instances students are prohibited from buying their own texts by the cost of these imported volumes. One or two are prescribed for each courses and others recommended are read in the libraries. An American text of the type used commonly in U.S. schools of journalism costs a sum equal to one-fourth the year's tuition. Texts do not often find their way into the professional newsroom as they do sometimes in other countries. Most practising journalists are unacquainted with the scant literature of Indian journalism and have only slight knowledge of that of other countries.

Few books on journalism are in either university or public libraries; it is easier to find such literature in the United States Information Service libraries than elsewhere. This is explained by the fact that there are approximately 4,000 volumes on the journalism and journalists of the U.S.A. and education in this subject is an established programme. Perhaps the largest single collection on the journalism of India, the U.S.A., and the U.K. is held by the libraries of Hislop College and Nagpur University, which between them possess about 700 volumes, the majority of them published in the past two decades.

To make up for the lack of textbooks, the Indian Association of Education in Journalism planned in 1960 a series of volumes for university use, to be written by the various teachers. At this writing these were still in production.

Attitude of the Profession

The attitude towards journalistic education of the professional journalistic world, as already noted, is somewhat like that existing in the United States early in the century, except that the sceptics are disconcerted by the success of the idea in the U.S.A. This might be summarized to range from outright antagonism (a minority view) through indifference (a majority attitude) to enthusiasm (a minority position). One antagonist was a practising newsman who had written a short book on journalism. He included a brief chapter attacking the idea of teaching journalism in a university, declaring that American journalistic schools are possible only because they are subsidized by millionaires. When he heard of the new department to be opened at Nagpur, however, he sent copies of his little book to three officials .suggesting its adoption as a text.

A more typical attitude, perhaps, was that of an Indian journalist who in 1959 made the categorical statement: "Great and renowned journalists of any country are not products of any university." It was not difficult to point out that certain of the leading journalists of the U.S.A. are not only products of a university but of the school of journalism at that university as well.

The indifferent are open to persuasion. Among the enthusiasts are certain officers and members of the national press associations, such as the All India Newspaper Editors'

Conference and the-Indian Federation of Working Journalists, as well as regional groups like the large Southern India Journalists' Federation. The AINEC, with about 200 members, appointed a committee in 1949 consisting of three Nagpur journalists "to prepare a scheme for the establishment of an All India Institute of Journalism for giving higher training to journalists and ... to submit its report to the Standing Committee within three months."

The proposed institute would be governed by representatives of the Ministry of Education of India, the AINEC, and other recognized journalists' associations. Five years' practical experience and two-years' college education are to be prerequisites of admission. The Central and State Governments would finance the plan, with some aid from AINEC. English and Hindi would be the media of instruction.

The suggested syllabus covers courses in news reporting and writing, news editing, editorial writing, public opinion and propaganda, pictorial journalism, ethics of journalism, law of journalism, the graphic arts, shorthand and typewriting, and some background work in economics, politics, civics, and history.

AINEC members would be expected to co-operate on an internship or practical training plan; laboratories would be set up for certain courses.

The report, on which no action has as yet been taken, ends on a hopeful note not often heard in writings about Indian journalism:

> "With democracy, adult franchise and increasing literacy there is great scope for the development of newspapers which will need trained personnel in increasing number."

If the few departments and courses did a better job of promotion there would be less indifference or opposition to them. Journalists in India rarely know the extent of journalistic education in their country. An example of the damage that ignorance can do is an article printed in April, 1952, in the *Hindustan Times* of Delhi which declared that the Punjab department was unsuccessful because the press never hired any of its diploma holders.

Professor Singh, although he had published the facts in his catalogue, forthwith listed a host of press people who are his graduates, including some on the staff of the *Times* itself.

What are the answers to sceptics who say that university education in journalism works well in the United States or other countries but will not function in India ?

To begin with, the Indian journalists or educators who take this view are discovered, usually, to know almost nothing about what has been done in their own country in this area of study and to have only the barest understanding of what has taken place elsewhere in the world. At best they conceive of a school of journalism as no more than a trade school. They know nothing of the research aspects, the opportunities for self-expression, the chance to orient the student, the teaching of responsibility and proper use of communications media, and the possibilities of making the whole educational experience more meaningful and more interesting to the student.

Nevertheless the opponent's arguments are not all pointless. His strongest is the existence of language difficulties. Hindi is gradually is displacing English in education, government, and business. Yet it will be many years before most of India's people can use it in addition to their regional language. D.R. Mankekar, while editor of the Delhi edition of *The Times of India* and a friend of journalistic education, nevertheless had to tell the Punjab students of journalism that "...when one talks of the future of Indian journalism one does not mean English language journalism. For all the good and noble work it has done, English journalism is doomed. The future is all with Indian language journalism, and particularly with Hindi journalism. In fifty years' time, perhaps, when Hindi has sufficiently developed as the all-India language, our dreams of six-digit circulations for Indian newspapers might at last be realized."

It is true that the student who is taught his basic journalistic techniques in college can learn them most readily if universities in all the provinces or linguistic areas offer such work. A programme entirely in English or any one other language for the present is handicapped by being unable to accept brilliant students with insufficient mastery of English or another language not their mother-tongue and by being unable to help place graduates in journalistic occupations requiring excellent command of some regional language unknown to them. A Malayali, for instance, cannot serve out his full internship in Nagpur or New Delhi because there are no publications in his language in these cities. This is a real difficulty but it is not insurmountable, inasmuch as regional departments can be set up and run by experienced journalists in at least the major languages.

E. B. Brook, while news editor of India's only remaining important British-owned daily. *The Statesman* of Calcutta and New Delhi, expressed a second objection from the field when he said: "I am afraid the principal problem will be for those who have been educated in journalism to find adequate employment."

His ground for this statement is his knowledge that India has only about 8,500 newspapers and magazines of all types and in all languages and that many are one-man jobs. However, he overlooks All India Radio, with its nearly three dozen stations, whose news coverage increases constantly; the mounting number of trade journals and other specialized periodicals; the developing public relations and publicity business the news agents the new field of preparation of journalistic materials for adults just become literate; and numerous non-journalistic areas where the journalist's skills are needed.

A third contention is less easily dealt with: the relatively low pay scale, poor working conditions, and lack of future for practising journalists which are real conditions in the newspaper and magazine worlds. U. Bhaskar Rao, when editor of the *Indian Express,* Delhi, told Punjab students not to look forward to "a life of ease and luxury. The work is tough, the spiritual rewards are very satisfying, but alas there is not much monetary reward in this profession. It will be a life of struggle, asceticism, in some cases of downright poverty."

But for many talented and ambitious people such circumstances are not insurmountable barriers. These people will put up with almost any hardships for the sake of remaining in their chosen field of journalism. And there are signs that conditions are being bettered. The rank and file newsmen have solidified their ranks slightly more and formed the Indian Federation of Working Journalists; numerous regional groups have been organized as a consequence. These organizations are asking for training. Furthermore, the era of unquestioning acceptance of policies and action of the Congress Party, which led India to freedom, is over and this group, now in the seat of government, is being pressed for stronger social reforms, certain of which will benefit the Indian journalist.

The Future

When, as the late Devadas Gandhi, managing editor of the *Hindustan Times,* pointed out in several speeches and articles, the rate of illiteracy decreases sufficiently and newsprint once again is available in adequate quantities, there will be a growing demand for publications in India. The number of papers and magazines will increase still more rapidly, and the circulations will mount swiftly. He anticipates a flood that must be met, when the time comes with many well-prepared publications These will need trained personnel in abundance.

India's present four or live departments and courses obviously will be totally inadequate to the situation. They will be insufficient not only because the future demands for staff will be great but also because the spread of Hindi and the necessity for knowledge by most journalists of at least two languages will further complicate the problem.

This country, it would seem, should plan for 25 schools and departments of journalism connected with universities in all the principal linguistic areas of the nation. Hindi, Marathi, Urdu, Bengali, Malayalam, Gujerati, Telugu and Tamil journalisms, for example, are so strong and well-developed that they will continue to exist for many years within India. University study of journalism in Hindi or English, while it will help greatly in preparing journalists for necessary service, will not be as valuable for the time being as study in the student's mother-tongue.

An instance supporting this contention occurred at Hislop College. Long before coming to India, I searched for a history of India's press. The best one I could find was Margarita Barns' *The Indian Press,* which is not satisfactory, because it carries only through the 1930's and because it deals, as do most studies of India's press history, primarily with the conflicts between the press and the government. It ignores most of the important technical and professional developments.

One day, however, the college librarian came upon what appears to be a much more useful book for general study of the role the press plays in India, *History of*

Newspapers, by V.K. Joshi and R.K. Lele, published in 1951 in Bombay. But it is in Marathi — and was, therefore, unreadable not only for the American faculty members of the Department of Journalism of Hislop, but also for more than half of the students in their classes, who come from various states. At Punjab, Calcutta, and Madras, the students of journalism would be under even greater handicap in using this volume.

The suggested 25 schools and departments should be organized with co-operation between universities, colleges, governments (state and central), and journalists' organizations. They are necessary and feasible, because literacy is increasing, newsprint supplies are returning to normal, India's journalistic organizations are becoming stronger and more nearly national in scope, and teaching personnel is available.

Just as has happened in my own country, the United States, the existence of sound schools and departments of journalism will help improve the standards of the press, better the working conditions for journalists, and enrich the educational background of students, professional journalists and readers.

What should these schools and departments teach ? Here there are legitimate differences of opinion among teachers of journalism and practising journalists who do acknowledge the need for university training.

Thus, far, the courses offered in India have been of two kinds. One emphasizes technical preparation (Punjab and Nagpur) easily within reach of all. Such a graduate programme would work out variously depending upon the student's background. The other stresses along with journalism such general studies as law, history and economics (Madras and Calcutta). Neither is sufficient for India's needs, present and future, for under both these plans the student receives inadequate technical training and usually does not master the general subjects required by the journalist.

It is possible for Indian students to obtain their B.A. without studying political science, psychology, or sociology, all of which are essential for proper preparation for modern journalism, especially in this country where social development is dynamic. In their journalistic education they are able to obtain a diploma without studying more than superficially, if at all, the business side of journalism.

Little, if any practical instruction is given in printing and typography, press photography, radio and television journalism, specialized journalism, and journalistic and communications research. Although almost all courses at present are at the post-graduate level, few are of graduate calibre. On this basis journalistic instruction in India cannot acquire depth.

Journalistic instruction at its best should begin not later than the first or second year of undergraduate college work.

This does not mean that students should take nothing but classes in journalism for four years. What it does mean is this: they study for their B.A. as visual, but their B.A. programme is carefully planned to give them the broad general education necessary in all walks of life, plus selected courses in journalism, taken one or two at a time each year for the four undergraduate-years. A student's time might be divided thus:

First year: Language, natural sciences, mathematics, social sciences and an introductory course in journalism (the latter might be one pre-professional class meeting once or twice a week during the year).

Second year: Continuation of the general studies, including economics, history, and other social studies, more language, art, science etc., plus a course in news reporting and writing (not as handled by the newspaper alone) and one in printing and typography for the journalist.

Third year: Further general studies, with municipal organization, government, and constitutional law, (imperative), plus technical and non-technical courses in editing, article writing, history, ethics, and problems of journalism. Press photography, radio-television journalism and a few free-choice subjects.

Fourth year: Completion of the general studies; to which are added courses in press law, specialized journalism, business aspects of journalism, and contemporary affairs.

Not more than 25 per cent of the courses should deal with journalism, so that the student is sure to study all basic general educational subjects. Mastery of shorthand and typewriting would be essential as a technical subject to be completed privately. A period of practical experience would be included.

This course of study would lead to a new degree for India: a Bachelor of Arts in Journalism, or to a simple Bachelor of Arts with journalism and some social study as the principal concentration of courses.

Students with either degree, as well as regular college-degree-holding professionals who wish advanced training would be eligible then for genuine graduate work, which might be offered at a selected few of the 25 universities offering undergraduate journalism. These institutions should be well distributed graphically so as to be easily within reach of all. Such a graduate programme would work but variously depending upon the student's background.

Graduates of schools and departments of journalism would spend from one to two years taking advanced study in the various phases of journalism already begun in their undergraduate days. They might concentrate on magazine journalism, newspaper journalism, on the business aspects, or on research phases. Those who undertake to write a thesis as part of their work would need two years and would receive a master's degree that reflects such effort. The non-research degree might be called Master of Arts in Journalism; the research degree Master of Science in Journalism.

Graduates of recognized universities who did not study journalism while at college would spend from two to three years taking similar advanced courses. If they lacked the proper study of government, law, history, economics, sociology, or other subjects already indicated, they would require two or three years to obtain the master's degree, depending upon whether they produced a thesis.

Graduates of recognized universities who did not study journalism but have had at least five years of professional experience in the field on accepted publications and in areas related to journalism would obtain the master's degree in from one to two years. The time would depend upon their general study and upon how much of their professional work could be accepted in lieu of classes (to be determined by examinations of a practical nature).

By the time such programmes can be developed, it is assumed that Hindi will have become more nearly India's national language and advanced instruction in that medium will be feasible.

All this, of course, presumes adequate staff and equipment. These schools, therefore, should be associated with universities in the biggest cities or in cities where the fields of journalism, printing and broadcasting have been highly developed, so as to provide living laboratories.

An estimate of the annual cost of operation of an average undergraduate school of journalism would reach

Rs. 1,50,000. This sum would be needed for four or five full-time teachers, several part-time lecturers from the field, maintenance of a small professional library, purchase of supplies, and other basic costs.

REFERENCES

1. Report of the Press Commission, pp. 483-85.
2. Umrigar, K.D., *Lest I Forget,* Popular Book Depot, Bombay, 1949.
3. Report of the Sub-Ccmmittee on Establishment of an All India Institute of Journalism, All India Newspaper Editors' Conference, 1949.
4. D.R. Mankekar, "Post Independence Trends in Indian Journalism." Report of his presidential address on the occasion of the Fourth Journalism Day Conference of the Punjab University Department of Journalism, New Delhi, 14 July 1950.
5. Letter to the author, 18 April 1952.
6. U. Bhaskar Rao, "Inaugural Address," delivered at the Fourth Journalism Day Conference of the Punjab University Department of Journalism, New Delhi, 14 July 1952.

[*Courtesy:* Ronald E. Wolseley]

6

The Elements of Journalism

> We need all the technical training we can lay hold of. But let us not mistake qualification for ability; it is the use of a tool rather than the possession of it which get a job done.
>
> —*Vincent Taylor*

As anthropologists began comparing notes on the world's few remaining primitive cultures, they discovered something unexpected. From the most isolated tribal societies in Africa to the most distant islands in the Pacific, people shared essentially the same definition of what is news. They shared the same kind of gossip. They even looked for the same qualities in the messengers they picked to gather and deliver their news. They wanted people who could run swiftly over the next hill, accurately gather information, and engagingly retell it. Historians have pieced together that the same basic news values have held constant through time. "Humans have exchanged a similar mix of news . . . throughout history and across cultures," (Mitchell Stephens).

How do we explain the mystery of this consistency? The answer, historians and sociologists have concluded, is that news satisfies a basic human impulse. People have an intrinsic need — an instinct — to know what is occurring beyond their direct experience. Being aware of events we cannot see for ourselves engenders a sense of security, control, and confidence. Mitchell Stephens has called it "a hunger for human awareness."

One of the first things people do when meeting a friend or acquaintance is share information. "Have you heard about . . . ?" We want to know if they've heard what we have, and if they heard it the same way. There is a thrill in a shared sense of discovery. We form relationships, choose friends, make character judgments, based partly on whether someone reacts to information the same way we do.

When the flow of news is obstructed, "a darkness falls," and anxiety grows. The world, in effect, becomes too quiet. We feel alone. John McCain, the U.S. senator from Arizona, writes that in his five and a half years as a prisoner of war in Hanoi, what he missed most was not comfort, food, freedom, or even his family and friends. "The thing I missed most was information — free uncensored, undistorted, abundant information."

Awareness Instinct

Fundamentally, we need news to live our lives, to protect ourselves, bond with each other, identify friends and enemies. Journalism is simply the system societies generate to supply this news. That is why we care about the character of news and journalism we get: they influence the quality of our lives, our thoughts, and our culture. Writer Thomas Cahill, the author of several popular books on the history of religion, has put it this way: you can tell "the worldview of a people . . . the invisible fears and desires . . . in a culture's stories."

At a moment of revolution in communications, what do the stories we tell say about our worldview, our fears, desires, and values?

The public, in turn, increasingly distrusted journalists, even hated them. And it would only get worse. By 1999, just 21% of Americans would think the press cared about people, down from 41% in 1985. Only 58% would respect the press's watchdog role, a drop from 67% in 1985. Less than half, just 45%, would think the press protected democracy. That percentage had been nearly ten points higher in 1985.

"In the newsroom we no longer talk about journalism," said Max King, then editor of the Philadelphia Inquirer. "We are consumed with business pressure and the bottom line," agreed another editor. News was becoming entertainment and entertainment news. Journalists' bonuses were increasingly tied to the company's profit margins, not the quality of their work. Finally, Columbia University professor James Carey offered what many recalled as a summation: "The problem is that you see journalism disappearing inside the larger world of communications. What you yearn to do is recover journalism from that larger world."

Implied in that was something more important. If journalism — the system by which we get our news — was being subsumed, what would replace it? Advertising? Entertainment? E-commerce? Propaganda? Some new hybrid of all these? And what would the consequence be?

The answers matter, the group thought, to the public and news-people both. Journalism provides something unique to a culture — independent, reliable, accurate, and comprehensive information that citizens require to be free. A journalism that is asked to provide something other than that subverts democratic culture. This is what happens when governments control the news, as in Nazi Germany or the Soviet Union. We're seeing it again in places like Singapore, where news is controlled to encourage capitalism but discourage participation in public life. Something akin to this may be taking root in the United States in a more purely commercial form, as when news outlets owned by larger corporations are used to promote their conglomerate parent's products, to engage in subtle lobbying or corporate rivalry, or are intermingled with advertising to boost profits. The issue isn't just the loss of journalism. At stake is whether, as citizens, we have access to independent information that makes it possible for us to take part in governing ourselves.

Now a plan engage journalists and the public in a careful examination of what journalism was supposed to be. We set out to answer two questions. If newspeople thought journalism was somehow different from other forms of communication, how was it different? If they thought journalism needed to change but that some core principles needed to endure, what were those principles?

We learned, among other things, that society expects journalists to apply this theory, and citizens to understand it, though it is seldom studied or clearly articulated. This lack of clarity, for both citizens and newspeople, has weakened journalism and is now weakening democratic society. Unless we can grasp and reclaim the theory of a free press, journalists risk allowing their profession to disappear. In that sense, the crisis of our culture, and our journalism, is a crisis of conviction.

There are, we have distilled from our search, some clear principles that journalists agree on — and that citizens have a right to expect. They are principles that have ebbed and flowed over time, but they have always in some manner been evident. They are the elements of journalism.

The first among them is that the purpose of journalism is to provide people with the information they need to be free and self-governing.

To fulfill this task:

- Journalism's first obligation is to the truth.
- Its first loyalty is to citizens.
- Its essence is a discipline of verification.

- Its practitioners must maintain an independence from those they cover.
- It must serve as an independent monitor of power.
- It must provide a forum for public criticism and compromise.
- It must strive to make the significant interesting and relevant.
- It must keep the news comprehensive and proportional.
- Its practitioners must be allowed to exercise their personal conscience.

Why these nine? Some readers will think items are missing here. Where is fairness? Where is balance? After synthesizing what we learned, it became clear that a number of familiar and even useful ideas — including fairness and balance — are too vague to rise to the level of essential elements of the profession. Others may say this list is nothing new. To the contrary, we discovered that many ideas about the elements of journalism are wrapped in myth and misconception. The notion that journalists should be protected by a wall between business and news is one myth. That independence requires journalists be neutral is another. The concept of objectivity has been so mangled it now is usually used to describe the very problem it was conceived to correct. It has happened each time there is a period of significant, social, economic, and technological change. It occurred in the 1830s and 1840s with the arrival of the telegraph, in the 1880s with the drop in prices of paper and the influx of immigrants. It occurred again in the 1920s with the invention of radio and the rise of the tabloids and the culture of gossip and celebrity. And it occurred with the invention of television and the arrival of the Cold War.

It is occurring now with the advent of cable followed by the Internet. The collision this time may be more dramatic.

For the first time in our history, the news increasingly is produced by companies outside journalism, and this new economic organization is important. We are facing the possibility that independent news will be replaced by self-interested commercialism posing as news. If that occurs, we will lose the press as an independent institution, free to monitor the other powerful forces and institutions in society.

In the new century, one of the most profound questions for democratic society is whether an independent press survives. The answer will depend on whether journalists have the clarity and conviction to articulate what an independent press means, and whether, as citizens, the rest of us care.

REFERENCES

1. Mitchell Stephens, *History of News: From the Drum to the Satellite* (New York: Viking Press, 1988), 34.
2. Harvey Molotch and Marilyn Lester, "News as Purposive Behavior: On the Strategic Use of Routine Events, Accidents and Scandal," *American Sociological Review*, 39, February 1974, 101-112.
3. John McCain, with Mark Salter, Faith of My Fathers (New York: Random House, 1999), 221.
4. Thomas Cahill, The Gift of the Jews: How a Tribe of Desert Nomads Changed the Way Everyone Thinks and Feels (New York: Nan A. Talese/Anchor Books, 1998), 17.

7

Journalism: Views on Performance

> Wickedness is a myth invented by good people to account for the curious attractiveness of others..
>
> —*Oscar Wilde*

The overall quality of news coverage — including issues ranging from decreased accuracy to increased sensationalism — remains the most important problem area in journalism today, according to the press. But its relative seriousness has plummeted compared to the loss of credibility with the public.

On being questioned the validity of various criticisms of the press, a significant minority of the news media agree that news reports are increasingly full of factual errors and that too little attention is paid to correcting mistakes. Further, large majorities in the business say the line between reporting and commentary has blurred, as has the line between entertainment and news. The latter problem is particularly troubling to reporters and editors in the newsroom.

"People don't trust us the way they used to, and they have good reason not to," says a local television news assignment editor. "A lot of stuff now is slanted toward sensationalism."

Standards

When asked to describe in their own words the most

important problem confronting journalism today, half of journalists and news media executives mention issues related to quality, such as sloppy reporting, an erosion of standards and the trend toward sensationalism. While news quality remains the top concern, it no longer dominates as it did a decade ago when an overwhelming 70% in the news media said it was the most important problem facing the profession.

Today, growing numbers of the news media say that business and financial pressure is the most important problem confronting journalism: 40% in national markets and 37% in local, compared to 31% overall in 1989.

Looking at problems in journalism thematically, loss of credibility continues to rank third. But concern about it has almost doubled over the past 10 years, and it is the single problem most often cited by the press. Roughly one-in-three members of the national and local media now say that a decline in public trust, confidence and credibility is the most important problem facing journalism; 17% said this in 1989.

> "Journalists are down among used car salesmen in credibility," says a network news producer.

The print media are particularly concerned about the public's attitude towards the press. More than four-in-ten print journalists and executives cite this as a major problem for journalism, compared to roughly 20% of those in television news. By contrast, more of those working in television than in print feel that the quality of news coverage is the most important problem facing journalism today.

Although younger members of the news media agree with their older colleagues' concerns about the quality of reporting and economic pressures, fewer of those under the age of 35 mention problems associated with credibility than do those 55 and older (19% vs. 43%, respectively).

Criticisms of the Press

Overall, journalists and news media executives see plenty of room for improvement in the press. More than two-in-three agree that charges of paying too little attention to complex issues and the mixing of commentary and reporting are valid criticisms. More than half of the news media agree that journalists are too focused on internal dynamics (like getting the story first), out of touch with their audiences and too cynical.

This disconnect is obvious to Americans: two-thirds of them say the press doesn't care about the people it covers.

Compared to 1995, more journalists and news media executives believe that the distinction between reporting and commentary has seriously eroded (69% of the national news media and 68% of local media agree that this is a valid criticism, compared to 53% and 44%, respectively, in 1995).

> "I'm concerned about the blurring of the lines between the kind of-fact-based journalism that I grew up with — and which I hope to continue to practice — and the proliferation of celebrity pundits who are constantly barraging the public with views that aren't fact-based," says a reporter for a national newspaper.

Similarly, the number who agree with the charge that news reports are increasingly full of errors is up in the national media to 40% from 30%, and up to 55% from 40% in the local media. Those in local television are even more critical of the inaccuracy of news reports: 62% say it is a valid criticism.

Americans agree that the press is sloppy: 58% say news stories and reports are often inaccurate, a jump from 34% in 1985.

On the upside, fewer members of the news media today believe that the press fails to cover positive developments adequately than they did in 1995 (down to 49% from 58% in the national media, and to 44% from 51% in the local markets). The Internet news media are particularly positive in this regard, with only one-in-three agreeing with the charge. The African-American journalists and executives surveyed, however, say just the opposite, with a 78% majority agreeing that positive developments are under-reported.

Entertainment vs. Hard News

The news media are also concerned that pressure to attract audiences is pushing their industry too far in the direction of infotainment. Two-thirds of those in national, local and Internet news say that efforts to attract readers or viewers take them too far in this direction. This criticism is especially strong among news staff members: Three-quarters of those in local and national news markets say this is so — a significantly larger number than the 57% of national executives and 54% of local executives who agree.

> "Journalists feel the need to entertain people as opposed to the need to inform them," says a sports reporter for a national newspaper.

When it comes to covering complicated stories, the news media generally agree that television faces greater obstacles than print. Solid majorities of top brass, middle management and newsroom staff acknowledge at least a fair amount of difficulty inherent in television news' attempts to inform the public about complicated topics. There is little consensus among the different media about the extent of this challenge, however.

About six-in-ten of those in the print press say that it is very difficult for television to cover complicated news stories, but less than one-third of those in television agree. Instead, most in television news say that this is fairly difficult for them to do. The Internet press falls in between these other two, with 51% saying very difficult and 39% saying fairly difficult.

The Watchdog Role

A narrow majority of journalists and news media executives now believe that by covering the personal and ethical behavior of public figures, news organizations often drive controversies rather than simply report the news.

"Anything is fair game for the media today," says the president of a midwestern television station. "There are no restraints."

This reflects a dramatic shift in opinion on this issue since the mid-1990s, particularly among those in local news. In 1995, 61% of the local media believed news organizations were simply reporting the facts in their coverage of politicians' personal and ethical behavior; only 33% said they were actually driving the controversies. Today those numbers are nearly reversed: 39% say news organizations are reporting the facts; 56% say they are driving the controversies.

The shift is more pronounced in television news than print. Six-in-ten in national television news now think news organizations drive controversies about public figures; in 1995, 37% held this view. Similarly, 59% in local television now think news coverage drives controversies, compared to 32% in 1995.

It follows that journalists and media executives are critical of the way national news organizations covered the Clinton-Lewinsky scandal. More than half say the scandal received too much coverage; roughly four-in-ten say the quantity of coverage was about right. The national and local press have nearly identical views on this issue. Among those in national news, 57% say news organizations made too much of the scandal; among those in local news, 60% make the same judgment.

Reporters and editors are among the most critical of the Clinton-Lewinsky coverage. Two-thirds of national news staff think the scandal was overcovered, a view shared by 65% of local staff. This compares with only 44% of national executives and 48% of local executives.

> Two-thirds of the American people agree, and after the impeachment trial ended, 59% gave the press a "C" grade or worse for its coverage of the scandal.

In spite of this widespread self-criticism, journalists and media executives still strongly adhere to the value of the watchdog role. Nearly 90% say that criticism of political leaders is worth it because it keeps those leaders from doing things that should not be done. Less than 10% think that such criticism keeps political leaders from doing their job. This holds true across markets and mediums.

Opinions on Polls

More than six-in-ten in the news media believe polls are right most or all of the time, and a majority say polls have a positive impact on society. Those in the national press express slightly more faith in the accuracy of polls than the local media (69% compared to 61%), but no greater belief that they work in the best interest of the country.

The American people are more skeptical of polls' accuracy, but they are also more supportive of their good. Just 26% of the public believe polls are right most or all of the time, while 66% say they are beneficial.

Thus, to conclude, it may be safely inferred that almost universality can be traced in findings of this study and the views on performance of journalism are more or less same everywhere in the present age.

8

Journalism: Case Study Curriculum

> The most original authors are not so because they advance what is new, but because they put what they have to say as if it had never been said before.
>
> —*Johann Wolfgang Von Goethe*

The case study method of inquiry, and the Socratic dialogue that goes along with it, have a long and distinguished history. We generally identify them today with training in the law. Indeed, the subject matter of the law comes predigested in the form of cases, and thus the method fits as naturally into the classroom as into the courtroom. Similarly case study method has also been used in schools of business, where the cases must be created through the distillation of actual commercial and industrial experiences into a realistic case format.

Notably, the case study method has not been widely used in journalism schools, with the exception of teaching press or communications law and, to a lesser extent, in classes in advertising or media management. One area that lends itself naturally to the case study method and Socratic dialogue is the teaching of ethics, a subject often subsumed under the heading of "critical issues" or "contemporary problems" in journalism. The case study method can also be used to teach news judgment, editing, and a number of other subjects. However, journalism issues and problems, unlike legal ones, do not deliver themselves neatly packaged as teachable cases. They must be created from scratch. This can be done hypothetically; a method pioneered by the Fred Friendly seminars on the Public Broadcasting System. Yet such cases frequently suffer from a studied lack of reality, or else age quickly—or both. Instructors can, of course, create their own cases—real or hypothetical—but faculty are quick to point out that they lack the time, resources, and, sometimes, access to original materials that are necessary to make such cases definitive. Valuable ethics books exist that pose cases or, less satisfactorily; stage arguments on opposing sides of controversies. However, the cases presented are brief and contain only modest detail. Staged arguments suffer from the problems common to, well, staged arguments: they are a little too neat, and no obvious means are available for reconciling the conflicting views.

Yet these cases, as carefully developed as they are, still do not teach themselves. Unlike cases in law, cases in journalism do not have a clear procedure for adjudication; unlike business cases, they do not have an obvious and quantifiable goal in view, namely the maximization of profit. First, they must add a standard of judgment against which to test proposed solutions to the cases, or else classroom discussion will collapse into mere opinion or an unprincipled relativism. Second, these cases demand that careful thought be given to the procedures for reasoning them through, from the initial facts to the principles governing their resolution.

What standard of judgment is appropriate in journalism cases? Clifford Christians, in Media Ethics: Cases and Moral Reasoning, has outlined the most important and traditionally invoked of such standards: the Golden Mean and the Golden Rule, otherwise known as the Categorical Imperative—for example, the greatest happiness of the greatest number. However, I suggest that the standard of judgment to be used in attacking these cases is the ethics of democracy. Without a free press there can be no political democracy. It is equally true that without the institutions of democratic life there can be no journalism. No journalism, no democracy. And equally: no democracy, no journalism. Journalism and democracy share a common fate, for journalism is identical with or simply another name for democracy. When democracy falters, journalism falters, and when journalism goes awry, democracy goes awry.

This is a controversial principle, for it seems to commit journalists to the defense of something-to compromise their valued independence or nonpartisanship. The principle claims that journalists can be independent or objective about everything but democracy; for to do so is to abandon the craft. About democratic institutions, about the way of life in a democracy; journalists are not permitted to be indifferent, nonpartisan, or objective. It is their one compulsory passion, for it forms the ground condition of their practice. Without the institutions or spirit of democracy; journalists are reduced to propagandists or entertainers. The passion for democracy is the one necessary bond journalists must have with the public.

We do not need much evidence to support the principle. There were people in the former Soviet Union who called themselves journalists, who worked for things called newspapers, broadcast stations, and magazines. Such people were not journalists but propagandists; their organizations did not constitute a press but the apparatus of a state and a party. Soviet journalism was an oxymoron. Without the institutions of democracy-including freedom of expression protected by law and tradition-it was a sham. However, forces other than the Totalitarian State can destroy journalism; the Entertainment State can also destroy it. When journalists measure their success or their ethics by the size of their readership or their audience, by the profits of their companies or by their incomes, status, and visibility, they have caved in to the temptation of worshipping false gods. They have sold their heritage for pottage, as completely as those who cynically convinced themselves they were serving democracy by acting as the mouthpiece of a putatively revolutionary party.

Democracy requires more than a free press. It also requires a high level of trust among citizens, a healthy judiciary, an effective legislature, a strong; presidency, and a balance of powers among these institutions. The ethics of journalism is a matter of judging the consequences of stories, actions, and investigations for the vitality of these institutions and the continued capacity of people to act as citizens.

Doing good journalism, like writing good prose, is always a matter of judgment. What is right may change from situation to situation. Still-as anyone who has done journalism or who has read or watched closely knows-there are good choices and bad choices.

The key for journalists and for democratic societies is the process those who produce the news go through in making their decisions. Once a journalist begins to develop a disciplined, thoughtful way of making choices, he or she will build on it and refer to it over and over again, much the way a musician continues to practice scales or an athlete continues to perform calisthenics. Like most valuable talents, the ability to make intelligent choices is refined through continued practice. Without an inbred process of critical decision-making, journalists in the minute-by-minute world of news are doomed to lean on less reliable pillars: peer pressure, fashion, convention, the fear of being scooped, the toss of a coin, or, most damagingly, the pressure of competition.

The concept of learning by case study is about how to make reasoned decisions when reason is tied to the needs of a democratic polity. In preparing it, journalists and teachers joined together. We thought about what decision-making areas we could cover in ten or so cases. The cases might be taught as a single course or used individually as elements in several different courses. On our list we included such areas as the discipline of verification, competitive pressure and commercial influence, political imperatives, the timing of stories, the use of sources, and the impact of new technology. We sought out distinguished journalists to serve as authors, for we believed that the creation of cases that would ring true depended on deep and systematic reporting to retell as fully as possible the thinking of the journalists in the case. Though any of these cases may raise various issues, each of them was designed to focus on one or two key ideas. Once written, each case was "lab taught" at journalism schools around the country before being edited again.

Some of these cases raise questions concerning such practices as the mutual manipulation of press and government that leaves citizens as increasingly powerless and cynical spectators. Other cases lend themselves to discussion of some very general issues: What is the role of the press in a democracy? Is it to be a watchdog? Where does such a concept come from? Who enunciated it? How well does the press play the role of watchdog? Are there other roles, even more ennobling, that the press can play?

There is no mystery behind the case study method. The point of it is to get students to think through problems in a public forum, to make and defend judgments against the criticisms brought to bear by the instructor and other students. Each case is subject to multiple interpretations, and each raises more than one issue and advances more than one principle. The creativity emerges in laying out the questions that take the student from the facts to the principle and to the debate that ensues about the validity of the principle and the degree to which it fits the facts in question. Others who teach by the case study method in different fields offer other advice. Professor Robert Bruner, distinguished professor of business administration at the University of Virginia, claims the following advantages for the case study method:

- Students learn best the lessons they teach themselves.
- The case study method builds the capacity for critical thinking.
- It helps students weigh the practical implications of their decisions.
- It teaches risk taking, respect, trust, and tough-mindedness.
- It helps establish inductive, continuing learning habits.

The skills enumerated are precisely those desperately needed in modern journalism: critical thinking rather than habitual reaction; trust and respect rather than cynicism and contempt; tough-mindedness rather than sentimentality, timidity, and closed-mindedness; and most of all the realization that journalism is a craft depending on lifelong cultivation of intelligence and discipline.

Beyond that, the case study method is a pleasure to use in the classroom- a pleasure for both teacher and student. Enjoy!

9

News and Sales

> I do not believe you can do today's job with yesterday's methods and be in business tomorrow.
>
> —*Nelson Jackson*

To attract both viewers and advertisers, television news must be credible. Protecting the integrity of the news product has become increasingly challenging, however, as stations seek new revenue sources in a difficult economic climate. Good journalism and a station's economic goals can sometimes conflict. But stations risk damaging the foundation of their business if they produce or avoid news stories to please sponsors, or solicit or place advertising in a way that weakens the integrity of their news operation.

Overview

The following general principles should serve as the basis for all decisions affecting news and sales:

- News content should be determined solely through editorial judgment.
- News sponsors should not dictate or influence news content.
- News content should be clearly distinguishable from advertising content.

Guidelines

Written guidelines help to manage the relationship

between news and sales. Managers must decide—and then clearly articulate to the newsroom, sales department, and sponsors—what is and what is not for sale. In past instances, people have been fired and companies have been subjected to national embarrassment because specific guidelines were not in place or not properly communicated. Among other issues, guidelines should clarify:

- What is content and what content can be sponsored.
- Whether newscasts in different day parts or on different days of the week are subject to different rules and if so why.
- Whether the news department will create content specifically as a vehicle for advertising and if so under what terms.
- How news and sales people communicate, especially about story ideas or sales suggestions.
- ho must see and approve sponsorship proposals.

Useful Questions for all Situations

To develop guidelines and to work through most situations involving news and sales, answering these four basic questions will help:

- What are the short-term and long-term consequences of making or not making this sale or arrangement?
- What will viewers think when they see this on the air? For example: Could this sponsorship influence or appear to influence the content of the story in any way? Could this sponsorship affect the station's brand, image or reputation?
- How will you explain this decision to viewers, critics and station personnel, and are there any details you would be uncomfortable making public?
- Should this arrangement be in writing?

Management

The general manager should be directly involved in developing station guidelines, and ultimately is responsible for ensuring that sales proposals do not "cross the line" and jeopardize the station's integrity.

- The general manager should personally review any sales or promotional agreements that could affect the credibility of the newsroom or its employees, or the station's image.
- The general manager should be the final arbiter of disputes involving news and sales.

Communication

Everyone in the station has a stake in the credibility of the news and the success of the business. Stations can foster understanding between news and sales employees in various ways. Here are some examples:

- General managers can bring all department heads together to watch and discuss newscasts.
- The news director can speak to groups of clients to explain in general how and why editorial decisions are made.
- News managers can hold periodic meetings for sales personnel, trainees and others to explain the newsgathering process.

In addition to the questions listed above for developing guidelines, the following questions may be helpful when deciding specific cases, such as:

- Story or Franchise Sponsorships
- Station Campaigns and Partnerships
- Billboards and Logos
- Coverage of a Sponsor
- News Personnel

- Outside Experts
- Online/New Media Issues

Story or Franchise Sponsorships

- What are we selling with this sponsorship?
- Will the sponsor provide or expect to provide experts on this topic, exclusive or otherwise?
- Does it make a difference if the idea for the franchise or story came from the newsroom, the station sales office or the advertiser?

Station Campaigns and Partnerships

- Will you co-sponsor an event or activity with just one sponsor?
- Will you handle campaigns differently if the outside sponsor is non-commercial?
- Will the partner provide or expect to provide experts or guests, exclusive or otherwise?
- What role will news personnel play in the event or activity? (For example, will they endorse or appear to endorse any products or services and what effect will that have on their ability to report on this topic or sponsor?)
- How will you respond to requests for news coverage of an event the station is co-sponsoring?

Billboards and Logos

- Where in the newscast will you place billboards? How often can they run?
- Where in the newscast and where on screen will you place sponsor logos? (For example, will you allow sponsor logos to appear over news content?)
- Will sponsors be able to brand or title elements of your newscast?

- Will sponsor logos or billboards also include audio mentions, and if so, by whom?

Coverage of a Sponsor

- How and when will the newsroom inform other station management that a story about an advertiser is in the works?
- How and when will the newsroom inform co-owned stations about a story involving one of their advertisers?
- Who will respond to questions from the advertiser?

News Personnel

- What can news personnel do on your air, outside of news programming?
- What can news personnel do for air on other stations?
- What can news personnel do off the air? (For example, appearances, speeches or endorsements.)
- What can news personnel do for pay and what can or should they do pro bono?

Outside Experts

Will you disclose the expert's associations on the air? How, and how often? If not, why not?

- Can an expert sponsor his or her own on air appearances?
- What product or company endorsements or mentions, if any, will be allowed during the expert's on air appearances?
- What will the expert be allowed to do outside of on air appearances?

Online/New Media Issues

- Do the same guidelines applied to broadcast content apply to online content and sponsorships?

- Can the user clearly tell the difference between news and other content online?
- Who owns and who benefits from any database created by online signups?
- What are the privacy rules on your Web site and how do they apply to sponsor information?
- Do you disclose these rules? Why or why not?

Several broadcast organizations already have developed guidelines on news and sales that can serve as a starting point for discussion for stations wanting to draft their own.

10

Professional Values and Motivations

> A man should learn to detect and watch that gleam of light which flashes across his mind from within, more than the lustre of the firmament of bards and sages. Yet he dismisses without notice his thought, because it is his. In every work of genius we recognize our own rejected thoughts: they come back to us with a certain alienated majesty
>
> —*Ralph Waldo Emerson*

Nearly all journalists and media executives say they are proud of what they do for a living, and they express general satisfaction with the values, leadership and ethics programs of their own news organizations. This may reflect some of the common motivations that draw people to journalism: writing, communicating and providing information to the public.

But despite an overall sense of shared professional values, divisions within the press emerge across markets and job types. The distinctions are clear when looking at whether news media professionals say that colleagues share their values "a great deal" or "a fair amount." Generally, those at top levels of national news express more affinity for their staff's values than do those in local news. But national news owners and upper level managers see themselves as sharing more with their staffs than the news staff says is so.

Fully 53% of national news executives and managers

say that reporters in their organizations share their professional values a great deal; 38% of national news staff reciprocate this view. Among local news executives and managers, 30% say their staffs share their professional values a great deal; only 26% of local staff members feels similarly connected.

While the national news media express greater levels of shared professionalism than do their local counterparts, a sense of shared values is particularly weak among those working in national television news. In this group, less than half of the executives say they share a great deal of the professional values of the reporters in their organizations; just 29% of staff members say the same of the owners and top editors in their news organizations. This is significantly less than the 60% of national print executives who feel this tie, and the 47% of national print staff who express a strong connection to the top bosses.

Rating Quality of Leadership

Overall, most of the news media rate the quality of leadership in their own newsrooms as good, and a substantial minority give their leaders excellent marks. Fully 44% of those working in national news say their newsroom leadership is good and another 36% say it is excellent. Similarly, among local news organizations, 51% rate the quality of leadership in their newsroom as good and an additional 24% give their leaders top marks.

Those closest to leadership positions are the most complimentary. On the national level, news media executives are twice as likely as staff to rate their organization's leadership as excellent (52% vs. 25%, respectively). On the local level, the gap is as great: By a ratio of 42%-to-13%, executives give leaders excellent marks. There are no significant differences in the way those working in print and broadcast view their leadership.

Dealing with Ethics

Most media professionals attest to the existence of a concerted effort to address ethical issues by their news organizations, and they express general satisfaction with such programs. Fully 81% of those working in national news, 72% of those in local news outlets and 79% of those involved in online news say that such ethics programs exist.

In spite of those responsible for creating or directing such programs are the most likely to report their existence. Almost all (98%) of national media executives and nearly as many (88%) executives in local news acknowledge a concerted program to address ethics. Somewhat smaller majorities of national and local news staff are aware of such ongoing efforts in their organizations (74% and 60%, respectively).

Despite these minor differences in perception as to the actual existence of ethics programs, both news media executives and working journalists generally agree on their evaluations of the current state of such programs. A majority of almost every group says that their newsroom's current effort toward addressing ethics is about right. Staff members working in local news are the only group in which a majority expresses support for heightened efforts: 53% want more of an organized effort, compared to about one-third of those in higher positions or national markets.

Some of the greatest differences in attitudes toward ethical issues are generational in nature. Those under age 35 are the least likely to say there is an official program and the most likely to want more of an organized effort. The opposite is true for those age 55 and older: This group overwhelmingly acknowledges an on-going program and strongly supports the current level of effort.

Finally, when it comes to discussing specific ethical

concerns, journalists working in both the national and local news media express a fair amount of trust in senior management. Over half of both national and local staff say they would turn to their immediate supervisor if they had a problem or question about ethics. This inclination is somewhat greater in the national print than the national television media. Approximately 20% of the news media say they would turn to top editors or producers and an equal percentage favor turning to their colleagues.

Why Are They in the Newsroom?

More than anything else, those in the news media say that being able to write or communicate for a living was a very important reason for entering journalism. Nearly as many identify the promise of an exciting career as critical to their choice of work, although somewhat more in the national media consider this a very important reason (62%) than in the local press (53%).

More than two-thirds of the news media say that providing people with information they need is a very important reason why journalists work in news.

> "You can make a worthwhile contribution to society," says the managing editor of a local newspaper.

A slim majority think that uncovering wrongdoing is very important to their colleagues. More members of the print press than television hold this view. More in national than local news say that being a witness to history is very important (55% vs. 36%).

> "It's a ringside seat to breaking news events of our time," says a national newspaper reporter.

Nearly one-in-five members of the local television news media believe that their colleagues are motivated by a desire to become famous or well-known, compared to only 2% in local print.

Proud of What They Do

More than nine-in-ten journalists and news media executives say they feel proud when they meet someone for the first time and tell them where they work; less than 10% say they feel somewhat apologetic in this situation.

In a recent survey of government officials, fewer members of Congress (75%) and the senior executive service (81%) say they feel proud when they tell people what they do. However, just as many presidential appointees (92%) as journalists and media executives say they are proud of their work.

11

Journalism & Right to Information

At any journalism convention of consequence, a resolution vowing to fight to the bitter end for FoI, to use the characteristic headline abbreviation for the Cause, is bound to be submitted with a flourish and unanimously agreed upon as quickly as possible. After all, who can be against virtue in journalism?

In many ways, it is a pity that so important a matter is usually discussed in cliches appropriate for a Fourth of July celebration at Center Moriches, N.Y. For the issues that are lumped together under the symbol, FoI, are real and vital and very much worth careful examination. Contrary to the rather bored public impression of this long and persistent exercise of journalistic rhetoric, its is no sham battle that is being waged by self-appointed crusaders for murky and ill-defined goals. Practical ends are being sought—and in part achieved—by perfectly hardheaded, tough-minded men.

What they seek, when they talk about "the public's right to know" as opposed to the military intelligence standard of "the public's need to know," is more access to information of public concern and more legal protection for the journalist. Judged by any form of measurement, their achievements have been impressive. Through the passage of laws of varying effectiveness, "open records" are available in many states. In addition, a national "freedom of information" law has taken effect amid cautious testing by government and news media alike to determine what its long-range effect is likely to be. However, the journalist is very far from achieving the almost universal status of confidentiality for his sources that is accorded to the lawyer for his client, the physician for his patient, and the clergyman for his flock.

Moreover, it is unlikely that he will ever be given access to all public records or admitted to all meetings having to do with public business. Nor are these ultimate goals as desirable as some perfectionists believe they are. For if the journalist is given such privileges, it follows as a matter of public policy that he will be asked in return for some such manifest of responsibility as the licensing that is required of the physician, the examination and character study to which lawyers must submit before admission to the bar, and submission to the higher ecclesiastical authority that usually regulates the clergy.

Remarkably, There are other disturbing elements about FoI. What makes the campaign truly remarkable is that the supposed beneficiary, the American public, seems to have shown no all-consuming interest in the movement and certainly has done little to support it. The burden has been carried almost entirely by a comparatively small group of dedicated editors, plus a few interested publishers and broadcasters. They have done the hard—and often thankless—job of speaking, writing, and lobbying on behalf of such illustrious organizations as the American Society of Newspaper Editors, National Editorial Association, Sigma Delta Chi, Associated Press Managing Editors, American Newspaper Publishers Association, National Association of Broadcasters, and other groups of lesser renown.

It is no great secret that the prime movers for FoI have had to contend with an almost monumental apathy inside the profession as well as outside it. Frequently, they have complained of lack of support. However, they have persisted despite an increasing tendency to question the value of their total effort and slowly rising opposition within government and the legal profession. In effect, they hold that by incessant lobbying for legal enlargement of their rights they will surround the journalist with sufficient safeguards that will be a substitute for an aroused public opinion.

The rationale for FoI, consequently, is thus almost entirely defensive. Editor of the *Washington Post* and one of the most devoted FoI campaigners, recognized the danger of an apathetic public when he wrote: "The requirements of freedom are not satisfied in a climate, where only the rich, powerful, resourceful and courageous dare assert the right to utter what is unpopular. There must be encouragement, in an affirmative way, for those who seek knowledge and desire to use it. The indifference, indolence and ignorance of great numbers of citizens will be a serious barrier to the full realization of mankind's greatness. Where a state is hostile and the population prejudiced against freedom of expression, this freedom and every other freedom will not long survive."

If there were a latter-day with a great cause around which journalists could rally in an appeal to public opinion, they might not have so much difficulty in arousing sympathy for their campaign of self-defense. But for the most part, the cases that have come to public attention in recent years are based on issues that do not readily make an impression either on the public or even the news media themselves. As early as 1896, Maryland recognized by law the journalist's right to a certain amount of professional secrecy. New Jersey became the second state to pass a law protecting the confidentiality of sources in 1933 and ten others have followed since.

In most states of the nation, however, journalists who defy the courts by refusing to reveal their sources have to face up to the contempt power. One of the most celebrated in this century was Martin Mooney, a reporter for the *New York American,* who wrote a series about "policy racket" gambling operations in 1935. When he refused to tell a New York County Grand Jury who the gamblers were, he was held in contempt of court, fined $ 250, and sentenced to 30 days in jail. Upon appeal, his conviction was affirmed.

In a more recent case, a 20-years-old college newspaper editor, Annette Lesley Buchanan of the University of Oregon, was fined $300 for contempt of court in 1966 because she refused to reveal her sources for an article on campus marijuana smoking to the Lane County Grand Jury, Eugene, Ore. She won national publicity and sympathy for her appeal, making her for a brief time one of the minor heroines of American journalism.

However, the courts have been careful not to create too many martyrs, or to make examples out of the illustrious except under extreme provocation. It is an easily observable truth that most reporters are not usually challenged for their sources, even in states where there is no legal immunity for journalists. In fact, the whole structure of investigative journalism is based on the assumption that law enforcement authorities will generally seek to cooperate with the press in the exercise of its "watch dog" function instead of trying to obstruct an inquiry.

In Illinois, for example, the lack of statutory protection for journalists did not stop George Thiem, a reporter for the *Chicago Daily News,* from unmasking thefts of state funds by Orville E. Hodge, the State Auditor, who was subsequently convicted and jailed. Thiem was never asked for the name of the young woman clerk in a state office who referred him to the necessary records on condition that she would never be identified.

The Position of the Press

Curiousl, despite the demonstrated ability of journalists to take care of themselves without legal protection in most cases, there should be so passionate a resort to the comparatively less effective. For statutes where they exist. Furthermore, those journalists who have the best records for achieving success in gathering information by traditional methods are generally the ones who insist on new-laws protecting confidentiality and access, as well, on the apparent presumption that every little bit helps. Mollenhoff, for example, argued, in the Buchanan case that the prosecutor should have proceeded with vigor against narcotics peddlers instead of trying to "harass a journalist." But if the protest was intended to stimulate interest in an Oregon law to protect the confidentiality of journalistic sources, it failed.

Most lawyers, including a committee of the American Bar Association, have consistently opposed the extension of such confidentiality statutes. They argue that a policy of martyrdom by the journalist—of accepting punishment rather than to reveal sources—is likely to be a greater service to society, whatever, the journalist himself may think of such a proposition. Basically, the legal profession doubts that freedom of the press actually is involved in most of the cases in which journalists shout from every conceivable platform that their liberties are being endangered. The lawyers also argue that the general principle governing the administration of justice in the United States, as elsewhere, is that judicial and legislative bodies have a right to demand and obtain complete information.

Finally, they warn that laws protecting the confidential nature of journalistic source might encourage some reporters, admittedly a minority, to fake stories on the basis of nonexistent, confidential evidence. James E. Beaver, associate professor at the University of Washington Law

School, wrote with particular reference to the Buchanan case: "Whether or not the 'special position' sought for newspapers is secure, reporters are going to continue protecting their sources of information, and judges continue to deal very lightly with contemptuous journalists..... The public's interest is better served by the newsman's code which means something to him, than by creation of a privileged status to shelter him against standing on his own hind legs."

The contrary view was posed by Robert C. Notson as president of the American Society of Newspapers Editors, who concluded that any requirement that forced journalists to reveal sources would seal off information which, if published, would be likely to have a beneficial public effect. "The pledge of confidentiality is not to be made lightly," he wrote, "but, once made, should be kept by the editor and respected by the court, barring an overriding public interest....."

In the long run, society will be more satisfactorily served if the various media of public information are privileged to determine when a source should be withheld and when a source should be revealed. Granted that the instruments of government should have access to all relevant information in the majority of cases, the relationship between the journalist and his sources is of such importance to our society that it should be protected by law."

The sort of arguments as Dr. Siebert's, however, have not made a perceptible dent in the opposition of bench and bar to expansion of the body of protective laws for the benefit of the journalist. Nor has he swayed all the doubters in the ranks of journalism itself; despite their somewhat reserved demeanor, they do amount to a considerable minority and can make their influence felt if they wish. Basically, they believe that the news media are actually hurting themselves by repeatedly raising the issue of confidentiality without sufficient cause and thereby creating the public impression that they are continually sounding the alarm when there is no fire. If freedom of the press is really in jeopardy, then the minority would like the apply Justice Holmes's test of a "clear and present danger".

The same feeling, to an even broader extent, applies to the drive for more access to public records and meetings by representatives of the news media. Not every journalist believes that he has an inherent right to see everything and hear everything that pertains to the public's business. In fact, considering the breadth of the restrictions and the fairly obvious reasons for most of them, it is difficult to say exactly where the line should be drawn. For example, the confidential records of executive departments of government on a wide range of subjects from military secrets to diplomatic correspondence and law enforcement are generally held to be of a non-public nature. In addition, there are federal or state statutes imposing either mandatory secrecy or limited access at best to many nonjudicial records including data pertaining to criminal identification, fire prevention, industrial relations, narcotic drugs, juvenile delinquency, public welfare, health, and even motor vehicles in some cases. Some tax records, particularly income tax, also are not generally open for public inspection. Nor is there a uniform policy for so ordinary and useful a field as vital statistics.

There are many instances as for police records and judicial proceedings in which there is no right of public inspection. A despairing reporter in the New York State Supreme Court. Manhattan, once exclaimed after learning that a judge had impounded papers in a divorce case: "There are more secret records in this place than there are in the Pentagon!"

It has seemed so to many a reporter who was denied access to public records in instances that appeared to him and to his news organization to be both arbitrary and unreasonable. The responsible news media, in consequence, are torn between a desire to respect the processes of government that clearly demand a certain amount of confidentiality and to check the growth of such objectionable official practices as holding unnecessary executive sessions and maintaining unnecessary secrecy over public records. It is one thing for a President to insist on the right of executive privilege in his dealings with other branches of the government, or for other executives to safeguard government proceedings in the national interest.

It is quite another for town councils and school boards to go behind closed doors primarily to spare themselves the inconvenience of public questioning of their decisions. In between lies the vast grey area in which there are interminable wrangles over whether secrecy is the best policy—or the worst. When in doubt, quite understandably, the press plumps for full disclosure and not even the moderates pose many objections.

'Disclosure' of misconduct in public office, is another reason for the outward strength of the press policy on "open records" and "open meetings". The government is not in a good position to defend a policy of secrecy in public offices if it can be shown that either wrong doing or partiality may be possible by-products. Nor can sympathetic editors he expected to champion the government's cause in such circumstances. And when the press is able to demonstrate that innocent persons have been convicted of crimes they did not commit, as Gene Miller of the *Miami Herald* did in 1966 when he helped free two persons who had mistakenly been found guilty of murder, the legal profession cannot contend that all virtue resides in the courts.

When Stephen J. Roth was Attorney General of Michigan, he once suggested to reporters: "I think the less concern you have with what you're entitled to under the law, the better off you're going to be.... I think reporters.... get a lot more cooperation than the law requires public officials to give them in the matters of automobile accidents, arrests, criminal prosecutions, etc." Harold L. Cross, one of the foremost authorities in the land on the law as applied to the press, argued that this was a profoundly realistic view, although he conceded that the right of access to public documents is not always adequate. "It indicates," he wrote, "the wisdom in the preponderant majority of cases and circumstances of present newspaper practice in placing primary and major reliance on the processes mentioned rather than the law. Sugar, plus judicious admixtures of strength and determination, catches more 'police news' than vinegar."

Those who campaign under the slogan of the "People's Right to Know" are seldom impressed with the notion of a compromise that leaves the decision on access to public records entirely in the province of government. One of the most ardent of FoI advocates, Virgil M. Newton, Jr., managing editor of the *Tampa* (Fla.) *Tribune,* argued: "Theoretically, an informed public opinion is supposed to direct the people's representatives in their law-making. That is the very lifeblood of free legislative government. But if the people are uninformed, through bureaucratic secrecy, and confused, through bureaucratic propaganda, on the major issues of government, how can a citizen make an unprejudiced decision and let his Congressman know how he feels about any one measure?"

The Federal Law

This, basically, is the rationale that has resulted in federal as well as state legislation to support the continuing FoI campaign. No one can be sure of the eventual effectiveness of the federal "freedom of information" law which became operative on July 4, 1967, but every government officeholder is well aware of it. In form, it is an amendment of a 20-year-old Administrative Procedures Act (5 U.S.C. 22) under which federal records could be withheld "in the public interest" or if they related "solely to the internal management of an agency." In substance, it is similar to the state laws already enacted that limit official secrecy. But its comparatively untested procedures make it an uncertain quantity.

President Johnson's somewhat ambivalent attitude toward the federal legislation is an indication of the government's own strong doubts. For while the President expressed *pro forma* approval of the law, he also gave fair warning that it "in no way impairs the President's power under our Constitution to provide for confidentiality where the national interest so requires." This was a reference to the doctrine of executive privilege under which Presidents have repeatedly asserted the right to withhold certain types of information in the national interest, even from Congressional investigating committees. The Congressional sponsors of the information bill to date have never disputed the President on this point. Even more bluntly, the President insisted that government officials "cannot operate effectively if required to disclose information prematurely or to make public investigative files and internal instructions that guide them in arriving at decisions." This, to some extent, took the edge off his rather routine statement of support. "No one should be able to pull curtains of secrecy around decisions which can be revealed without injury to the public interest."

As always, it appears certain, the government and the news media are going to have differing estimates of what constitutes the public interest—and this is going to make for an interesting time. Typically, lawyers and business people seeking information on government contracts have been far more eager than journalists to use the newly opened public reading rooms in federal agencies to study various types of records. But the law has also made possible some advances in the gathering of news. At the Pentagon, for example, the Defense Department finally dropped its system of monitoring all interviews granted to journalists in 1962. Moreover, on request, such information as records bearing on federal pardons granted to prisoners in federal jails have been granted to the *Cleveland Plain Dealer* and background on public welfare operations in Mississippi have been made available to the press of that state. However, it is clear that the journalist will encounter dogged opposition in nine specific areas in which the new law provides exemption from disclosure. These include such categories as national security, foreign policy data in which the government requires secrecy, trade procedures within the province of government that should be kept secret, personnel files and medical data concerning government employees, bank reports, and intergovernmental data that might be used in litigation against the government.

The most important part of the new statute is its establishment of the principle of review by the courts of any decision by the federal government to withhold records. While this is in effect an open invitation to the press to institute judicial action to pry records loose from reluctant federal officeholders, the courts—with voluminous internal records of their own to safeguard—are scarcely likely to create a reporters' holiday.

Resultantly, the press's customary attitude of self-congratulation over the slightest indication of progress in the FoI campaign is not really warranted. The ever aggressive Clark Mollenhoff warned his colleagues soon after the adoption of federal legislation: "The new federal records law will be meaningful if it is understood by the press and the public and is used as a device to force government agencies to produce documents. It will be meaningless if it is not used, or if political appointees or career bureaucrats are permitted to twist its nine exemptions into an unintended authority to withhold... To be realistic, we must accept that a change in the law does not change the attitudes of those bureaucrats who have tried to claim personal proprietary interests over documents in their custody. Neither will it change the tendency of bureaucrats and political appointees to try to impose secrecy to avoid disclosures of corruption or mismanagement."

The prospect, consequently, is for a continuing struggle. In some respects, the resort of the press to legal action to obtain more information is like swatting Uncle Remus's Tar Baby. The more legislation there is, the more involved the press is likely to become in expensive and time-consuming lawsuits which may make news in themselves but not the most desirable kind. Unhappily, a very large section of the public is even less interested in the press's legal adventures than it is in the inordinately dull accounts of how routine news must be gathered from a maze of sources. What the public wants, primarily, is the news; like editors, the people as a whole have scant patience with alibis or voluminous reasons why information is not available.

The Future of FoI

If anything has been oversold inside and outside journalism, it is FoI. The symptoms are plain enough. The evidence of public and professional boredom with the issue is so apparent that it needs no further documentation. Despite Clark Mollenhoff and his cohorts, it is very difficult for most people to believe that the government at any level can successfully withhold for any appreciable time the kind of information to which the public is entitled. The very success of the reporters, as shown in the news media day by day, completely overshadows the FoI campaign in the public mind. For quite truthfully, a decent balance has been achieved between the government's legitimate effort to safeguard sensitive information in the public interest and the press's equally necessary function as the public's "watchdog" over the governmental process.

If the balance should ever shift appreciably in the direction of government, then the press will be in deep trouble because of the violent and—in some respects—premature appeals that have been made in the cause of FoI. Then the penalty for overselling will have to be faced. For it will be very difficult to appeal to an inert public, its senses dulled by an overreacting press, if there should be real danger of regulation of the news media. Then there will be no escape for those editors who yearn to remain impartial spectators in the never ending struggle for control over the news. Whether they like it or not, they are the central figures in one of the most important contests of the era and they cannot escape the consequences in time of crisis.

Virtually, no one in journalism would want to see the FoI campaign abandoned, although some more appropriate symbol and more realistic nomenclature may be found. To drop the campaign after so much effort has been invested in it would be a confession of futility; whatever may be said of FoI, it is most certainly not a futile effort. What can and should be done is to scale the intensity of the effort to the needs of the news media and the times instead of crying "Woe!" on all occasions. It would also be helpful if the base of the activity could be broadened, relieving the handful of hardened press veterans and distributing the burden in more equitable fashion among all elements of the news media. Television, for example, should have a role commensurate with its responsibilities and its special problems should be attacked by the press with the same vigor that it uses to espouse its own cause. There can and should be no separation of the news media in such matters, for what affects one affects all.

But most important of all, the issues that affect the freedom of the press—which means all news media—should not be discussed in symbols and platitudes that obscure rather than enlighten. The blunt and hardheaded attitude with which the journalist approaches the news is equally appropriate for the consideration of his own fate. It will also help if he can abandon both self-interest and self-adulation, admittedly a difficult task for a journalist but not beyond his talents.

The private commercial organizations in the United States whose principal enterprises consist of the news media should never forget that it is their privilege, but not necessarily their inalienable right, to give the news exclusively to the American public. As long as the public is convinced of both their professional skill and their good faith, excesses and errors may be forgiven and quickly forgotten. But once the news media fail to justify public confidence in their independence and their credibility, then the whole system of gathering and distributing news by private hands is in danger. This is the primary reason for abandoning crude caricature and overblown peril in discussing such things as FoI.

12

The Codes of Ethics for Journalism

"Not only all arts and sciences but all actions directed by choice aim at some good."

—Aristotle, Nicomachean Ethics, I. 1.

OREGON CODE OF ETHICS FOR JOURNALISM[1]

Preamble

We believe in the teaching of the great ethicists that a general state of happiness and well-being is attainable throughout the world; and that this state is the chief end-in-view of society.

We recognize an instinct in every good man that his utterances and his deeds should make a reasonable and continuous contribution toward this ultimate state, in the possibility of which we reiterate our belief, however remote it may now seem.

We believe that men collectively should also follow the principles of practice that guide the ethical individual. For whatever purpose men are associated, we believe they should endeavour to make the reasonable and continuous contribution that distinguishes the ethical man. And all the agencies and instrumentalities employed by men, singly or collectively, should be based upon the best ethical practice of the time, so that the end-in-view of society may thereby be hastened.

Of all these agencies the printed word is most widely diffused and most powerful. The printed word is the single instrument of the profession we represent, and the extent to which it is shaping the thoughts and the conduct of peoples is measureless. We therefore pronounce the ethical responsibility of journalism the greatest of the professional responsibilities, and we desire to accept our responsibility, now and hereafter, to the utmost extent that is right and reasonable in our respective circumstances.

Accordingly we adopt for our guidance the following code, which shall be known as the Oregon Code of Ethics for Journalism.

1. Sincerity; Truth

The foundation of ethical journalism is sincerity. The sincere journalist will be honest alike in his purposes and in his writings. To the best of his capacity to ascertain truth, he will always be truthful. It is his attitude toward truth that distinguishes the ethical from the unethical writer. It is naturally not possible that all writing can be without error; but it can always be without deliberate error. There is no place in journalism for the dissembler; the distorter; the prevaricator; the suppressor; or the dishonest thinker.

The first section of this code therefore provides that we shall be continuously sincere in professional practice; and sincerity as journalists means, for example, that:

1. We will put accuracy above all other considerations in the written word, whether editorial, advertisement, article, or news story.
2. We will interpret accuracy not merely as the absence of actual misstatement, but as the presence of whatever is necessary to prevent the reader from making A false deduction.
3. In an ethical attitude toward truth, we will be open

at all times to conviction, for the sincere journalist, while fearless and firm, will never be stubborn; therefore we will never decline to hear and consider new evidence.

4. If new evidence forces a change of opinion, we will be as free in the acknowledgment of the new opinion as in the utterance of the old.
5. We will promote a similar attitude in others toward truth, not asking or permitting employees to write things which as sincere journalists we would not ourselves write.

2. Care; Competency; Thoroughness

Inaccuracy in journalism is commonly due more to lack of mental equipment than to wilfulness of attitude. The ill-equipped man 'cannot be more competent as a journalist than he can as a doctor or engineer. Given an ethical attitude, the contribution that each journalist makes to his community and to society is nearly in ratio to his competency. We regard journalism as a precise and a learned profession, and it is therefore the second part of this code that:

6. By study and inquiry and observation, we will constantly aim to improve ourselves, so that our writings may be more authentic, and of greater perspective, and more conducive to the social good.
7. We will consider it an essential in those we employ that they not merely be of ethical attitude, but reasonably equipped to carry out their ideals.
8. We will make care our devotion in the preparation of statements of fact and in the utterance of opinion.
9. We will advocate In our respective communities the same thoroughness, sound preparation, and pride of craft, that we desire in ourselves, our employees, and our associates.

10. We are accordingly the active enemies of superficiality and pretense

3. Justice; Mercy; Kindliness

Liberty of the press is, by constitution, statute, and custom, greater in the United States than anywhere else in the world. This liberty exists for our press so that the liberty of the whole people may thereby be guarded. It so happens that at times the liberty of the press is exercised as license to infringe upon the rights of groups and of individuals: because custom and law have brought about certain immunities, it happens that in haste or zeal or malice or indifference, persons are unjustly dealt by. Yet the freedom of the press should at all times be exercised as the makers of the constitution, and the people themselves through their tolerance, have intended it. The reputations of men and women are sacred in nature and not to be torn down lightly. We therefore pronounce it appropriate to include in this code that:

11. We will not make "privileged utterance" a cloak for unjust attack, or spiteful venting, or carelessness in investigation, in the cases of parties or persons.
12. We will aim to protect, within reason, the rights of individuals mentioned in public documents, regardless of the effect on "good stories" or upon editorial policy.
13. We will deal by all persons alike so far as is humanly possible, not varying from the procedure of any part of this code because of the wealth, influence, or personal situation of the persons concerned, except as hereinafter provided.
14. It shall be one of our canons that mercy and kindliness are legitimate considerations in any place of journalism; and that if the public or social interest seems to be best conserved by suppression, we may suppress; but the motive in such instances must

always be the public or social interest, and not the personal or commercial interest.

15. We will try so to conduct our publication, or to direct our writing, that justice, kindliness, and mercy will characterize our work.

4. Moderation; Conservatism; Proportion

Since the public takes from the journalist so great a proportion of the evidence upon which it forms its opinions, obviously that evidence should be of high type. The writer who makes his appeal to the passions rather than to the intellect is too often invalid as a purveyor of evidence because his facts are out of perspective. By improper emphasis, by skillful arrangement, or by devices of typography or rhetoric, he causes the formation in the reader's mind of unsound opinion. This practice is quite as improper as and frequently is more harmful than actual prevarication. Through this code we desire to take a position against so-called sensational practice by acceptance of the following canons:

16. We will endeavour to avoid the injustice that springs from hasty conclusion in editorial or reportorial or interpretative practice.
17. We will not overplay news or editorial for the sake of effect when such procedure may lead to false deductions in readers' minds.
18. We will regard accuracy and completeness as more vital than our being the first to print.
19. We will try to observe due proportion in the display of news to the end that inconsequential matter may not seem to take precedence in social importance over news of public significance.
20. We will in all respects in our writing and publishing endeavour to observe moderation and steadiness.
21. Recognizing that the kaleidoscopic changes in news

tend to keep the public processes of mind at a superficial level, we will try to maintain a news and an editorial policy that will be less ephemeral in its influence upon social thought.

5. Partisanship; Propaganda

We believe that the public has confidence in the printed word of journalism in proportion as it is able to believe in the competency of journalists and have trust in their motives. Lack of trust in our motives may arise from the suspicion that we shape our writings to suit non-social interests, or that we open our columns to propaganda, or both. Accordingly we adopt the following professional canons:

22. We will resist outside control in every phase of our practice, believing that the best interests of society require intellectual freedom in journalism.
23. We will rise above party and other partisanship in writing and publishing, supporting parties and issues only so far as we sincerely believe them to be in the public interest.
24. We will not permit, unless in exceptional cases, the publishing of news and editorial matter not prepared by ourselves or our staffs, believing that original matter is the best answer to the peril of propaganda.

6. Public Service and Social Policy

We dispute the maxim sometimes heard that a newspaper should follow its constituency in public morals and policy rather than try to lead it. We do not expect to be so far ahead of our time that our policies will be impractical; but we do desire to be abreast of the best thought of the time, and if possible to be its guide. It is not true that a newspaper should be only as advanced in its ethical atmosphere as it conceives the average of its readers to be. No man who is not in ethical advance of the average of the community should be in the profession of journalism. We declare therefore as follows:

25. We will keep our writings and our publications free from unrefinement, except so far as we may sincerely believe publication of sordid details to be for the social good.
26. We will consider all that we write or publish for public consumption in the light of its effect upon social policy, refraining from writing or from publishing if we believe our material to be socially detrimental.
27. We will regard our privilege of writing for publication or publishing for public consumption as an enterprise that is social as well as commercial in character, and therefore will at all times have an eye against doing anything counter to social interest.
28. We believe it an essential part of this policy that we shall not be respecters of persons.

7. Advertising and Circulation

We repudiate the principle of "letting the buyer beware." We cannot agree to guarantee advertising, but we assume a definite attitude toward the advertising that we write, solicit, or print. We believe that the same canons of truth and justice should apply in advertising and circulation as we are adopting for news and editorial matter. We therefore agree to the following business principles:

29. We will cooperate with those social interests whose business it is to raise the ethical standard of advertising.
30. We will discourage and bar from our columns advertising which in our belief is intended to deceive the reader in his estimate of what is advertised. (This clause is intended to cover the many phases

of fraud, and unfair competition, and the advertising of articles that seem likely to be harmful to the purchaser's morals or health.)

31. We will not advertise our own newspaper or its circulation boastfully, or otherwise, in terms not in harmony with the clauses of this code of ethics. (This is intended to cover misleading statements to the public or to advertisers as to the whole number of copies printed, number of paid-up subscribers, number of street sales, and percentage of local circulation.)
32. We will not make our printing facilities available for the production of advertising which we believe to be socially harmful or fraudulent in its intent.

To the foregoing code we subscribe heartily as a part of our duty to society and of our belief that the salvation of the world can come only through the acceptance and practice by the people of the world of a sound and practical ethical philosophy.

SOUTH DAKOTA CODE OF ETHICS[2]

We of the profession of journalism, especially of that department which has to do with the publication of newspapers, deem it fitting that a code of ethics be set down to embody those ideals of service and that sense of propriety and honor which should imbue the motives and guide the actions of all who enter upon this profession.

This code of ethics is founded upon the basic principle of truth and justice. It is to be kept as nearly inviolate as is possible in the alignment of human aspirations with the golden rule of conduct, "Whatsoever ye would that they Ho unto you, do ye so unto them."

Service

The profession of journalism occupies the place of an essential service in its relations to the public. Its implied contract with the reader invites trust and accepts the responsibility of dependence. To merit this mutuality of interests the newspaper owes and must give adherence to high standards and these recognized ideals of motive, heart, and conduct.

Truth and Honesty

The foundation stone of the profession of journalism is truth. Unwavering adherence to "whatsoever things are true, whatsoever things are honest," must be the constant aim of men and women who publish newspapers.

News should be uncolored report of all vital facts accurately stated, insofar as it is possible to arrive at them.

Editorials should be sincere discussion based upon true statements in the premises from which honest argument may be developed by orderly deduction.

Advertising should be decent and honest in its selling intent and free from misleading or untrue statement.

Fairness and Accuracy

The profession of journalism must be fair in all its dealings with the public. Society exists and our laws are made under a government deriving its powers from the people and depending upon their approval for its stability and continued existence.

To the end that this continue to be justly so, it is of first importance that the whole people be kept fully and fairly informed.

The printed word is the most widespread and useful

medium of contact with the human mind, and the newspaper the most powerful agency for broad-casting information. Upon those who practice this profession rests the sacred duty of keeping these mighty means of communication among mankind pure at the source, undefiled of intent, and free of bias.

The profession of journalism is the greatest force in influencing human judgment. It is of first importance therefore, that judgments be formed after a fair presentation of all facts, accurately stated. This accuracy is not only to be an absence of misstatement, but the orderly presence of ill the pertinent truths.

In accuracy partisanship or the taint of propaganda has no part and cannot be present in fair journalism.

Sincerity and Decency

Sincerity of purpose as well as of writings characterizes the ethical journalist. Honest convictions inspire his written words. Back of them is the sincerity of desire that actuates all high intent.

With full realization of this, the members of the South Dakota Press Association accept their responsibility in truthfully reporting, in directing the thoughts, and shaping the conduct of society. In all sincerity and to the utmost extent that is right and reasonable in our respective communities, we pledge our efforts to this end.

Guaranteed the freedom of its press, the profession of journalism recognizes liberty is not license. It therefore reserves to itself the right of decision in what shall be printed and what shall be omitted.

This is done to safeguard our publications from unrefinement, to protect within reason the rights and reputations of individuals, and to free our papers from sordidness, except as we sincerely believe publication to be for the good of society.

We deem suppression to be a righteous function of ethical journalism to enforce omission of undue matter based upon an honorable intent to serve public good, and not selfish purpose.

Advertising, indecent in word or motive, the aim of which is to defraud, or which serves no useful purpose, has no part in the publications of the sincere member of the profession.

Honor

The honor of the profession is above the publication of an untruth upon an unworthy motive or upon a biased discussion based upon the false premise of a half truth entered upon for personal gain or party advancement.

The honor of the profession should be dear to all in a realization that individual character and conduct reflect good or ill upon the profession. If then, private honor never be smirched by private act or omission, the honor of the profession remains unsullied.

Recompense and Respect

As the servant is worthy of his hire, journalism is entitled to fair recompense in proportion as it serves. This must be evidenced by a demand which should be sufficient to establish all useful publications upon a sound business basis.

This is a prime essential because it is a fact that the publication, successful through honest endeavor and free of entanglements of financial obligation and political debt, has broader scope toward service, freer acceptance of its opinions and a larger opportunity for usefulness. Success in service is the end sought. And it is only to be obtained rightfully through integrity, industry, and a clear vision of the function of the true journalist.

As the profession of journalism demands of its members that they be honest, fair, and just to all, they in return shall demand fair treatment, justice, and respect from those with whom they deal.

MISSOURI DECLARATION OF PRINCIPLES AND CODE OF PRACTICE[3]

Preamble

In America, where the stability of the government rests upon the approval of the people, it is essential that newspapers, the medium through which the people draw their information, be developed to a high point of efficiency, stability, impartiality, and integrity. The future of the republic depends on the maintenance of a high standard among journalists. Such a standard can not be maintained unless the motives and conduct of the members of our profession are such as merit approval and confidence.

The profession of journalism is entitled to stand side by side with the other learned professions and is, far more than any other, interwoven with the lines of public service. The journalist can not consider his profession rightly unless he recognizes his obligation to the public. A newspaper does not belong solely to its owner and is not fulfilling its highest functions if devoted selfishly. Therefore the Missouri Press Association presents the following principles as a general guide, not as a set form of rules, for the practice of journalism.

Editorial

We declare as a fundamental principle that Truth is the basis of all correct journalism. To suppress the truth, when it properly belongs to the public, is a betrayal of public faith.

Editorial comment should always be fair and just and not controlled by business or political expediency. Nothing should be printed editorially which the writer will not readily acknowledge as his own in public.

Control of news or comment for business considerations is not worthy of a newspaper. The news should be covered, written, and interpreted wholly and at all times in the interest of the public. Advertisers have no claim on newspaper favor except in their capacity as readers and as members of the community.

No person who controls the policy of a newspaper should at the same time hold office or have affiliations, the duties of which conflict with the public service that his newspaper should render.

Advertising

It is not good ethics nor good business to accept advertisements that are dishonest, deceptive, or misleading. Concerns or individuals who want to use your columns to sell questionable stocks or anything else which promises great returns for small investment should always be investigated. Our readers should be protected from advertising sharks. Rates should be fixed at a figure which will yield a profit and never cut. The reader deserves a square deal and the advertiser the same kind of treatment.

Advertising disguised as news or editorial should not be accepted. Political advertising especially should show at a glance that it is advertising. It is just as bad 'to be bribed by the promise of political patronage as to be bribed by political cash.

To tear down a competitor in order to build up one's self is not good business, nor is it ethical. Newspaper controversies should never enter newspaper columns. Good business demands the same treatment to a competitor that one would like for the competitor to give to one's self. Create new business rather than try to take away that of another.

Advertising should never be demanded from a customer simply because he has given it to another paper. Merit, product, and service should be the standard.

Subscription

The claiming of more subscribers than are actually on the paid list in order to secure larger advertising prices is obtaining money under false pretenses. The advertiser is entitled 'to know just what he is getting for his money, just what the newspaper is selling to him. Subscription lists made up at nominal prices or secured by means of premiums or contests are to be strictly avoided.

Our Code

In every line of journalistic endeavor we recognize and proclaim our obligation to the public, our duty to regard always the truth, to deal justly and walk humbly before the gospel of unselfish service.

KANSAS CODE OF ETHICS FOR THE PUBLISHER[4]

In Advertising

Definition.—Advertising is news, or views, of a business or professional enterprise which leads directly to its profits or increased business.

News of the industrial or commercial development of an institution which in no way has a specific bearing upon the merits of its products is not advertising.

Besides news which leads to a profit, advertising also includes communications and reports, cards of thanks, etc., over the space of which the editor has no control.

Charges for the latter become more in the nature of a penalty to restrict their publication.

Responsibility.—The authorship of an advertisement should be so plainly stated in the contract or at the end that it could not avoid catching the attention of the reader before he has left the matter.

Unsigned advertisements in the news columns should either be preceded or followed by the word "advertisement" or its abbreviation.

Freedom of space.—We hold the right of the publisher to become a broker in land, loan, rental, and mercantile transactions through his want and advertising columns, and condemn any movement of those following such lines to restrict this right of the publisher to the free sale of his space for the purpose of bringing buyer and seller together.

This shall not be construed to warrant the publisher as such in handling the details, terms, etc., of the trade, but merely in safeguarding his freedom in selling his space to bring the buyer and seller together, leaving the bargaining to the principals.

Our advertising is to bring together the buyer and the seller, and we are not concerned whether it is paid for and ordered by the producer, the consumer, or a middleman.

Acceding to any other desires on the part of traders is knocking the foundations out from under the advertising business—the freedom of space. We hold that the freedom of space (where the payment is not a question) should only be restricted by the moral decency of the advertising matter.

We hold that the freedom of space denies us the right to sign any contract with a firm which contains any restrictions against the wording of the copy which we may receive from any other firm, even to the mentioning of the goods of the first firm by name.

Compensation.—We condemn the signing of contracts carrying with them the publication of any amount of free reading matter.

We condemn the acceptance of any exchange articles, trade checks, or courtesies in payment for advertising, holding that all advertising should be paid for in cash.

We condemn the giving of secret rebates upon the established advertising rate as published.

Rates.—All advertising rates should be on a unit per thousand basis and all advertisers are entitled to a full knowledge of the circulation, not only of the quantity but also of the distribution. Statements of circulation should show the number of bona fide subscribers, the number of exchanges, the number of complimentaries, and the number sold to newsdealers, and if possible the locality of distribution, in a general way.

Position.—Position contracts should he charged a fixed percentage above the established rate of the paper, and no contracts should be signed wherein a failure to give the position required results in a greater reduction from the established rate than the position premium is greater than the established rate.

Comparisons.—We consider it beneath the dignity of a publisher to place in his columns statements which make invidious comparisons between the amount of advertising carried or the circulation of his paper and that of his competitor.

Press Agents and Unpaid Advertising.—The specific trade name of an article of commerce, or the name of a merchant, manufacturer, or professional man *with reference* to his wares, products, or labors should not be mentioned in a pure news story.

We condemn as against *moral decency* the publication of any advertisement which will obviously lead to any form of retrogression, such as private medical personals, indecent massage parlor advertisements, private matrimonial advertisements, physician's or hospital's advertisement for the care of private diseases, which carry in them any descriptive or suggestive matter of the same.

In Circulation

Definition.—Circulation is the entire list of first-hand readers of a publication and comprises the paid readers, complimentary readers, exchange readers, and advertising readers.

Compensation.—Subscriptions should be solicited and received only on a basis of cash consideration, the paper and its payment being the only elements to the transaction.

Newsdealers.—The purchase of a quantity of papers should be made outright, allowing for no return of unsold copies.

Gambling.—We condemn the practice of securing subscriptions through the sale or gift of chances.

Complimentaries.—Complimentary copies should not be sent to doctors, lawyers, ministers, postal clerks, police or court officials for news or mailing privileges.

In Estimating

Definition. -Estimating is the science of computing costs. Its conclusion is the price.

Basis.—We do not favor the establishment of a minimum rate card for advertising which would be uniform among publishers, but we do favor a more thorough understanding of the subject of costs, and commend to our members the labors of the American Printers' Cost Commission of the First International Cost Congress recently held in Chicago. Let us learn our costs and then each establish a rate card based upon our investment and the cost of production, having no consideration for the comparative ability of the advertisers to pay, or the semi-news nature of the advertisement.

Quantity Discount.—We consider it unwise to allow discounts greater than 10 per cent from the rate of first insertion for succeeding insertions.

News

Definition.—News is the impartial report of the activities of mind, men, and matter which do not affend the moral sensibilities of the more enlightened people.

Lies.—We condemn as against truth:

1. The publication of fake illustrations of men and events of news interest, however marked their similarity, without an accompanying statement that they are not real pictures of the event or person, but only suggestive imitations.
2. The publication of fake interviews made up of the assumed views of an individual, without his consent.
3. The publication of interviews in quotations unless the exact, approved language of the interviewed be used. When an interview is not an exact quotation it should be obvious in the reading that *only* the thought and impression of the interviewer is being reported.
4. The issuance of fake news dispatches, whether the same have for their purpose the influencing of stock quotations, elections, or the sale of securities or merchandise. Some of the greatest advertising in the world has been stolen through news columns in the form of dispatches from unscrupulous press

agents. Millions have been made on the rise and fall of stock quotations caused by newspaper lies, sent out by designing reporters.

Injustice.—We condemn as against justice:

(1) The practice of reporters making detectives and spies of themselves in their endeavors to investigate the guilt or innocence of those under suspicion.

Reporters should not enter the domain of law in the apprehension of criminals. They should not become a detective or sweating agency for the purpose of furnishing excitement to the readers.

No suspect should have his hope of a just liberty foiled through the great prejudice which the public has formed against him because of the press verdict slyly couched in the news report, even before his arrest.

We should not even by insinuation interpret as facts our conclusions, unless by signature we become personally responsible for them. Exposition, explanation, and interpretation should be left to the field of the expert or specialist with a full consciousness of his personal responsibility.

(2) The publication of the rumors and common gossips or the assumptions of a reporter relative to a suspect pending his arrest or the final culmination of his trial. A staff of reporters is not a detective agency, and the right of a suspect to a fair and impartial trial is often confounded by a reporter's practice of printing every ill-founded rumor of which he gets wind.

Indecencies.—Classification: For the sake of clearness and order, crimes with which we will be concerned may be divided into those which offend against the *public trust* (such as bribery, defalcation, or embezzlement by a public official); those which offend against *private institutions* or *employers* (which are also often defalcations and betrayals of confidence), and crimes which offend against *private morality,* most often centering around the family relation.

(1) In dealing with the suspicions against *public officials* or trustees we urge that *only facts* put in their *true relation* and records be used in the news reports.

No presumption or conclusion of the reporter should be allowed to enter, even though it has all the elements of a correct conclusion.

Conclusions and presumptions should be placed in interviews with the identity of their author easily apparent.

If an editor desires to draw a conclusion on the case, let him sign it. Do not hide behind the impersonality of the paper with your personal opinions.

(2) In dealing with the suspicions against agents of private institutions, facts alone, put in their true relation, should again be used.

But in this class of stories suspicions and conclusions should be confined to those of the parties directly interested, and no statement of one party to the affair reflecting upon another should be published without at the same time publishing a statement of the accused relative thereto.

The comment of those not directly involved should not be published previous to the arrest or pending the trial.

(3) In dealing with the offenses against private morality, we should refuse to print any record of the matter, however true, until the warrant has been filed or the arrest made, and even then our report should contain only an epitome of the charges by the plaintiff and the answers by the defendant, preferably secured from their respective attorneys.

No society gossips or scandals, however true, should ever be published concerning such cases.

However prominent the principals, offenses against private morality should never receive *first-page position* and their details should be eliminated as much as possible.

Certain crimes against private morality which are revolting to our finer sensibilities should be ignored entirely; however, in the event of their having become public with harmful exaggerations, we may make an elementary statement, couched in the least suggestive language.

In no case should the reckless daring of the suspect be lionized.

(4) Except when the suspect has escaped, his picture should never be printed.

FOR THE EDITOR

Views

Definition.—Views are the impressions, beliefs, or opinions which are published in a paper, whether from the editorial staffs of the same, outside contributors, or secured interviews.

A Distinction.—We hold that whenever a publication confines the bulk of its views to any particular line of thought, class of views, or side of a moot question, it becomes to that extent a class publication, and insomuch ceases to be a newspaper.

An Explanation.—You will note by our definition of news that it is the impartial portrayal of the decent activities of mind, men, and matter. This definition applied to class publications would be changed by replacing the word *impartial* with the word *partial.*

In this section we will deal with *impartiality* in the presentation of the decent activities of the mind of the community—with the views or editorial policy of a paper.

Responsibility.—Whereas a view or conclusion is the product of some mind or minds, and whereas the value and significance of a view is dependent upon the known merit of its author or authors, the reader is entitled and has the right to know the personal identity of the author, whether by the signature in a communication, the statement of the reporter in an interview, or the caption in a special article, and *the paper as such* should in no wise become an advocate.

Influence (Editorial).—We should avoid permitting large institutions or persons to own stock in or make loans to our publishing business if we have reasonable grounds to believe that their interest would be seriously affected by any other than a true presentation of all news and free willingness to present every possible point of view under signature or interview.

Influence (Rcportorial).—No reporter should be retained who accepts any courtesies, unusual favors, opportunities for self-gain, or side employment from any factors whose interests would be affected by the manner in which his reports are made.

Deception.—We should not allow the *presumed* knowledge on the part of the interviewed that we are newspaper men to permit us to quote them without their explicit permission, but where such knowledge is certain we insist upon our right to print the views unless directly forbidden.

Faith With Interviewed.—An interview or statement should not be displayed previous to its publication without the permission of the author.

Bounds of Publicity.—A man's name and portrait are his private property and the point where they cease to be private and become public should be defined for our association.

EXTRACTS FROM RULES AND SUGGESTIONS PREPARED BY NEWSPAPERS FOR THE GUIDANCE OF THEIR STAFFS

THE BROOKLYN EAGLE[4]

Eagle Policy

1. *The Brooklyn Eagle* is primarily a home newspaper. It prints all the news, but aims to emphasize what is helpful rather than harmful. It believes in enterprise, but not in sensationalism. As a 3-cent newspaper it must uphold the highest standards of newspaper making. In particular it must always be truthful, accurate and fair.

2. "Brooklyn -First" is a cardinal principle of *Eagle* policy. This newspaper is a Brooklyn institution. It is also a public service institution. Whatever helps Brooklyn helps *The Eagle.* The more you know about Brooklyn and about *The Eagle* the better you will serve both.

3. *The Eagle* ranks as one of the world's greatest newspapers. The world is its province and its interest extends to the activities of human-kind everywhere. It is through being liberal and cosmopolitan that you can best contribute your share to preserving *The Eagle's* reputation as a broadly representative newspaper.

General Rules

The cardinal principle of good newspaper work is accuracy. *The Eagle* demands it and will insist on getting it. Verify your facts. Don't depend on some one's say-so, but go to the reference books.

Get names right. Nothing does a newspaper more harm than misspelled names. A list of names frequently used in *The Eagle* is included in this book. Supplement this with a list of your own. Carelessness in this connection always bars promotion and has led to dismissal.

Be fair. *The Eagle* wants to make friends, not enemies. Don't suppress any part of the truth for fear of spoiling a good story. Get both sides. Don't let any one use *The Eagle* to vent a grudge. Give the man or institution under attack a chance to make out a case.

When a person is charged with crime or has done something immoral or discreditable do not intrude the names of prominent relatives who are in no way involved. In writing obituaries do not emphasize unfortunate incidents in the lives of well-reputed persons.

Beware of the seekers after free publicity. Remember that space in *The Eagle* is worth twenty-five cents a line. What you give away *The Eagle* cannot sell. Don't help press agents cheat the advertising department.

Always hesitate to write anything that will offend the members of a race or sect. You may offend 20,000 *Eagle* readers with a single word. Do not mention the nationality or religious belief of a person under arrest unless that is an essential and inevitable feature of the story. Don't emphasize locality in fire or burglary stories or in news reports which give a special section an unsavory reputation.

Read *The Eagle* from the first page to the last. Only in that way can you become familiar with its style, its policy, and its special hobbies. If you discover errors, report them; if you have suggestions, make them. Read the other local papers and note how they handled your story. If you notice any important difference of fact, length or emphasis, call it to the City Editor's attention. To be known as a "live wire" is to be in line for promotion.

Beware of your own prejudices. Your personal likes or dislikes have no place in a news story. If you feel strongly on some subject try your hand at an editorial or write a letter for the Forum Page. But keep your news reports free from editorial comment.

Never promise to suppress a news story. News which you secure as an *Eagle* employee is *The Eagle's* property, and your superiors are the final judges of what shall or shall not be used. Requests for suppression or omission must always be carefully reported and reasons given, but your answer to the request must be nothing more than the promise that you will transmit it.

Always accept news items or suggestions from outsiders gratefully. Some may be worthless, but an attitude of encouragement ultimately wins help that will prove invaluable to you and to *The Eagle*.

REFERENCES

1. Written by Dean Collin V. Dyment, University of Oregon, and adopted by the Oregon State Editorial Association in 1922.
2. Written by a committee composed of J. H. McKcever, H. A. Sturges, Paul W. Kieser, and J. A Wright, and adopted by the South Dakota Press Association in 1922.
3. Written by William Southern, Jr., and adopted by the Missouri Press Association in 1921.
4. Written by Willis E. Miller and adopted by the Kansas Editorial Association in 1910—apparently the earliest code of ethics adopted by any association of journalists.

13

Towards Future of Indian Journalism

Journalism consists in buying white paper at two cents a pound and selling it at ten cents a pound.

—*Charles A. Dana*

Speeches that are measured by the hour will die with the hour.

—*Thomas Jeferson*

The rapid strides which the newspaper industry in India has made during these few years after freedom came are an earnest of vast possibilities which the Press Commission rightly calls "very bright". Today the Press stands on the threshold of a promising era of fairly rapid expansion promoted as much by the rise in income and the growth of education as by the vast development of democratic institutions and wider interest in public affairs.

The developing economy of India is steadily proceeding along the highway to the take-off stage. Nine Five Year Plans have been successfully completed.

Since the end of the war and since India became free, there has been, as the Press Commission of 1954 notes with evident satisfaction, "a welcome increase" in the number and circulation of newspapers. The Registrar of Newspapers for India in his report for 1961 records that there were 8,026 papers in 1960 as against 7,651 in the previous year. The total average circulation of 4,651 newspapers for which the Registrar could collect figures was 182.19 lakhs in 1960.

The rapid growth of this institution that plays a vital role in popular governance may be considered satisfactory, particularly in comparison with what existed, say, when India became free. Fifty eight years of freedom and 53 years of Planning have seen, among other things, a great growth of the press that in this largest democracy in the world as in other democracies, mirrors and moulds public opinion.

This growth, comparatively great as it has been, has not taken India anywhere near the advanced nations like the United States. There 1855 papers, according to a report prepared by the USIS in 1959, sold over 57 million copies every day to a population of 180 million. In India with her 430 million people, 318 newspapers sold in that year a meagre 4.2 million copies. Nor has this increase been consistent with the growth of political consciousness in the country, improvement in economic conditions and advance in literacy. On the basis of 16 per cent literacy, there are more than 65 million literates in the country with the minimum prospect of literacy increasing at the rate of 5 per cent every year. True, some of those taken as literates are still in the school stage who form newspaper readers only potentially. And true indeed, every adult literate cannot afford to buy a newspaper. Making allowance for all these factors, effective circulation of just over four million copies among 65 million literates must cause some concern.

The concern becomes more, when competent authorities claim, as does a memorandum on newspaper circulations prepared by an advertising agency, that "there are surprising sales of what are virtually luxury goods to relatively poorly-paid people in this country". The popularity of cinema and other luxuries or semi-luxuries would not suggest that "the cost of a daily or even a weekly newspaper is beyond the means of half so many people as one might imagine".

Into this vital aspect were conducted careful inquiries. The National Sample Survey revealed that the households in urban areas spent a little over 30 nP. a month on newspapers while for those in the rural areas the figure was less than 3 nP. The per capita income at the time of the survey was Rs. 280.

Many other reasons may be listed for this inadequate growth: Concentration of papers in towns, metropolitan location of distribution centres, inadequate communication facilities, insufficient distribution arrangements and consequent failure to penetrate into rural areas, where the bulk of the population lives. Newspaper circulation is mainly urban. From all this, the Press Commission came to this disappointing and depressing conclusion : "Unless there is a substantial change in the trend disclosed by the survey, as for instance a diversion of a part of the amount spent on ceremonials to heads like amusements, education or newspapers and periodicals, no significant expansion of the press can be expected". This is not particularly helpful. And that is perhaps why Dr. N.B. Parulekar, in his Presidential address to the 1961 session of Indian and Eastern Newspaper Society, called for a "fresh study of the press by the press itself" to find out the causes for the stunted growth of the newspapers and suggest right remedies. The problem in India is not one of manicuring into a well-tended garden a luxuriant growth of jungle vegetation but of finding out how this tender sapling can grow into a giant tree.

That this tender sapling can and must, in national interests grow into a giant tree admits of little doubt. The great scope for expansion pertains inevitably to language newspapers. The advertising agency memorandum to which reference has been made believes that the language press based on present rate of progress of literacy, standards of living wage etc. can hope for six times its present circulation. A progressively expanding language press is an inevitable and intimate part of the mass movement when papers will look beyond the leisured class and cater to the common man.

The Place of English Press

The Press Commission feel that "the scope for expanding the circulation of English newspapers is definitely restricted." To a certain extent it is so. But the statement would seem to be rather over-cautious. Rapid growth has been common to both the English and the language Press. A leading English paper increased its circulation by nearly 70 per cent during the ten years after 1950. Other English papers have registered during the same period a rise of about fifty per cent and more. English journalism would continue to take its share in the progress that journalism will make in India.

The confidence is based on solid facts. English that was threatened with dethronement after freedom came will now continue as the associate official language for an indefinite period. This is no small gain. The publication of a large number of books in English is evidence of its continuing influence. More evidence comes from the that the Indian National Congress proposes to start an English newspaper from New Delhi. The Communist Party proposes to emulate the example. These may be only blades of grass. But they show the way the wind blows.

What sort of press, whose future we have assured ourselves is bright, are we likely to have ? As a general proposition it may be said that the press of the future will be what the public want it to be. A democratic country deserves the press it gets as it deserves the government it gets. If the people get the press they deserve, it becomes the responsibility of the people to see that they help build up a free, independent and prosperous press. The responsibility is equally that of government in a democracy and of the press itself to see that the Fourth Estate grows up as a palladium of popular rights. It must so grow up and then we could say with Thomas Jefferson: "Were it left to me to decide whether we should have a government without newspapers or newspapers without government, I would not hesitate for a moment to prefer the latter.

The press should not be a Beggars' Opera. A servile press is a sure invitation to disaster. A free, democratic nation cannot for long maintain its freedom or its democracy without a free press. The moral is obvious. There should be ever-increasing public support for newspapers, not by subsidies or spoon-feeding, which are pernicious for all concerned, but by a steadily growing, paid readership.

Stake of Society

Society has a far greater stake in good journalism than it realizes. The people must be fully and completely informed and given all the material necessary for the continuing development of man's personality in a welfare State

The press fights by itself alone but not for itself alone. It fights the battles of the people who must realize and give evidence of that realization that the newspapers are the eyes and cars of the community.

A democratic government must realize that it has a duty, in the interest of democracy and ordered government itself, to help build up a free and independent press. One of the ways in which it can render this help is to resist the temptation to have on the Statute Book Press laws that terrorize the less timid editors. The press has no more rights than the ordinary citizen and has no special privileges. Why then seek to impose separate laws and special penalties

? Some of these have continued long after the emergency ceased to be ; some others are unknown to law in other countries. In any case their existence is itself a stigma on the Indian press. The press laws must go. And with them must go the Press Advisory and the Liaisoning system.

Scrupulous adherence to the principle of propriety in the matter of distribution of government advertisements will remove one cause for complaint. Another cause will go if prompt steps are taken to ensure availability of adequate quantities of newsprint which is the basic raw material of the newspaper industry and of democracy itself. There is one newsprint factory, the Nepa Mills, in the public sector in the country with an installed capacity of 100 tons. With full production it will meet about one third of the country's requirements of 90,000 tons of newsprint per annum. The decision to double the capacity of the mill and also to establish two new mills is welcome. The stringent foreign exchange position is a serious headache. But adjustments must be made with regard to vital sectors of national life like the press. More efforts, as the Indian and Eastern Newspaper Society has repeatedly emphasized, are called for on the part of government to secure for the press adequate quantities of this raw material, which in the view of a leading editor should receive, in the order of national values, a place next only to food. Also steps must be taken to encourage manufacture of press equipment and printing machinery in India and make them available at reasonable cost. There is a strong case for further concessions in postal, telephone, telegraphic and teleprinter charges for the press. Cable and wireless rates are considerably high. Substantial reduction in international telegraph charges is essential for the development of the press in this country.

The responsibility of the press to society is tremendous. That responsibility becomes greater in a society such as ours where there is not sufficient volume of public opinion to assert itself or to react to the performance of the press. A pervading sense of social purpose is the basis and bedrock of all good journalism. The New York *Times* gave, in short, the aim of honest journalism when it adopted, the news that is fit to print", as its motto. The London *Times* the objective of decent and purposeful journalism when its own aims in the following shining words, "To be the first but not the hastiest with the news; to persuade and not to dogmatize to be emphatic without being hysterical, to be graphic without sensationalism ; to give the story and to reject the stunt, to miss nothing that is amusing and to keep the trivial in proportion, to give the news faithfully and fully without featuring the worst side of human nature.' It may be a far cry to this golden ideal. But it is a goal worth working for.

The ultimate goal of the Indian society is clearly defined in the directive principles of the Constitution — and that is to secure and protect a social order in which justice, social, economic and political shall inform all the institutions of national life. The press as a responsible part of democratic society must engage itself in presenting a clear picture of the goal and the progress of the journey to it. On the whole it has been doing so. The standard and performance of the Indian press have, according to the findings of the Press Commission, been in general "fair and accurate".

Standard Maintenance

This does not mean that there are no instances of deplorable lapse from these standards. Nor does this mean that there can be any relaxation of continuous effort at improvement. The outlines of a code of conduct for journalists were sketched when C.R. Srinivasan, a former President of the Editors' Conference, said that the Ten Commandments provide perhaps the negative basis for it, while our own scriptures emphasize the positive aspects in the twin rules, "Satyam vada, Dharma chara" (Tell the truth and do your duty). The establishment of a Statutory Press Council, like the Bar Council and the Medical Council, has been suggested by many, to serve as an instrument for safeguarding the freedom of the press and for helping in the maintenance of standards.

The Press Commission made a recommendation in this behalf. Little has been done about it all these seven years. Prime Minister Nehru in his message to the 1961 Conference of the Indian Federation of Working Journalists, wanted them "to lay down standards to which the journalists should conform". The Conference could do no better than request the Prime Minister to implement the recommendations of the Press Commission and constitute the Press Council. The Press Council is expected to enable the Press to function as a self-governing, self-disciplined, self-sustaining, autonomous body that will take care of standards of journalism.

One factor, perhaps more than others, makes difficult the maintenance of such standards. And that is the lamentable decline in the status of editors. This decline to which the Press Commission drew painful attention was mentioned in his address to the 1961 session of the All India Newspaper Editors' Conference by Prime Minister Nehru, who noted with regret that "the editors had lost their old position and count for a little less now than they used to do in the past". And one result is that their "rather platonic writing becomes duller and duller". There are other and more disastrous results of this eclipse of the editor by the manager that has been brought about by the economics of production of newspapers.

It is a wholly deplorable development. The future of journalism, as the Press Commission emphasize, depends upon the independence of the editor. It is only a valiant crusader who can fight the evergrowing battle against pressures, internal and external on the newspaper and maintain its integrity. The never-ending war for safeguarding the people's divine right to know can hardly be waged by a deflated, devalued editor. For maintaining the status of the editor who in America "holds a position that exceeds that of most college presidents", the Press Commission has made certain recommendations. On the position of the editor, his personality, force and character depends the newspapers' role in society, a point that was ably underlined by Frank Moraes, editor of the *Indian Express,* at a Seminar on the Press and Public Opinion held in 1958 in Bombay. Norman Issacs, editor of The *Louisville Times,* contested the proposition, saying "a newspaper's role and stature can be determined by the editor but *only* if the proprietor is willing to permit the editor the necessary freedom. It is the character and intent of ownership that is the dominant factor."

A Potential Danger

Out of this trend of ownership arises a potential danger to the development of good journalism. Examining what that veteran journalist Pothan Joseph calls "chain stores in newspaper industry," the Press Commission found that out of a total of 330 dailies, five owners control 39 papers and 31.2 per cent of the circulation. Fifteen owners control 54 papers and 50 per cent of the circulation. Considerable degree of concentration which is the result of what Earl Attlee calls "Cannibalism" in the world of newspapers, already exists. The 1961 Conference of the Commonwealth Press Union discussed with concern this monopolistic tendency in the newspaper world. This tendency, in the words of Mr. Nehru, comes in the way of a free press. We are warned against further concentration even though it may not be due to evil designs but largely attributable to economic and technological factors.

Commercialization is inevitable. And the profit motive may easily become a great danger. The remedy may come as many fondly hope it will come, when the journalist will function as the-self-respecting member of a great profession. This is true so far as it goes. But it does not go far enough. The right and the real remedy may be formation of public trusts for the newspapers and voluntary agreements of owners to limit their sovereignty, a trend that was approvingly noted by the Press Commission of the United Kingdom.

The Indian Press Commission have suggested diffusion of ownership and control so that there are few impediments to the free flow of news and a wide variety of opinion finds scope for expression. They have also suggested annual publication of ownership details and a watch over the trend by the Press Registrar. These have been implemented. If the results are not satisfactory, strength will be added to the demand for a high power commission to go into the structure of newspaper industry and concentration of ownership.

The News Agencies

An offshoot of concentration of newspaper ownership, namely the emergence of two news agencies controlled by "the press barons", is a source of anxious concern. Of the two old agencies, the United Press has gone into liquidation and the Press Commission has recommended that the other one, the Press Trust of India, should be converted into a public corporation.

Meanwhile, these two new agencies have come up. The Federation of Working Journalists views this is seriously threatening the freedom of the press, affecting the objective distribution of news and harming the growth of small papers. There is a demand that only such news agencies as are developed as public trusts should be recognized and given facilities for operation. The demand is legitimate.

The newspapers of the future have to be better and

brighter and pleasanter to the eye and easier to the mind. They should give better, more varied and specialized coverage. The papers have to be an integral part of the normal mental and moral requirements of the people. The press has to come down to the market place in the service of the common man. It follows that the language used must be simple, direct and easily understood. A survey conducted in Britain showed that school girls of II years of age reading editorials of mass circulation adult newspapers failed to understand only two words in every hundred. A similar survey in India will not yield such satisfactory results. The moral cannot be missed.

This applies to metropolitan papers and more so to district newspapers. In fact, as I said in my presidential address at the Convention of the Working Journalists of Madhya Pradesh, held some time back, the future is with small newspapers. Small papers even in America where newspaper chains are thick and long, are, as E.S. Friendly, former President of the American Newspaper Publishers Association, says "a grass-roots foundation of journalism which gives strength and virility to all newspapering". More than 1,500 papers out of America's 1,855 daily newspapers are published in towns with less than 50,000 population and truly reflect the life and answer the needs of the American people. There are many towns in India with more than a lakh of population which do not have a daily paper. District journalism aiming at restricted and local readership offers vast scope. The growth of small newspapers is also an antidote in some measure to newspaper chains, the dangers of winch have been discussed earlier in this chapter.

The Future of Indian Journalism

Magazines and periodicals with brightly coloured covers which one sees in the bookstalls have a rich field before them. They are not newspapers but they are part of the press.

There are nearly 2,600 of those in this country ranging from the *Astrological Magazine* to *Zamindar's Bulletin,* dealing with different trades and technical matters, different professions and occupations embracing every aspect of life under the Indian sun. As fuller and ampler life develops under democracy, the scope for these magazines, as for journalism in general, will become immense.

Scope is also substantial for the development of syndicates for the supply of features, short stories, special articles, cartoons and comic strips. The progress of regional journalism for which I foresee a great future will demand the services of and will in return be helped by such syndicates. The small town newspapers may not have the resources to employ whole-time staff for preparing these features which can well be supplied by syndicates that are in a position to engage specialists for the purpose. Cartoons and comic strips transcend linguistic barriers and get clients all over the country. Some syndicates have been functioning in India for some time now. Some have recently come into existence. More enterprise joined to greater resources will be able to exploit this vast field.

Radio and television as competitive institutions for public education, are fast coming up. They constitute competition, as Roy L. Matson, editor of the *Wisconsin State Journal* declared at the Bombay Seminar. But he did not consider them rivals because "they have failed in their mission to serve the same purpose as newspapers in society". When radio came in America and again when television came there, the newspaper proprietors, we are told, "wailed in the anguish of the prophet of doom". Actually however, far from heralding the doom, radio and television became the harbingers of new newspaper readership, by whetting the appetite of listeners and viewers.

Radio and Television

The radio and television do compete for the advertise'

money and the readers' time. To a certain extent the average reader spends less time today than he did before, on his favourite newspaper. But all this has not reduced the number of newspaper readers ; it has increased them. The ghost that the radio and television are rivals to the press was laid long ago.

In India, radio is a government monopoly that has already celebrated its silver jubilee. The number of radio stations has gone up to 28. There are 2.1 million licensed radio sets. The hours of broadcast in a year have increased to 122,000. All this marks noteworthy progress.

Here again, the possibilities are vast. Illiteracy, which is a chink in our armour, is no obstacle in the case of the wireless as in the case of the press. The far-flung areas of the countryside are being opened up and brought under the educative influence of radio, by installing a large number of community sets. There is emphasis on rural programmes which must become more pronounced.

Radio-mindedness is limited mainly by the paying capacity of the people. Today radio sets are costly. Manufacture of cheaper radio sets is engaging the attention of the authorities. Small sets for local reception will go a long way to answer most of our requirements and enable the public to derive fullest benefits from the All India Radio.

The celebration in 1961 of the silver jubilee of AIR was an occasion for renewing the demand to convert it into a public corporation. Today it is a government department subject to all the irksome restrictions, routine, and red tape associated with such departments. Complaints about its news service are not a few. Opinion in India favours modelling AIR on the BBC. There is not much enthusiasm for the American example of commercial radio enterprise. The golden mean of a public corporation is accepted even by those in authority, but only as a distant ideal. That distance must be reduced and AIR set up as a public corporation as early as possible.

Education for Journalism

Journalists may be born ; but they are made. And it is necessary to produce an army of skilled craftsmen who will answer the mighty challenges of the times. For the amateurish inefficiency one sees most of the newspapers in India, the mode of recruitment of staff and the virtual absence of training are responsible. A realization of this fact is slowly dawning. The evidence of it is that more than five universities have introduced journalism courses, of which the best and the most scientific is the one conducted by the Hislop College affiliated to the Nagpur University. The Hislop project, started in 1952 under the leadership of Prof. Roland Wolseley, who is the General Editor of this volume, has done notable work.

The newspaper office with its plentiful stains of the printer's ink, it has been argued, is the best school of journalism. True, but the training given by a journalism course will greatly add to the efficiency of the craftsman. N. Raghunatha Iyer, then assistant editor of *The Hindu* who inaugurated the Hislop project, went to the extent of suggesting that education for journalism should be among the basic cultural equipment that goes to make the new society.

In this new society, the journalistic craftsmen may not be "honoured guests at a Barmecide feast" It is a happy sign that journalists have organized themselves. While some have accepted, the professional basis for organization, others have adopted trade union methods. There may be differences of approach but all of them strive for securing better conditions of work for this class of public servants. The Working Journalists (Conditions of Service) "Act and the constitution of the Wage Board have served to secure for the journalists minimum wages and conditions of work. They have got to go a long way. A start has just been made.

A new era unfolds itself in the world press. And this brings with it what the International Press Institute calls "new tasks, new professional demands and new moral demands in order to satisfy the needs of the People living in complex and rapidly expanding world. "The great: unanswerable challenge of our times", as Mrs. Vijaialakshmi Pandit, while India's High Commissioner in London, said in addressing the Commonwealth Press Union to which reference has been made earlier, "faces us here on earth and not in space or the high heavens."

The press which has effectively served India in her fight for freedom and in her development in the post-Independence period will, play a worthy part in the ampler life that is opening up in the country and fulfil a definite purpose in the economy of the nation. This definite purpose includes among other things keeping the people, in a dynamic economy and an evolving democracy, informed about local and world developments and promoting a live interest in the national plans.

Pandit Nehru charges the press with the additional duty of helping in correcting "the gradual extension of what is vulgar in life and help, not only in building up a better and brighter social conscience, but a social behaviour on the little things of life."

[*Courtesy:* K.P. Narayanan]

14

The Journalism Law

Between the great things we cannot do and the small things we will not do . . . the danger is that we shall do nothing.

—Henry G. Weaver

The survival of the fittest is the ageless law of nature, but the fittest are rarely the strong. The fittest are those endowed with the qualifications for adaptation, the ability to accept the inevitable and conform to the unavoidable, to harmonize the existing or changing conditions.

—Dance E. Smalley

"A man who speaks in a newspaper has no greater right than he who speaks out of it. A newspaper is no sanctuary behind which a person can shield himself for breaking the laws of the land."

Newspaper is regarded as an institution from which favour and reprimand go out. In a democracy the free press is exhibit No. 1. It is the most important medium of public opinion which pulsates and invigorates the democratic system of government. And the freedom of press in pursuance of that, is firmly set in the constitutional structure of India and is guaranteed.

"All citizens shall have the right to freedom of speech and expression" [Art. 19(a) Constitution of India]. And this right fundamentally includes the "freedom of the press".

In a recent judgement, Sakal Papers (Private) Ltd., vs. Union of India, the Supreme Court of India states, "The right to propagate one's idea is inherent in the conception of freedom of speech and expression. For the purpose of propagating his ideas every citizen has a right to publish them to disseminate them and to circulate them." He is entitled to do so either by word of mouth or by writing. The right guaranteed thus extends, subject to any law competent under article 19(2), not merely to the matters which he is entitled to circulate but also to the volume of circulation. In other words a citizen is entitled to propagate his views and reach any class and number of readers as he chooses ....." While the right to freedom of press is so guaranteed yet this right is not a licence. It is fortified by such reasonable restrictions as the legislatures may deem necessary in the interest of the security of the state, friendly relations with the foreign states, public order, decency of morality or in relation to contempt of court, defamation or incitement to an offence [Art. 19(2)].

As was pointed out in Ramesh Thappar vs. State of Madras [1950 S.C. 124], "Very narrow and stringent limits have been set to permissible legislative abridgment of the right of free speech and expression and this was doubtless due to the realization that freedom of speech and of the press lay at the foundation of all domestic organizations for without free political discussion no public education, so essential for the proper functioning of the process of popular government, is possible. A freedom of such amplitude might involve risks of abuse. But the framers of the Constitution may well have reflected with Madison, who was the 'leading spirit in the preparation of the First Amendment of the Federal Constitution', that it is better to leave a few of its noxious branches to their luxuriant growth than, by pruning them away, to injure the vigour of those yielding the proper fruits."

It is the court that fairly interprets whether the

restrictions imposed on the press by the Parliament or the State Legislatures are reasonable within the meaning of Art. 19(2). The Court has been assigned the role of a sentinel on the *quivive.* Thus a journalist must fully understand the implication of the "freedom of the press". He can write and report as fearlessly and independently as his wisdom or conscience might dictate but limits are set and he must operate within that. No sooner you trespass, the protecting hand of the Liberty of Press would be withdrawn. The "freedom of the press" in effect is a "limited freedom" not only in India but also in other older democracies like the U.S.A. and the United Kingdom. The liberty of the press, as Lord Mansfield said in R. V. Dean of St. Asaph (1784) S.T.R. 428 at p. 431, consists in printing without any previous licence, subject to the consequences of law.

Freedom of expression is guaranteed to the press as to an individual, but it affords, no special privileges or right to unlimited publication of comments or news in violation of the Constitutional prohibitions and the statute. There is no freedom of press without co-relative obligations and responsibilities [Art. 19(2)]. Those engaged in journalistic work of any kind should, therefore, understand the principle of some of the important phases of the law of the press. It may be divided into: (i) Libel and Defamation; (ii) Contempt of Court; (iii) Copyright; (iv) Law of Privacy; (v) Regulatory provisions, like Security of State, Friendly Relations with Foreign State, Public Order, and Decency or Morality.

Libel and Defamation

The press is free but subject to the law of libel; defamation committed by the press has at all times been considered the main offence, one that overshadows all other infringement of rights of which a newspaper may render itself guilty. Everyday a journalist deals with the reputation of individuals, in stating facts, allegations and charges, in making editorial comments, writing "scoops" and framing headlines, and in many more ways. It is, therefore, imperative that journalists should arm themselves with the knowledge of this branch of law to avoid involving the newspapers concerned in any embarrassing position and irksome and sometimes damaging litigation.

"Defamation" is a broader term applied in reference to defamatory statements made by word of mouth or by writing. The term "libel" applies to the defamatory statements published by the press or otherwise. "Slander" refers to oral defamation.

Libel is the chief terror of newspapers. It is the *publication* of a false and defamatory statement, expressed in writing, printing, or by signs, pictures or in some form which is permanent, published without lawful justification or excuse, concerning a person and which injures his reputation. It is calculated to convey to those to whom it is published an imputation on the person or injurious to him in his trade, profession, or business or holding him up to hatred, contempt or ridicule or tending to induce evil opinion of him in the minds of right-thinking persons. Such a statement is libellous and actionable whatever the intention of the writer may have been.

Any written words are defamatory which impute to the plaintiff that he has been guilty of any crime, fraud, dishonesty, immorality, vice, or dishonourable conduct, or has been accused or suspected of any such misconduct, or which suggest that the plaintiff is suffering from any infectious disorder; or which have a tendency to injure him in his office, profession, calling or trade.

And so too, are all words which hold the plaintiff up to contempt, scorn, or ridicule, and which, by thus engendering an evil opinion of him in the minds of right-thinking men, tend to deprive him of friendly intercourse and society. The essence of the libel is that there must be a false imputation either on the character of the plaintiff or on the mode in which he carries on his business or trade.

Libel is a false statement about a person to his discredit. It may be about a reference to an individual or a firm or a company. There is no codified law of libel in India. It is based on precedents drawn from English law.

The Ingredients of Libel

Ingredients of libel are: (i) The statement must be false; (ii) The statement must be defamatory (iii) The statement must have been published; (iv) The statement must be in some permanent form; (v) The statement must be concerning the plaintiff.

Generally, Libellous statements are divided in the following group: (i) Exciting hatred, contempt, scorn or ridicule; (ii) To be shunned or avoided by society; (iii) Affecting profession, calling or office; (iv) Affecting trade or business.

Statements that are damaging to the personal reputation of a person hold him up to ridicule, hatred or contempt. A person is exposed to hatred, contempt or scorn if dishonourable conduct or character is attributed to him and if such imputations are false.

To publish falsely of a person that he has killed his mother, that he has robbed a bank, that he is a drunkard that he beats his wife, that he is suffering from leprosy or some other infectious disease, that a woman is unchaste, that a lawyer knows no law, that a physician is a quack, is libellous.

To call a person a liar, a scandal monger, an infernal villain, a frozen snake, perjurer, a block-head, or a fool, a counterfeiter, a house thief, vile person, a very opposite of pious, a poor ungrammatical ignoramous, scoundrel, insane fanatic, low, mean, coward, paranoiac, low degraded person, lewd and depraved, or a man with impaired mental faculties are all instances where they were held libellous. It is libellous to impute any dishonourable conduct to another.

To compare a person with animals whose habits or characteristics are treacherous, odious, disgusting or offensive, like calling him "black sheep", "snake in the grass", "jackal" or "swine" is libellous. It has been held libellous to publish in a magazine under the name of the plaintiff who in fact was a writer of great repute, a story of inferior quality of which the plaintiff was not the author; to publish in a newspaper a story in which the plaintiff is made to appear ridiculous, even though he himself had narrated the story in the first instance, is libellous. To impute to any one who holds an office, or carries on a profession or trade, that he is unfit therefore, or that he has acted improperly, there, is libellous. Instances can be stated *ad infinitum*. The writer should ask himself, are the words calculated to injure the reputation of the person to whom they refer?

To charge a person with bad faith, treachery, and hypocrisy is to impute a conduct which would be condemned by any just, fair minded and reasonable citizen. To refer to a person as one who sympathized with crime is libellous.

Comparison to Persons in History

Libel may be committed by comparing persons to the characters in history, fiction, or mythology, if the persons with whom comparison was made were dishonourable, odious, contemptible, or otherwise known for undesirable characteristics.

Such statements and imputations as stated above are all known as libel *per se*. Any report that falsely imputes crime to an individual is a statement libellous *per se*.

Libel per *se* maybe defined as the false and privileged

publication by letter, newspaper or other form of writing, of unfounded statements or charges which expose a person to hatred, distrust, contempt, ridicule, or obloquy, or which tend to cause such person to be avoided or which have a tendency to injure such person in his office, occupation, business or employment, and which necessarily cause injury to the person concerned, in his personal, social, official or business relations of life, so that legal injury may be presumed or implied from the bare fact of the publication itself.

Absence of any intention or malice in the publication of such a report is no defence. A publication to be libellous *per se* does not need to contain the technical statutory language and phrases essential to a good indictment of the crime charged. Stories and statements that make readers believe that the person is guilty of a crime, although no specific offence is indicated, are libellous *per se.*

An imputation of a criminal offence, in order to be actionable *per se,* may be couched in any words, but the inference must be clear and unequivocal. [Mitha Rustomji vs. Nusserwanji Engineer. A.I.R. 1941 Bom. 278: 196 I.C. 503: 43 Cr. L. J. 17: Bom. L. R. 631: 14 R. B. 135.]

> "... So strict is the rule that a mere statement in a newspaper or publication that a person named is suspected of murder, that grounds for suspicions are said to exist, or that there is rumour of his confession, is actionable without even an allegation of special damages."

Public opinion is not static, and changes in the views of ordinary reasonable citizens as to what is creditable or discreditable may make words which are very damaging to a person's reputation at one time perfectly harmless at another and vice-versa.

When an authorized publication is libellous *per se,*

malice and damage are presumed from the fact of publication and no proof is required as to any resulting injury. The law presumes that general damages actually, proximately, and necessarily result from an unauthorized publication which is libellous *per se* and they are not required to be proved by evidence since they arise by inference of law, and are allowed whenever the immediate tendency of the publication is to impair plaintiff's reputation, although no actual pecuniary loss has in fact resulted.

Test

How the "public" reacts to the publication of a statement or a picture is the test of a charge of libel. It is not necessary that the statement should be calculated, to call forth hatred, contempt, or ridicule from the entire public. The Supreme Court of United States declared that the alleged defamation need not be universal consent be considered defamatory, but that it is libellous if it would hurt one's standing with a considerable and respectable class in the community. The standard of understanding is that of the ordinary reasonable man having the intelligence, knowledge, education, and experience of the average man in the class of the people to whom the words were published.

A person has a right to the enjoyment of his reputation and of the moral and material advantages to which it may entitle him in his relationship with the people including what L.J. Slesser, in Uouson Poff's case—(1934) 50 T.L.R. 681—calls, "the opportunities of receiving respectful consideration from the world". Any imputation which tends to infringe this right, and if published, is libellous.

Innuendo

Under certain circumstances, a publication that is not libellous *per se* and seems on its face innocent of defamatory meaning, may cause injury to the reputation of an individual, when the surrounding circumstances are taken into consideration. In these cases, the circumstances that surround the incident or its publication make it libellous rather than words themselves or their meaning. *This is libel by innuendo* or *libel per quod.*

Such a publication apparently may seem to be innocent of defamatory meanings but may cause injury to the reputation of an individual when the surrounding circumstances are taken into consideration. The words may be defamatory in a secondary sense, i.e. the words, though not defamatory in their ordinary sense, are used with special libellous meanings. That is *libel per quod* or *libel by innuendo.*

In these cases, the circumstances that surround the incident or its publication rather than the words themselves or their ordinary meaning make it libellous. Even the name of the person concerned (plaintiff) may not be specifically mentioned. But if the accusing fingers are judged by others to have been pointed at him—action lies.

To 'drop a hint' is to stab a reputation. The innuendo or libellous matter may be hidden among cleverly beautiful words. In that famous case Cassidy vs. Daily Mirror Newspapers Ltd. [1929 2. K.B. 331], the engagement of a gentleman and lady was announced by a photograph. The gentleman was already married. His lawful wife brought a suit for damages, alleging that by this announcement her friends understood to mean that she was not lawfully married but had been living an immoral life with her husband. The newspaper concerned had to pay damages of £500. [Also see an earlier case Jones vs. E. Hulton & Co., 1910. A.C. 20. Youssoupoff vs. Metro Goldwyn Mayer Picture Ltd. (1934), 50 T.L.R. 581.]

It is the duty of the journalist dealing with the copy concerned to detect any such objectionable material and save himself and the newspaper he has the honour to work for from any claim of damages.

Thus in a libel action it must be proved by the aggrieved person that the publication refers to him and that it conveys defamatory meaning and is capable of bearing the meaning which he seeks to put upon it and that is false. The standard to be applied is: what would reasonable people understand by the alleged libel ? It is not what the author of the libel wanted people to understand. His intention is immaterial.

A concert was announced in a newspaper and the name of the plaintiff, a widely-known public singer, was placed third in a list of four. In the statement of claim the plaintiff averred that by so doing the defendant showed the plaintiff as inferior to Nos. 1 and 2, the first and second places were the sign of superior reputation, and placing of her name as third in order was calculated to injure her reputation. Judgement was passed for the plaintiff.

.A defamatory imputation may be conveyed not merely by direct statement but also indirectly by ironical remarks, idioms, figures of speech and the like. With the headline, "How Lawyer B Treats his Clients" there appeared a report of a particular case in which one of the clients of B had been badly treated. The case was correctly reported but the headline was held to be libellous, innuendo being that lawyer B always treats his client badly.

To make a ironic statement about an attorney ("An honest lawyer" ?) is actionable. "You will not play the Jew or the hypocrite" is actionable if made ironically.

Where the libel consists of picture or caricature the libellous nature of the representation must be stated by innuendoes and it should be stated in the statement of claim and that it referred to the plaintiff. The use of a photograph of a person in connection with a libellous story will be liable of that person even if his name is not mentioned in the story or with the photograph. The publication of a caricature of a person the effect of which is to hold him up to contempt is libellous because the effect is the same as if his name were used in connection with libellous matter.

Other Libels

Erroneous announcements of personal notices, births, deaths, engagements, marriages, such as the marriage of a woman of high social position to a man of low caste or reputation, are libellous. The libel may result from an error or inaccuracy, by a simple mistake of using one incorrect initial or by even misspelling a name by one letter whereby an entirely different person may be damaged.

Accordingly it is of utmost importance to maintain a high standard of accuracy in reporting and sub-editing. Libelknis headlines are as bad as the libellous contents of the story. Libellous headlines may destroy the privilege. There is a growing tendency to take chances with headlines which may any day be a source of trouble to a newspaper. Wrong lines under the photograph may become libellous. The publication of a libellous story with such words as "it is reported" and "it is alleged" affords no protection. It only helps in the mitigation of damages. It is immaterial that the libel is couched in a form of hearsay.

Publication Explained

Publication consists in making known the libellous statement after it has been written or communicated to some person other than the person for whom it is written. It is the communication of the defamatory statement to a person or persons other than the person defamed. The publisher, although he is not the author of a libel nor in any way connected with or responsible for its being composed or written, is liable as a publisher. Every sale or delivery if the written or printed copy of a libel is a fresh publication.

Publication of a libellous statement takes place not only at the office of the publication of the newspaper and not only in the city in which it is published but also where it circulates. Each particular sale of a newspaper containing a libel constitutes legal publication and is a distinct cause of action. Publication includes a subsequent re-publication or translation thereof.

A person by repeating the libel, makes it his own and is responsible for the repetition. If the original publication was privileged, a person who repeats such a libel is responsible for the repetition. Privilege is something distinct from publication. It does not negate publication, but it excuses it.

A libellous statement to be actionable must contain an imputation concerning some particular person or persons whose identity can be established. Even if no name is mentioned, it must be proved that the imputation was directed against a particular person or persons who can be identified. Intention as affecting libel or motive with which the words are written is, as a rule, immaterial.

If the writer has in fact injured the plaintiff's reputation, he is liable even if he did not intend to do so and had no such purpose in mind when he wrote the words. Publication is false and defamatory, although if published accidentally or inadvertently with honest belief in the truth of the statement, those circumstances may, however, do much to mitigate the damages. A newspaper publishing libellous matter does so at *its own* peril.

Defences

The following are the important defences that may be urged in any action for libel: (i) Proof of the truth of the statement; (ii) Privilege (absolute and qualified); (iii) Fair comment or criticism.

Privilege

There is no absolute privilege available to the press.

This is available only to members in the legislatures, to the judges, lawyers, witnesses or parties in court, or to acts of states or state communication, Technically publication of the same is not absolutely privileged.

"The journalist's reports of such proceedings do not carry with it the immunity that the law grants to the participants."

Qualified Privilege

However, publication of such privileged proceedings or judicial proceedings after a long chequered history are now accepted as a "qualified privilege" and they can be published with immunity even if they were libellous.

To perform some public, legal, moral or social duty, or in other ways to protect his own interest, a person has been permitted by law to express opinions or make statements or publish reports, which, although, they may be defamatory, yet, the maker or the publisher believes it to be justified; provided the person making the statement is honest and is not actuated by malicious motives. Such communications have been defined as "statements fairly made by a person in the discharge of some public or private duty, whether legal or moral, or in the conduct of his own affairs—is fairly warranted by any reasonable occasion or exigency and honestly made."

Such communications are protected for the common convenience and welfare of society, and the law has not restricted the right to make them within any narrow time. A privileged occasion is, in reference to qualified privilege, an occasion where the person who makes a communication has no interest or duty, legal, social, or moral to make it to the person to whom it is made, and the person to whom it is made has a corresponding interest or duty to receive it. This reciprocity is essential.

For newspapers, the publication of Parliamentary and judicial proceedings is the most important occasion when this dictum of qualified privilege is applied. People are entitled to know what is going on in the courts of law or in legislatures.

The rule of law is that where judicial proceedings are transpiring before a properly constituted judicial tribunal exercising its jurisdiction in open court the publication, without malice, of a fair and accurate report of what takes place before that tribunal is privileged. The privilege begins when the judge begins to function in court. No privilege attaches when the report of the contents of the complaint is make of to where plaint is first Newspapers generally ignore this important rule and sometimes pay the price.

Malice

No privilege attaches to a report, however fair and accurate, of judicial proceedings properly heard in *camera*. If it is proved that the publisher in publishing such reports is actuated by some improper motives, the privilege is lost. Qualified privilege is lost by proof of malice. Statements published on an occasion of qualified privilege are protected for the common convenience and welfare of society. The publisher is not entitled to the protection of the privilege if he uses the occasion for some ulterior or wrong motive. The proceedings published may be correct, the report may be fair and accurate, but if the publication is made with malice, the defence is lost. The purpose must be to publish the news and not to vent his personal ill-feelings.

It is open to feature only a particular portion of the proceedings which may tend to create a false impression. Partiality and inaccuracy might occur by suppression of true as well as by insertion of untrue matters. For instance, a report is not fair and impartial which give the statements of counsel on the one side, they being injurious, and not to publish the statement, on the other side in denial. To publish an attack made on a member and not to publish any rejoinder is unfair and is not privileged.

In the very nature of things the report is bound to be short, but the reporter must not "dip his men is gall"—the trends of his sympathies must not appear in the report. Newspapers must give substantially accurate accounts of what takes place. They may be abridged or condensed but should not omit any material fact, which action will make it unfair. Headlines must be fair and accurate as well as must the body of the report. If they are sensational or exaggerated, privilege may be lost.

For instance, headlines should not read "Murderer Arrested". Headlines containing words like "traitor", "perjurer" or "seducer" are comments and not reports. The report must not give the impression that the arrested person is guilty. Reports of trial must contain no comments. Comments are made only after judgement.

A counsel examining a witness asked whether the company he represented was not the biggest in the town—the witness replied *"yes"* and the pleader on the opposite side remarked "And it is also the most dishonest in the town", the remark was held to be defamatory of the company, being irrelevant, with no reference to the subject-matter of the proceedings in courts, and was outside the pleader's duty. Publication of any such remarks is not protected. (Rahim Bux vs. Bachha Lal, 51, All. 509).

A journalist must resist the temptation to make the report interesting by introducing a comment here or there. Press reporters are generally permitted to see First Information Reports, charge sheets, affidavits, plaints, etc. They should be used only to check names or addresses or other such particulars. They should never be referred to in the published reports unless they are read out and formally put in evidence.

Publication of parliamentary proceedings is placed on the same footing as the publication of judicial proceedings. The published report must be fair and accurate and should be published without any malice. A speech made by a member in the House is privileged even though it may be defamatory of another. Qualified privilege attaches to its publication in a newspaper provided it is done in the ordinary course of reporting. But if the defamatory portion of the speech is specially featured with an intent to glorify the member making the speech or to embarrass the person attacked, the privilege will be lost.

Protection is not afforded to the journalists in relation to the publication of the reports of the public meeting. But the publication of such reports is a daily feature. The journalist therefore in such reporting must be extremely careful and cautious in preparing his copy. All libellous or defamatory, indecent, or blasphemous references must be ignored and must not be published maliciously.

Fair Comment or Criticism

Those who fill the public positions must not be thick-skinned in reference to comments made upon them. It often happens that observations are made about public men —which they knew from the bottom of their hearts undesirable and unjust yet they must bear with them and submit, to be understood for a time because all knew that the criticism of the press was the best certainty for the proper discharge of public duties, as Chief Justice Cockburn declared.

The right of freedom of fair comment is "the brightest jewel in the crown of law to seek and maintain the golden means between defamation on the one hand and a healthy and robust right of free public discussion on the other." The essence of fair comment is that the subject-matter must be matter of public interest. It should be an intellectual appraisal, founded on fact clearly stated, and be free from any imputation of sordid or corrupt motives. The comment must be the result of honest opinion and should always be free from malice. A comment is privileged in the interest of public good and hot to gratify personal feelings. Do not criticise the individual but his act or performance. You may tear your subject to pieces even if it may seriously damage somebody's reputation, but remain within the boundary walls laid for such criticism. "Criticism cannot be used as a cloak for mere invectives." Criticism only deals with such things as invite public attention, or call for public comment. It does not follow a public man into his private life or pry into his domestic concerns.

Defamanation as a Criminal Offence

Defamation also is regarded as an offence, against the State and has been made punishable under the Indian Penal Code. Section 499 of the Code defines defamation. The ingredients of the offence are more or less the same. Under that section, to impute anything to a deceased person if imputation: would harm the reputation of that person, if living, and is intended to be hurtful to the feelings of his family or near relatives, is punishable. An imputation in the form of an alternative or expressed ironically or which imputation directly or indirectly, lowers the moral or intellectual character of the person in respect of his caste or of his calling, or lowers the credit of that person, or causes it to be believed that the body of that person is in a loathsome state, or generally considered as disgraceful, is punishable.

However, it is not defamatory under the I.P.C. if imputation is true, if it is an opinion expressed in good faith in respect of the conduct of a public servant, in discharge of his public functions, substantially true report of court proceedings, or touching any public question or to publish or to express in good faith any opinion in respect of the merits of the case, which has been decided, or the merits of any performance which its author has submitted to the judgement of the public, or the accusation by a person in lawful authority, over and for the protection of the interest of the person making it, or of any other person, or for the public good, or to convey a caution to one against another for the good of the person to whom it is conveyed, or some other person in whom he may be interested, or for the public good.

Section 500, Indian Penal Code, provides punishment for defamation which may extend to simple imprisonment of two years or with fine or both. No limit on the amount of fine is imposed.

In this connection, see the latest case, namely, Tharayil Chellappan Pillai, *Correspondent of Malayala Rajyam vs. R.K. Karanjia*, Editor, Printer and Publisher of *Blitz,* in which case on the complaint of Chellappan, Karanjia was convicted and fined by Kerala High Court. Their Lordships observed that to bring the publication of scandalous imputation under the penal law it was not necessary to prove that it was done out of any illwill or malice or that the complainant had actually suffered from it. It would be sufficient to show that the accused intended or knew or had reasons to believe that the imputation made by him would harm the reputation of the complainant.

STATUTES GOVERNING THE PRESS

Obscene Publications

When licentiousness begins, freedom of the press ends to that extent; for liberty is not licence. Sections 292, 293, and 294 of the Indian Penal Code deal with the obscene publications. If a publication is detrimental to public morals and is calculated to produce a pernicious effect in depraving and debauching the minds of the persons in whose hands it may come, it will be obscene publication, which the law suppresses. The publication of obscene advertisement is punishable. Passages contained in religious works, otherwise not punishable, may become punishable if published separately as divorced from the context. The question of intention of the writer is not germane to the consideration of the offence. The publisher will be deemed to have intended the natural consequences and effect that the publication does produce.

But publications of a serious character intended to give advice to young married people on how to regulate the sexual side of their lives have been held not to be obscene. [See Emperor vs. Harnam dass, 1947 Lah. 383.] Mere nudity in painting or sculpture is not obscenity. Determination of what is obscene comes within the range of ordinary intelligence and sense of social responsibility. Offence under this section is punishable with imprisonment of either description for a term which may extend to three months or with fine or with both.

Young Persons (Harmful Publications) Act (1956)

This has also been put on the statute books. It seeks to prohibit the production, distribution, and circulation in India of harmful publications like book, magazine, pamphlet, leaflet, newspaper, or other like publication which consists of stories with or without the aid of pictures or wholly in pictures portraying wholly or mainly the commission of offences, or acts of violence or cruelty or incidents of repulsive or horrible nature; in such a way which would tend to corrupt a young person. Whosoever puts that into circulation or publically exhibits it is liable to be punished with imprisonment up to six months or fine or with both and copies of such publications may be destroyed.

The notions of morality vary from country to country and from age to age. Not long ago birth control *per se* was regarded as immoral. Annie Besant was convicted for publishing literature advocating contraception. Yet the

Government has in the Third National Plan allocated considerable amount for propagating birth control.

But it is now being increasingly realized in the words of an American jurist: "Filthy literature is the great moral wrecker. It is creating criminals faster than jails can be built." And so these regulations by law. Apart from the offence under Indian Penal Code, Sees. 20-23 of the Post Office Act (1898) prohibit the transmission by post of obscene matter. Sec. 18(c) of the Sea Customs Act prohibits import of such literature. Sec. 3(c) of the Dramatic Performance Act of 1846 provides for the prohibition of dramatic performance which is likely to deprave and corrupt persons present at the performance. Any review in your newspaper criticizing such roles played would be an offence.

Forfeiture Under Code of Criminal Procedure

Sees. 99a to 99g of the Criminal Procedure Code were added by the Press Law Repeal and Amendment Act, 1922 (XIV). These sections are based on Sections 12, 17, 18, 19, 20, 21, and 22 of the Indian Press Act [1(i) of 1910] now repealed.

These *new* sections provide for the forfeiture of such publications winch are intended to promote feelings of enmity or hatred between different classes and which publications are punishable under Sections 124a and 153a or Sec. 295a of the Indian Penal Code. The aggrieved party, however, has been granted the right to apply to the High Court to set aside such order on the ground that the issue of the newspaper did not contain such matter. On the receipt of such application, the high court will constitute a special bench of three judges and may, if so satisfied, set aside the order of forfeiture. This provision has been proved to be of great help to the press and many executive wrongs have in the past years been righted by judicial decisions.

Sec. 144 of the Code of Criminal Procedure

The section has at times been resorted to enforce pre-censorship. This is a section which arms the magistrate with a power for temporary orders being passed in urgent cases of apprehended danger. The Supreme Court in the *Pratap* case impliedly upheld the pre-censorship order of the Punjab Government. But the matter is destined to be fully mooted in Parliament since the liberty to print without previous governmental or executive scrutiny is the essence of the freedom of the press.

Outraging Religious Feelings

Section 295a of Indian Penal Code penalizes the publication made with deliberate and malicious intention of outraging the religious feelings of any class of citizens of India or for offering insults or attempt to insult the religion or the religious beliefs of the class.

In this connection the provisions of Section 153a of the Code be also kept in view which deals with the same subject.

Sedition

Words spoken or written which bring or attempt to bring hatred or contempt or which attempt to excite disaffection towards the Government established by the law in India is an offence under Section 124a of the I.P.C. This section has a chequered history.

During the freedom struggle it was resorted to frequently. The then Federal Court of India held that mere criticism is no offence unless it is calculated to "undermine respect for the Government in such a way as to make people cease to obey it and obey law so that only an anarchy can follow. Public disorder is the gist of the offence." Privy Council, however, over-ruled this decision. The founding fathers of the Constitution, however, ignored this decision and the word "Sedition" was not included in Article 19(2). The High Court of Punjab decided that Section *1243,* was *ultra-vires* of the Constitution. After the Constitution (First) Amendment Act, 1951, however, the validity of Section *124a.* was restored. Yet the original Federal Court's decisions remains the basis of the offence under the Section.

Along with Section *1243.,* Section 505 dealing with statements conducing to public mischief may also be studied.

The Police Incitement to Disaffection Act, 122 (S.3)

This act makes it an offence to do any act which causes or is likely to cause "disaffection towards the Government established by law in India amongst the members of the police force or induces or attempts to induce.. . any member of a police-force to withhold his service or to commit a breach of discipline ..."

The Dramatic Performance Act, 1876 (S. 3B)

It empowers Government to prohibit the performance of a drama in a public place, if Government is of opinion that such performance is likely "to excite feelings of disaffection to the Government established by law in India."

The Security and Public Safety Act of the Various States

These acts, generally, punish the publication of any statement or report which incites the commission of any "subversive act" such as: *(a)* Prevention of illegal acquisition, possession or use of arms; *(b)* Suppression of subversive acts, endangering communal harmony or safety or stability of the Province, such as looting, sabotage, prejudicing the recruitment or attendance of members of the police force, fire brigade or other public servants or to temper with the loyalty of such persons.

The Official Secrets Act

This act contains stringent provisions prohibiting the communication of any official secret by any person for any purpose prejudicial to the safety or interests of the State. Apart from the question of publishing such information, journalists should be careful even in receiving voluntarily any such information from any one.

Indian Telegraph Act

Section 5 of the Act empowers the Government to take possession of telegrams and to order interception of messages in an emergency, like false or distorted or irresponsible news.

Indian Post Office Act

Under Sections 25-27 there is power to intercept postal articles. Under Section 27a, no newspaper printed and published without conforming to the provisions of the Press and Registration of Books Act can be transmitted by post. By Section 9, rules have been made for the registration of newspapers for transmission by post as registered newspapers.

Sea Customs Act

Sections 19, 181a, 181b, and 181c of the act confer powers to prohibit or restrict importation or exportation of goods including packages containing certain publications imported into India.

Juveniles

Various states have enacted legislations prohibiting the publication of the name, address, or other details of any child involved in any offence and being tried under those acts. [Also see the Reformatory Schools Act VIII of 1897].

Lotteries

Publication of lotteries as advertisement or otherwise except such as are previously permitted by the government is contained in Section 294a of the Indian Penal Code. The publication of any such proposal of lottery is punishable with fine which may extend to one thousand rupees.

Press and Registration of Books Act (1867)

The act originally was promulgated on March 22, 1867. During the nearly one hundred years since it has undergone a large number of changes and modifications. The act as it at present stands was amended in 1956.

The main object of the act is to set up a statutory machinery for the collection, and making available to the public, of authentic statistics regarding all aspects of the newspaper industry. It empowers the Government of India to appoint a Press Registrar who is required to maintain an up-to-date Register of Newspapers as prescribed under the act. The publishers of newspapers must furnish to the Press Registrar information, statistics, and returns required by him. The Registrar, or any gazetted officer authorized by him, has access to the relevant records maintained by the publisher for the collection or verification of the information. The Press Registrar is required to prepare an annual report containing a summary of the information supplied to him. Wilful disclosure of information supplied by a newspaper, other than that provided under the act, is a penal offence.

This deals with newspapers, books and printing presses. Every newspaper must contain the name of the person who is the editor and his name must be printed clearly on each copy of the newspaper as the editor of the paper. Before a newspaper is printed or published, the "Printer and the Publisher" of such a newspaper must make and subscribe before a competent magistrate, in duplicate, the following declaration: "I, A. B. declare that I am the printer (a publisher or printer and publisher) of the newspaper entitled *Nation* (and to be printed or published, and to be printed and published) as the case may be at 55, A, Jor Bagh, New-Delhi". The declaration is made on a prescribed form available from the Registrar of Newspapers' office and/or the competent magistrate in the respective district.

As soon as the place of printing or publication is changed, a new declaration must be made. But if a change is only for a period up to thirty days, no fresh declaration is necessary. However, intimation must be given to the magistrate concerned within 24 hours thereof.

Such a printer or the publisher having made the declaration, if he leaves India for a period exceeding 30 days, must make a new declaration from a new printer or publisher resident within the said territory.

Every declaration so made becomes void if within six weeks of the declaration in the case of a newspaper to be published (a) once a week or oftener (that means weekly to daily) or (b) within three months of the declaration in the case of any other newspaper (that means bi-monthly, monthly, quarterly), the relevant newspaper is not published. A new declaration for the like is necessary, if any such newspaper is to be published after the expiry of that period.

Where, in any period of three months any daily, tri-weekly bi-weekly, weekly, or fortnightly newspaper publishes issues the number of which is less than half of what should have been published in accordance with the declaration made in respect thereof, the declaration shall cease to have effect and a new declaration shall be necessary before the publication of the newspaper can be continued.

Where any other newspaper has ceased publication for a period exceeding twelve months, every declaration made in respect thereof shall cease to have effect, and a new declaration shall be necessary, before the newspaper can be re-published.

The person making the declaration and the editor of a newspaper must have attained majority. Minors can be neither a printer, publisher nor editor of a newspaper.

It is any time any printer or publisher having made that declaration ceases to be so, he must again appear before the competent magistrate and make the following declaration: "I, A. B., declare that I have ceased to be the printer or publisher or printer and publisher of the newspaper entitled *Nation*".

If the name of any person has appeared as editor while actually he is not he is entitled to within two weeks of his knowledge appear before the magistrate and make such a declaration, whereupon after due satisfaction the magistrate will certify accordingly.

Thus on the paper, the name of the editor, the name of the printer and the place of printing, the name of the publisher and the place of publication must be given which in common parlance is known as "Imprint Line". Imprint is the stamp of suspicion which has attended printed matters from the earliest times. This is to enable to proceed against the person responsible for the commission of any offence connected with the newspaper.

These are all regulatory provisions that have been held by the Supreme Court to be in conformity with the article 19(i)a of the constitution of India. [(In re Alavandar) (1957)—M.L.J.] ' Two copies of all newspapers must be delivered to the state Government and one such copy to the Press Registrar free of expense. It should be delivered within 48 hours;

The publisher of every newspaper in India is required

under the act to deliver, free of expense to the Registrar, one copy of each issue of the newspaper as soon as published. The rule provides that every publisher shall, within 48 hours of the publication of an issue of his newspaper, send to the Press Registrar one copy of the issue by post or by a messenger. In this connection, it has been provided that the copies of the issue of newspapers published in Hindi, Urdu, or English and of a newspaper published into languages, one of which is Hindi, Urdu, or English should be sent to the Press Registrar, New Delhi. Copies of the issues or newspapers published in any of the regional language (specified below) should be sent to the Officer-in-Charge of the Regional Office of the Press Information Bureau, Ministry of Information and Broadcasting, Government of India, at the place specified, who will receive it on behalf of the Press Registrar.

Punjabi: Jullunder; Bengali, Oriya and Assamese: Calcutta; Tamil and Telugu: Madras; Malayalam: Ernakulam; Marathi and Gujarati: Bombay; Kannada: Bangalore.

Copies of the issues of newspapers published in any other language or languages are to be sent to the Press Registrar, Delhi. Infringement of these provisions entails penalties.

The Delivery of Books 'and Newspapers' (Public Libraries) Act (1954)

The act provides for the development of four public libraries in different parts of India to encourage scholarship and dissemination of knowledge. By the Delivery of Books (Public Libraries) Amendment Act 99 of 1956, newspapers have been brought within the purview of this Act. So like all books, newspapers are also to be delivered free to libraries as mentioned by the Government.

They are: National Library, Kolkata; Connemara Public

Library, Chennai; National Central Library, Delhi; Central Library, Mumbai.

The Prize Competition Act, 1955

This act was enacted on April i, 1956. The act aims to prohibit advertisement of a prize competition except as provided in the act, and also prohibits the sale and distribution of tickets and also bans the offering of any inducement which may tend to encourage people to participate in such prize competition. The state Governments are empowered to forfeit copies of such newspapers, carrying any advertisement of prize competition in contravention of the act.

The act prohibits promoting or conducting any prize competition in which the total value of the prize or prizes whether in cash or otherwise to be offered in any month exceeds one thousand rupees and in every such competition the number of entries must not exceed two thousand entries. Licence is also needed under the act.

The Drugs and Magic Remedies (Objectionable Advertisements) Act, 1954

No person must take any part in the publication of any advertisement referring to any drug which may lead to the use of that drug for the procurement of miscarriage in women or prevention of conception in women or such other matter, or which advertisement gives a false impression of the drugs or is misleading in particular or advertisement referring to any magic remedy nor any document containing an advertisement of the nature can be imported into or exported outside India.

Working Journalists: "Conditions of Service and Miscellaneous Provisions"

This act aims to settle the service conditions of the working journalists pertaining to their salaries, provident, notice for termination, holidays, and other conditions. The act further prescribes 144 working hours during four consecutive weeks.

The Parliamentary Proceedings (Protection of Public) Act, 1956

The Act confers an immunity from any liability in respect of the publication in a newspaper of a substantially correct report of any proceedings of either House of Parliament unless the publication is proved to have been made with malice. The act permits the press to report defamatory statements in Parliament without committing a breach of the privilege of the Parliament and by implication no libel action for the publication of any such statement referring to any outsider would lie. This act applies only to the proceedings of Parliament and not of the state Legislatures, which are left free to enact their own legislation in that respect. It appears that legislation to that effect may be enacted soon by different state legislatures.

Thus for reporting the Parliamentary proceedings which otherwise include such matters as normally may be deemed defamatory, no action could be maintained.

Newspaper (Price and Page) Act, 1956

This was enacted to regulate the prices of newspapers in relation to their sizes and then to enable the Government to issue from time to time a price page schedule fixing a minimum price at which a paper of a particular size could be sold. The *vires* of the act were challenged in the Supreme Court of India. The court has declared the Act as *ultra vires of* the constitution. [Sakal Papers etc. Union of India] and that settles the question of control on circulation. According to the court the freedom of a newspaper to publish any number of pages or to circulate it to any number of persons is each an integral part of the freedom of speech and expression. A restraint placed on either of them will be a direct infringement of that fundamental right; it is so because freedom of speech and expression of opinion are of paramount importance under a democratic constitution, which envisages changes in the composition of legislature and government.

Assuming that the object of the impugned Newspaper (Price and Page) Act, 1956 and the Order of 1960 made thereunder, which sought to regulate the number of pages of newspapers according to the price charged, was to suppress unfair practice by newspapers and to prevent monopolies in order to protect small or newly started newspapers. Their Lordships pointed out: "The legitimacy or even the legality of the result intended to be achieved does not necessarily imply that every means to achieve it is permissible, for even if the end is desirable or permissible, the means employed must not transgress the limits laid down by the Constitution, and if the method employed directly impinges on any of the fundamental right guaranteed by the Constitution, it is no answer when the constitutionality of the measure is challenged that apart from the fundamental right infringed provision is other legal."

The Copyright Act, 1957

This act has now taken place of a former Copyright Act of 1914. The present act, as passed by the Indian Parliament, received the assent of the President in June, 1957.

Copyright is the product of labour, skill, and capital of one man which must not be appropriated by another, in the element, the raw material, if one may use the expression upon which the labour and skill and capital of the first have been expended [Lord Atkinsons in Macmillan Co. vs. Cooper, 51 Indian Appeals 109], but it has been further sufficiently established that a person can have no monopoly of knowledge and ideas and there is no copyright in the ideas. Copyright is in the written form of expression. It has reference to some literary form of composition and does not extend to ideas, schemes, or systems of methods. Copyright means the exclusive right in the case of the literary, dramatic, or musical work: (a) to reproduce the work in any material form, (b) to publish the work, (c) to perform the work in public, (d) to produce, reproduce, perform or publish any translation of the work, (e) to make any cinematograph form or a record in respect .of the work, (f) to communicate by radio diffusion or to communicate to the public by loud speakers or by any other similar instrument the radio diffusion of the work, (g) to make any adaptation of the work, (h) to do in relation to a translation or the adaptation of the work in all the acts specified in Section 14 of the Copyright Act.

As will now be seen, many exclusive rights have been included within the meaning of copyright, such as the publication of original work, its production, reproduction, or translation.

In respect of such works in which copyright subsists, Section 13 gives clear and precise answer. The copyright subsists in original, literary, dramatic, and musical and artistic works in any cinematograph films and records.

However, copyrights do not subsist in any work of the type referred to above unless either the right is extended under Section 40 to foreign works or unless in the case of a published work, the work is first published outside India, if the author on the date of such publication or if he were out at the time of his a citizen of India, the copyright would subsist. In the case of any published work other than an architect work of art, to claim right, the author must at the date of the making of the work be a citizen of India or domicile of India. If there were joint authors the same conditions would apply.

Regarding the ownership of the copyright, Sees. 17 to 21 define the rights of those in whom the copyrights subsist. The ownership of the copyright could be transferred, assigned, or relinquished. The term of copyright in published literary work, musical and artistic works under Sec. 22 is for the lifetime of the author and 50 years thereafter.

In respect of the photograph, the copyright subsists only for 50 years from the beginning of the calendar year next following the year in which the photograph is published (Sec. 25).

The act should be fairly, exhaustively and carefully studied by all journalists, especially those who are assigned responsible jobs for production of intelligent material. It would be seen that the act also has made provision giving sufficient protection to authors against damage being done to their reputation etc., by garbled reproduction of their works.

The act confers the right on the owners of copyright whose such right has been infringed to enforce remedies such as injunction damages etc. The government has been conferred the power to enter into international copyright relations on the basis of inter-national treaties in such manner as the Government may deem fit.

The following acts do not constitute an infringement of a copyright, namely: a fair dealing with literary, musical or artistic, work for the purpose of, (a) research or private study, *(b)* for criticism or review, *(c)* for the purpose of reporting current events in a newspaper, magazine, or similar periodical, or *(d)* for the purpose of judicial proceedings. The details in respect of such matters are stated in Section 52.

A newspaper is entitled to publish a summary of a copyright work, 'report of a lecture or speech delivered in public. Copying of reasonable passages for the purpose of comment and literary appreciation is permitted.

A mere copy prepared without any trouble or cost by a mechanical operation of scissors and paste is not protected. Neither is the abstraction of matter for the purpose of profit justified.

Basically news as such is not the subject of copyright. But apart from the bare recital of facts or statement of news, there is a copyright in the particular forms of the language or mode of expression by which the information contained in the news is conveyed and not the less so because the information may be with respect to the current events of the day. [See Walter vs. Steinkopff (182) 489; also International News Service vs. Associated Press (1918), 248 U. S. 215.] Mere acknowledgement of the source would not justify literary larceny.

The custom or practice of taking articles or extracts from different journals is not recognized by law.

Contempt of Court

In the course of multifarious duties carried on in a newspaper office, stories of civil or criminal cases, cases that are in the course of being filed or that are pending, are published. Sometimes the reporters or editorial deskmen review in detail facts before the trial begins. Evidence that may have to be produced is even sometimes anticipated and published in sensational headlines. Comments and editorials are put which sometimes unduly favour one side of a case and occasionally attempts are made to impugn the integrity of the judges and the courts. And there lies the danger for newspapers.

It is extremely difficult to define the term "contempt of court". Generally, however, contempt of court is constituted by any conduct that tends to bring the authority and administration of the law into disrespect or disregard or to interfere with or prejudice the parties litigating or their witnesses during litigation. Any act done or writing published calculated to bring a court of law into contempt or lower its authority or to obstruct or interfere with a due course of justice or the lawful process of the court, is contempt. Contempt is of two kinds: *(i)* Contempt committed in the face of the court, and (ii) Indirect contempt or Contempt out of court.

The reporter may be excluded from the court-room during a trial. But he may surreptitiously return to the court-room during the trial, thus violating the order of the court. A reporter may photograph an accused person in spite of the order of the court to the contrary. Publication of proceedings of a case being heard in camera, is a disobedience of the court's orders. These are instances of direct contempt.

But as newspapermen, we are more concerned with the contempt committed in the publication of reports, proceedings, and comments. Such a contempt is known as indirect contempt or contempt out of court.

The out of court contempt may be divided generally into: (a) false and grossly inaccurate report of court proceedings; (b) such publications that may have a reasonable tendency to interfere with the orderly administration of justice; and (c) publication that scandalizes the court, judges, counsel, parties, or witnesses.

Pending Cases

The courts will resent any comments or misreporting in pending cases, where these comments or misreporting could, in the least, be taken to have the effect of prejudicing the fair trial of an accused person. The golden rule is that no comment should be made and proper care should be applied in reporting when case is *sub judice. Do* not assume the role of investigator, counsel or witnesses or constitute yourself as tribunal, thus usurping the functions of the court of law. No extra-judicial opinion regarding a pending trial should be made. Paragraphs in newspapers having the effect of a comment on a case, written and published while it is pending, which prejudices or is calculated to prejudice any party, is contempt. There must be knowledge that the case is pending.

The question in every case is not whether the publication in fact interferes, but whether it tends to interfere with the due course of justice. If you publish pleadings, petitions, or evidence you must be careful to publish them on both sides or it will be a contempt and must not omit to publish the effect of the judgement of the court. If you report prosecution evidence, you must not omit to report defence evidence.

In the *Amrita Bazar Patrika* facts contained in a plaint instituted by a firm of merchants against amongst others a Tahsildar, appeared as statement of facts and not as facts alleged in the plaint. The High Court remarked that a special responsibility rests on the newspapers of seeing that everything is excluded from their columns in reference to pending cases, whether criminal or civil, which might possibly have the effect of prejudicing or prepossessing the mind of any judicial officer, juryman or potential witness who might be or become concerned with it.

Where it was contended that the article complained of was just a mere reproduction of a report given to the press by a police officer, and as such the publication could not amount to contempt, it was held that by itself will not take it away from the category of contempt of court, though regard may be had to it while awarding punishment.

The reports must not be partial or garbled. We have already dealt with these matters in considering libel.

No judge is immune from criticism. But the criticism must take the form of reasonable argument or expostulation. It must be made in good faith and must be free from the imputation of improper motive. Criticism of a judicial officer which takes the form of representation to the Government, expressed in terms which do not overstep the limits, is not contempt. It is contempt to criticize a judicial act so as to interfere with the administration of justice. But it is not contempt to criticize adversely the purely ministerial act of the court.

Newspapers may commit the contempt when publishing a report of the case and giving opinion when it criticizes the judges and the court and transgresses the limits of fair comment, thus interfering with the course of justice. It may take the form of scandalizing the court by attributing to the judge corruption, incompetency, and dishonesty irrespective of the fact whether the offending remarks are made in a case before trial, in a pending case or a case that has been decided.

A person may be guilty of contempt even though there was no intention of the publication of contempt. The question is not what was the intention of the publication, but what was the effect of the publication. The intention is to be inferred from the consideration of the natural meaning of the words used and the impression which they convey to an ordinary reader. Want of intention may, however, be considered as an extenuating circumstances.

Four stages of proceedings must be borne in mind while attempting to write anything about any judicial trial, viz. (a) before trial; (b) pending trial; *(c)* after the decision; and *(d)* when the appeal is pending.

It is left to the efficiency of the newspaper office to know exactly the stages of the case which, no doubt, is the duty of the staff to ascertain accurately. It should be noted that the right of a newspaper even to publish a faithful account of the proceedings before a court of law is subject to the condition that the publication does not tend to prejudice materially the fair trial of a case before a court of law. The publication of a document filed in a pending case would amount to contempt if it was published with the clear intention of causing prejudice to a trial which is pending.

Press photographers may not take photographs while the court is sitting, unless specifically permitted to do so. Judges sometimes allow pictures to be taken as was done in Mahatma Gandhi's murder case. But generally such a request is refused, specially in criminal trials where the publication of pictures may seriously prejudice the identification of the accused by witness.

Contempt by Cartoons

Comments, criticism, or ridicule by cartoons directed against a judge, parties to an action or others directly concerned in a trial that have a tendency to obstruct the administration of justice are contempt of court.

After Trial

Newspapers enjoy the privilege of fair comment. But the criticism in order to be fair must be on actual facts. Newspapers may review the facts of the law and express their opinion even if their opinion may be contrary to the decisions of the court. But personal attacks On the judges attributing incompetency, corruption, and partiality, judicial dishonesty, political bias and improper motives or "other considerations" are in contempt of court. The kind of contempt generally committed by the newspapermen after the trial is that Of scandalizing the court by speaking or writing contemptuously of the court or the judges acting in their judicial capacity and thus by destroying confidence in its judgment.

The Contempt of Court Act XXXII of 1952 says: "Save as otherwise expressly provided by any law for the time being inforce the contempt of court may be punished with simple imprisonment for a term which may extent to six months or with fine which may extent to Rs. 2,000 or with both.

"Provided that the accused may be discharged or the punishment awarded may be remitted on apology being made to the satisfaction of the court."

In this connection, Section 228 of the Indian Penal Code may also be considered which provides that intentional insult or interruption to a public servant sitting in judicial proceedings is punishable with six months' simple imprisonment and with a fine up to Rs. 1,000 or with both.

Apology

A full and qualified apology takes out the sting of the contempt. Courts shall take a very strict view where the apology is not tendered and refusal to apologize is considered an aggravation of the offence carrying deterrent punishment.

Law of Privacy

The right of privacy as applicable to the newspaper is a new development in contemporary life. In its legal interpretation nothing libellous is involved. The right of privacy is founded upon the claim that a man has the right to pass through this world, if he wills, without having his picture published, his business enterprises discussed, his successful experiments written up for the benefit of others, or his eccentricities commented upon whether in handbills, circulars, catalogues, periodicals, or newspapers.

The invasion by the journalists of the privacy of the members of the public has frequently been a subject of public complaint. It was suggested in the Report on the British Press that this relationship leaves much to be desired particularly on the point of intrusion into domestic privacy.

"People are rung up at nights by reporters, pestered for interviews and photographs, their gardens and grounds trespassed upon and every conceivable form of pressure exerted to extort the news and this invasion is extended whoever happens to be involved in simple incidents where there may be some suggestion of sensation or scandal."

The law of privacy is closely akin to the law of personal liberty or common law copyright in the protection of private thought, plans, and writings.

It is the personal right which is not without judicial recognition. It is the conferment of the right of immunity to one's person. The individual has always been entitled to be protected in the exclusive use and enjoyment of that which is his own. [See the case of Leo, a photographer for the London *Daily Mirror,* who was assaulted by a bridegroom, Captain Cecil, while attempting to take a photograph at his wedding party.] The report on the British press referred to above expresses the hope that press will itself take measures to redress the public grievance. If, however, the members of the public accept it as sound in principle it only remains for the legislature to bring a law in due course.

The present legal position is that invasion of privacy may amount to a libel and may entitle the plaintiff to compensatory damages or may mean civil or criminal trespass.

Contempt of Parliament and State Legislatures

The Parliament expects "a newspaper writer should be more cautious than a private citizen as his criticisms are widely published." Such comments in respect of Parliamentary proceedings or the performance of any member on the floor of the House, if they contain any personal attacks on individual members or if the language of the comments is vulgar or abusive, are not protected and cannot be deemed to come within the bounds of fair comment or justifiable criticism.

Such writing constituted a breach of privilege and contempt of the House, on the principle that, such acts tend to destroy the House and its members in the performance of their functions and duties by diminishing the respect due to them and by bringing them into odium, contempt, and ridicule. [See *Blitz* Case — Lok Sabha Debates of 20-4-61 and 18-8-61 and also see *Searchlight* Case, A. I. R. 1959, S. C. 395.]

Privileges of legislatures and the commission of its contempt is a subject which now is engaging the attention of all concerned and it appears sooner than later some sort of precise legislation may be put on the statutes governing these matters.

The Responsibility of Editor

Normally the responsibility of the editor depends on the terms of his contract with the proprietor. But whatever the terms of that contract may be, the editor is liable to respect of any libel, any matter which constitutes contempt of court, of legislature or is seditious, obscene, immoral, or illegal. His liability is there even if he is not directly concerned in the publication thereof.

The responsibility of the editor for the illegal contents of a newspaper is based upon the reasoning that the person who acts as editor of the paper and collects the material for the publication is in a better position than any other person to publish or refuse contributions. All manuscripts pass through his hands, he sifts them, sub-edits, according to the requirements of the paper, the contributions which he considers suitable, forwards them for composing, and allots the place where they should appear. He orders publication and therefore he is made responsible for the contents even if he has taken an indemnity bond from the author of the offending contribution.

Proprietors generally enter into contracts with the editors stating that after they leave the service they will not work as a proprietor or as an editor of a newspaper within a certain radius. Such restrictions are not valid. Section 27 (c) of the Indian Contract Act lays down that every agreement by which any one is restrained from exercising a lawful profession, trade, or business of any kind is to that extent void. An agreement by an editor to serve exclusively for a fixed period with the proprietor is not void.

Advertisement

It is open to the newspapers to accept or not to accept any advertisement. But the advertisements they accept must not be libellous, immoral, or indecent. Advertisement by lawyers and doctors, too, is not permitted and may not be accepted. Advertisement for lotteries and bettings are banned. Photos in advertisement should be carefully used.

News Collection

The Constitution does not confer any specific right to collect news. But there is no prohibition. The right to gather and secure news is guaranteed by inference. News is gathered because the events so reported are *publici juris.* [International News Services vs. Associated Press, 248 U. S. 215.]

The cooperation of the public with the newspapers and their accredited representatives places valuable, newsworthy material at the latter's disposal. But the reporter has no right to inspect government records that, in the first instance, are not strictly considered public records. A reporter cannot, for example, inspect diplomatic correspondence, or correspondence of government officials who are carrying on immediate business, or the records of a police department relating to the apprehension of criminals, or the plans for the prosecution of a criminal case, these are not strictly public records. The reporter has no right to gather news if to do so involves trespass. He cannot enter private property if given notice not to do so; he cannot assault others in order to obtain news; in short, he has no right to break the law in order to obtain information basic for a news story, information which if obtained, he is free from previous restraint to write and publish.

With the passage of time, new techniques have come up, many new laws for journalism have enacted. Yet the relevance of information, given in the present chapter is of perennial value.

[*Courtesy:* P.N. Mehta]

15

Setting Professional Standards

Whenever any scandal or even unpleasantness arises to ruffle the composure of the average American citizen as to government, civilization, or any such matter, he promptly fixes upon some individual or group of individuals whom he holds to be responsible, and asserts indignantly, "They ought to be put in jail." Or, in the event he realizes that there is no legal means whereby the culprits may be hurried to prison, he is prone to start his discussion, "There ought to be a law."

The faith of the American people in law is a problem for the psychologist rather than the journalist. That it exists as one of the facts of life in this country is not to be denied and must be faced by every public or quasi-public institution.

With this reliance of the public upon law it is not surprising that various laws have been proposed for the purpose of improving the press. Laws already in existence relate chiefly to libel, to obscene writing, and to the exclusion of certain types of advertising. In general these, as interpreted by the courts, are fair to the newspaper and to the public. The principal exception is in the case of laws relating to obscene writing, which have been stretched in some instances to cover works of great literary significance, but this has affected magazine and book rather than news paper publishers. Contempt proceedings against news paper workers by sensitive judges have been unfair to the persons directly involved and have at the same time rendered it difficult for the press to perform its rightful function.

Further proposals for legal restriction of journalism are intended to compel newspapers to be accurate and fair by process of law. The most drastic of such suggestions is a plan devised to secure "compulsory veracity" in newspapers. The proposer of this plan is Edward Paul, who advocates his plan in the following words:

> "Compulsory veracity in the newspapers is no more an infringement on our democratic rights than compulsory purity in foods. In maintaining that a pure news act would be interfering with the 'freedom' of the press, the press leads us to infer that Democracy is more interested in a healthy body than in a healthy mind. A healthy mind is dangerous to Democracy only in so far as that Democracy is shielding a minority in the enjoyment of privileges it is not worthy of enjoying. A healthier public mind would send more of such men to Washington as are now making things disagreeable for the packers and for those interests that thrive on the intimate friendship of railroads. The people having gained the vote, the last resort of Privilege is to deceive the voter, as it did last November. We have almost reached the *caveat lector* stage of social evolution.
>
> "It is of considerable importance that steps be taken before many years to bring about compulsory veracity in the newspapers. The pressure of economic circumstances may at any time make the masses aware of the fact that they cannot trust the organs for the dissemination of news. When they realize that, they are likely to inquire what sort of government it is which permits the overwhelming majority of the people to be tricked, while that majority, engaged in labor, has its back turned."

To obtain absolute accuracy a law is proposed that "whoever shall publish in a newspaper or other periodical a statement wilfully misrepresenting the facts, or shall publish as facts statements known to them to be untrue or erroneous through gross carelessness, shall be guilty of a misdemeanor."

In addition to this law there would be reserved in every paper a column for a public literary defender "elected by the people, who could give due importance to buried news and supply the point of view frequently omitted."

"With this system in vogue," asserts the editor of *The Arbitrator,* the paper responsible for the plan, "it would be possible to retain the freedom of the press. For there should be no objection to the appearance of any startling opinions of the editor, provided the correct ideas were given equal prominence in the same paper. If the policy of the paper was to oppose the conscription of men or of wealth, every issue could also contain the reason why such opinions were untenable and objectionable in the eyes of the government official answerable to the people."

"Another way," this writer goes on to say, "would be to have all complaints against the press submitted to various local commissions appointed for the purpose of punishing by fine, suspension, etc., the periodical which printed lies, or of compelling the offender to print a denial in a prominent column. Such a commission-would not only relieve the courts, but the term of office and personnel could be so arranged as to secure justice for the public."

While to the practicing journalist or the careful student of journalism such suggestions are obviously absurd, they are gaining adherents constantly among those who do not understand newspaper conditions and who are prone to grasp at legal solutions of all problems. The proposed law making it a misdemeanor to misrepresent the facts might be employed effectively in cases where there is certainty of record but where reporters disregarded the facts and published invented material of their own. This rarely happens, however, except through carelessness. Reports of cases in court, of municipal records, of legislative and executive proceedings, are reasonably accurate as to facts, and a reporter who habitually misrepresented in such matters through carelessness or design would not be retained on any important paper.

On other matters there is frequently room for difference of opinion an to what facts really are until some plan is devised whereby they can be carefully and competently investigated. With widely conflicting testimony presented, as would certainly be the case, a jury would rarely, if ever, convict. The same would hold true in the event of a prosecution for carelessness. Any one who has had experience in court knows that juries are exceedingly ready to accept extenuating circumstances, and carelessness would readily be adopted as such in a newspaper case, as it is accepted today in many court proceedings.

Already laws exist in certain states to punish all persons who knowingly and wilfully transmit to any publication false and untrue statements of fact. Such a law exists in New York as Section 1353 of the Penal Code. It has been very seldom invoked. So innocuous has it been that many newspaper men do not know of its existence. When a similar law was passed by the Minnesota legislature recently, certain New York newspapers referred to it as if it were a new legal departure. A Massachusetts statute, passed in 1922, imposes fine or imprisonment for publishing false statements about candidates for public office.

Granted that the proper means of establishing the veracity of the press is by law, it is obvious that the law proposed would be ineffectual. It would doubtless result in a number of prosecutions, mostly based on unimportant matters. These prosecutions would cover a short period of time after the law was adopted. Thereafter, the statute would become a dead letter, never invoked except for spite or in case of some flagrant violation, such as, however, is now covered by the laws punishing libel.

The suggestion of a public literary defender is still more absurd. Any one who has had experience as a newspaperman in dealing with public officials, from village council-men to high officials of the United States, knows how little reliance can be placed upon their objectivity of view or their fairness in any matter in which their personal interests or the interests of their party are concerned. It may be urged that a public literary defender would represent the point of view of a majority of the people on contested questions. In this country, however, the number of contested issues is so great that no elected officials necessarily represent the point of view of a majority of the people upon these issues. These officials were elected by a combination of factors. Some voters cast their ballots on one issue, others on another issue. Furthermore, as has been previously pointed out, the public is not always—perhaps is never—seeking the complete objective facts, the dissemination of which is the highest function of the newspaper. The proposer of the office of literary defender naively admits this in referring to "the correct ideas." Manifestly, he belongs to that group of careless thinkers who consider that correctness of opinion is to be established by majority vote. In considering this point of view, one may well reflect on what support the ideas of Socrates, of Galileo, of Darwin, to take but a few examples, had from the majority opinion of their times.

A still more drastic legal provision is suggested by W.T. Colyer, who advocates that every paper should be compelled to devote at least half a column in every issue to answering questions about its stockholders, employees, or contributors. He would make a requirement also that every paper print in each issue a list of the letters submitted for publication but not intended to be published, with a summary of the letters. It is evident, of course, that such proposals as Mr. Colyer's tend simply to confuse the issue of accuracy by introducing the question of personal bias on the part of editors or owners of the paper and by representing the newspaper to be a public forum, which, under the most widely social interpretation of its function, it is not. There is no obligation upon a newspaper to publish a letter which it receives, any more than there is an obligation upon the owner or lessee of a hall to open the platform for a reply to an appointed speaker. There is, of course, an obligation to correct errors of fact when brought to the newspaper's notice by letter or otherwise.

Upton Sinclair naturally urges law for the government of newspapers. He proposes in *The Brass Check* a law providing that newspapers shall not publish an interview with any one that has not been O.K.'d or concerning which they have not the permission of the person interviewed to publish it without an O.K. In point of fact certain newspapers make this requirement in the case of important matters. In not a few cases persons who know they will be interviewed on a matter prepare statements to be submitted to the newspapers to express their views. The Kansas Newspaper Code of Ethics, adopted in 1910, advocated the same proceeding that Mr. Sinclair advises.

Generally speaking, the rule which is thus urged would be impracticable because of limits of time in modern newspaper work. Suppose a reporter interviews a man in the Bronx in New York, then goes downtown to write his story or telephone it to the office to be written. In either event the sending of a messenger from downtown New York to the Bronx to obtain an O.K. on the interview would cause editions to be missed. Moreover, it would result in heavy expenditures of money which the importance of the matter would usually not justify. In some cases, for example, criminal matters, disappearance of the person interviewed would make an O.K. impossible.

Furthermore, the requirement of an O.K. on interviews would cause many written interviews, perfectly correct, to be destroyed and others to be altered, because upon reading them the person interviewed would feel that what appeared in black and white, while perfectly true, was contrary to his private interests. While undoubtedly interviews are sometimes faked or partly faked, every newspaper man knows that a considerable proportion of those concerning which complaint is made represent the actual statements of the persons interviewed. An individual denies the interview merely because upon its publication he has felt it to be unpopular or contrary to his own interests. Certain high officials have been notorious among newspaper reporters for denying interviews concerning which there was no question.

Mr. Sinclair also suggests "a law providing that when any newspaper has made any false statement concerning an individual and has had its attention called to the falsity of this statement, it shall publish a correction of the statement in the next edition of the publication and in the same place and with the same prominence given to the false statement."

The French practice with reference to corrections of errors and answers to attacks in newspapers is of interest here. The French law provides that when the official actions of public officers have been incorrectly reported or distorted, a newspaper is required to publish on the first page an answer of not more than twice the length of the injurious article. This answer must appear in the first issue following notification by the interested party. In case the answer is more than twice as long as the original, the newspaper may charge for the excess at the rate provided for legal notices.

With reference to private individuals named or designated in an untruthful news story, a newspaper must publish within three days after receiving it an answer twice as long as the original article. The answer must appear in the same place in the paper where the original article was published, and must be printed in the same type. "

In practice, the law is seldom invoked, as newspapers regularly publish the answers sent to them without waiting for any form of legal notice.

Another law advocated by Upton Sinclair is one putting the distribution of news to American newspapers under public control. Mr. Sinclair, who believes the. Associated Press to be a monopoly, desires that any one who wishes to publish a newspaper in any American city or town may receive the Associated Press service without any formality whatever except the filing of an application and the payment of a fee to cover the cost of the service. In view of the fact that Mr. Sinclair believes the public opinion of America to be "poisoned at the source" by this organization, it would seem anomalous that he should wish to extend its service. Laws of the sort advocated by Mr. Sinclair already exist in Kansas and Kentucky but have never been enforced, the handling of news being an interstate matter. Newspaper men, of course, know that the Associated Press is not a monopoly, the. United Press and the International News Service being vigorous general competitors, and several other services being competitors in limited fields.

None of the foregoing suggestions represents the serious thought of any one practically experienced in journalism. The only proposed law which does represent the point of view of the professional journalist to any extent is the suggestion of a state board of journalism which should issue and revoke licenses to practice the profession of journalism. Such a law would be intended to introduce into the journalistic profession standards similar to those now existing in the legal and medical professions. One of the earliest suggestions of this character was made by Barratt O'Hara, a practicing newspaper man, formerly lieutenant governor of Illinois. Mr. O'Hara's plan, proposed in 1913, contained the following provisions, according to the author's own statement:

> "A license should issue:
>
> "i. When the applicant had reached legal age;
>
> "2. Completed the equivalent of a high school education.
>
> "3. Studied two years in a recognized college of journalism, or passed the same period of time in a newspaper office as an apprentice reporter;
>
> "4, Furnished the Board with positive proof of good moral character; and
>
> "5. Successfully passed an examination, in writing, conducted by the State Board at regular intervals.
>
> "Adequate provision was made for the beginner, who might receive, on application to the board and proof of good moral character and an education equivalent to that of the ordinary high school, a certificate as an Apprentice Reporter. As such he might perform the usual work of a cub reporter, but would be disqualified from passing final judgment on his own and other persons' copy. That is, he might write the items, but the same would be read and possibly revised by a licensed journalist before reaching the printer. Two years of such training and restriction, with the natural looking forward to the examinations ahead and the constant preparing for them, could scarcely fail to bring out the very best newspaper qualities in the young aspirant. Or the same period might be spent with equal profit in an approved and practicable school of journalism.
>
> "A license, on the other hand, should be revoked: "i. Automatically, on the practitioner's conviction of a felony; or
>
> "2. After due filing of charges and trial by a jury of his fellow practitioners, for willful misrepresentation,

> malicious writing of scandal, acceptance of money or other prize tendered as bribe for the deliberate and unjustified coloring of news items, or other conduct unprofessional, reprehensible, and dishonest."

A somewhat similar bill was proposed in the Oklahoma legislature in 1923. It was strongly opposed by the newspapers of the state generally, which believed that it was inspired by a spirit of revenge rather than by a desire to improve journalistic conditions. The bill was defeated. The bill provided that the board should consist of the President of the State University, the Dean of the School of Journalism of the State University, and three members to be appointed by the governor. All of the appointed members were required to have had at least five years' active experience as newspapermen in Oklahoma. The revocation of licenses was made conditional on the following facts:

> "(a) When it shall be ascertained that any applicant made any false statements or representations in procuring his license.
>
> "(b) When any licensee is convicted of a crime against the laws of the State of Oklahoma involving moral turpitude,
>
> "(c) When any licensee becomes an habitual drunkard,
>
> "(d) When any licensee prints or causes to be printed, or permits the printing and publication of any story or news article about any citizen of this state or nation which is not true,
>
> "(e) When any licensee prints, or causes to be printed, or permits the printing and publication of any news article, story or editorial, which either directly or by insinuation, falsely charges any citizen of this state or nation with an act which hurts the standing or reputation of such citizen in the community or state or nation, either in a business or social way.
>
> "(f) When any licensee prints, causes to be printed or permits the printing and publication of any news item, editorial, or story which is immoral or degrading."

Similar bills have been introduced in the legislature of Connecticut and possibly those of other states.

It is altogether probable that in time admission to the profession of journalism will be made conditional upon passing certain requirements. This will come, however, as the result of a demand from practicing journalists rather than from the outside. In accordance with the practice in every profession, any examining board would be composed of members of the profession. Until the ethical standards of the profession are more definitely established than they are today, the tendency of examinations and other acts of the board might conceivably be to preserve the present status of journalism and to hinder development of higher standards. A professional consciousness and the ethical and social implications flowing from this are necessary before any legal enactment can improve the status of journalism as a profession.

ADDITIONAL READINGS

Hale, *The Law of the Press.*

Angel!, *The Press and the Organisation of Society,* pp. 76-89.

Sinclair, *The Brass Check,* pp. 403-407.

The Arbitrator, Vol. 2, No. *2,* July, 1919.

O'Hara, *A State License for Newspaper Men,* in Thorpe's

The Coming Newspaper, pp. 148-161. *Oklahoma Press Bill Is Doomed. Editor and Publisher,* March 17, 1923, p. 18.

REFERENCES

1. For a detailed discussion of laws governing the press, see Hales, *The Law of the Press.*
2. This and the following quotations are from *The Arbitrator* for July 1919 (Vol. 2, No. 2).
3. *General Laws of Massachusetts,* Chapter 55, Section 34a.
4. *Obligatory Answers,* in *The Arbitrator,* Vol. 2, No. 2, pp. 12-13.
5. P. 404.

6. See Appendix A, p. 206.
7. *The* Brass *Check,* p. 405.
8. The writer is indebted to Professor P. de Bacourt of Columbia University for authoritative data on the French law and practice
9. *The Brass Check,* p. 406.
10. *The Brass Check,* pp. 362-376.
11. Thorpc, *The Coming Newspaper,* pp. 154-156.
12. *Editor and Publiiher,* March 17, 1923, p. 18.

16

A Responsible Press

Free and Responsible Press

In December, 1942, Henry R. Luce of Time, Inc. suggested to President Robert M. Hutchins of the University of Chicago an inquiry into the freedom of the press: both its present state and future prospects. President Hutchins selected a dozen scholars to serve with himself on a Commission on Freedom of the Press. Their conclusions now published mark an important event in the history of American journalism.*

For the first time an examination of the performance of the press has been undertaken by a highly competent, independent body with adequate resources. They spent three years and $200,000 of Mr. Luce's money, then $15,000 more that President Hutchins dug out of the Encyclopaedia Britannica.

The variety of experience of the Commission membership lends weight to its findings. Besides President Hutchins, they were: John Dickinson, general counsel of the Pennsylvania Railroad; Bcardsley Ruml, then president of the Federal Reserve Bank of New York; Archibald MacLeish, formerly assistant Secretary of State; Reinhold Niebnhr of Union Theological Seminary; Gcorgc N. Sinister, President of Hunter College; Harold 1). Lasswell of the Yale

---

* Robert D. Leigh, *A Free and Responsible Press,* the report of the Commission on Freedom of the Press (University of Chicago Press, 1947).

Law School; John M. Clark, economist of Columbia University; Charles E. Merriam, political economist of the University of Chicago; Robert Red-field, Dean of Social Sciences at that institution; and three scholars of Harvard University. Zechariah Chafee of the Law School, Arthur M. Schlesinger, historian, and William K. Hocking, philosopher. As director of their staff they had Robert D. Leigh, former president of Bennington College, assisted by Llewellyn White.

Their extensive inquiry included all agencies of mass communication—books, magazines, movies, radio, newspapers. But with books they found little problem, and with magazines less than the other media. They are bringing out separate studies on the movies and radio. Their central report is largely concerned with the news-paper.

They considered freedom of the press in terms of a responsible press and they came out with the warning that only a responsible press can remain free. Failure of the press to meet the needs of a society dependent on it for information and ideas is the greatest danger to its freedom, the Commission finds.

Its answer to the question "Is the freedom of the press in danger?" is a flat "Yes." But the reasons do not echo the familiar assumption of the publishers that freedom of the press is their proprietary right I to act as irresponsibly as they please. The Commission's reasons are:

1. As the importance of communication has increased, its control has come into fewer hands.
2. The few in control have failed to meet the needs of the people.
3. Press practices at times have been so irresponsible that if continued, society is bound to take control for its own protection.

The citizen also has a right to truthful information on public affairs, the Commission asserts. "No democracy will indefinitely tolerate concentration of private power, irresponsible and strong enough to thwart the democratic aspirations of the people. 11 these giant agencies of communication are irresponsible, not even the First Amendment will protect their freedom from government control. The Amendment will be amended."

This is an urgent warning to the interests in control of the press. It is going to be a hard one to brush off or forget as so many criticisms of less weight have been brushed off and ignored.

The Commission recites the communications revolution that has made the press big business and shows it acting increasingly like big I business and increasingly in alliance with the interests of other big business. The vital necessity of the citizen to have access to clear channels of adequate informal ion on public affairs has never been more painstakingly presented. His right and obligation to secure such information is insistently put.

Then the Commission comes to a sticking point. How to protect the public right to access to truthful information is a complex problem. The Commission's remedy is less convincing than its diagnosis. That has been true of course of all earlier criticism of the press. The Commission shies away from public, regulation to make the press accountable, lest other freedoms be endangered. This is the dilemma of a modern society enormously dependent upon a press in private hands, inevitably controlled by large capitalists whose interests are not always the public interest.

It is easy to show that accountable service in communication is as essential as pure food, public, health, and fair trade practices. But these other needs are protected by law. If we accept the view that government regulation of the press is a danger to freedom, then the public is cut off from the traditional means of a democracy to protect its interests by public regulation.

That the Commission has not taken us out of that dilemma is both the weakness of the report and the riddle of the problem. If you refuse the public the sole public recourse to protect its rights, you haven't much left but hope and prayer. The Commission prays that the press may make itself more responsible. It urges that the press restore the professional status of journalism, long a captive to the publisher's business. It wants professional standards applied to the performance of the press. It insists that the press cease shielding its own miscreants by the device of refusing publicity to the malpractices and libel suits of its fellow members. It asks a sense of trusteeship by publishers. These are indispensable reforms.

But the only means to these ends that it finds to recommend are public concern, public appraisal, public criticism of press performance. It proposes an endowed agency to supply continuing appraisal of press performance. This is a very mild poultice to apply to the organic and spreading disorder of irresponsible giantism which it finds in the institution of the press.

But the report is not to be judged by failure to find the cure. Its value is in alerting the public and warning the publishers of the failure of the press to meet the public need. The definition of "common carrier of public discussion" as the function that a responsible press must accept is one for all journalism to paste in its hat.

The great strength of the report is its pernetrating examination of the performance of the press. It has the courage to challenge the whole rigamarole of press cliches as to what is news and the silly game of scoops and headline hunting. "The news is twisted by emphasis on the novel and the sensational . . . Too much of the regular output consists of a succession of stories and images that has no relation to the typical lives of real people anywhere. The result is meaninglessness, flatness, distortion and perpetuation of misunderstanding." It finds the press preoccupied with the sensational and trivial "to such an extent that the citizen is not supplied with the information and discussion he needs to discharge his responsibilities to the community."

Every newspaperman knows how generally this is so. With a few notable exceptions which the Commission might well have emphasized move than it did, newspapering in the United States is pretty sloppy business, casual, trite, almost ritualistic in its cliches, and so stereotyped that the individual differences among newspapers in widely differing communities are hardly more distinctive than among the different brands of canned corn. The easy flow of such stuff as comes from the police blotter gets so much of the attention of the press as to squeeze out most of the information on public affairs that makes any sense. The giant modern press has exploited our high literacy and the rapid technology of communication. But its own contribution in serving the one with the other remains for the most part as primitive as the hand press and post rider. It is directly because newspaper publishers as a class are among the most conservative- groups in America that newspaper performance is as uninspired, as unoriginal, and uniformed as it is. It makes its own definition of news which is often so peculiar and parochial as to exclude most information that has any use or any meaning. The value of this report lies in its jolt to the mentality of those who control most of the press to their own profit.

The honorable exceptions are easily identified. The public stake-in the issue runs parallel to its stake in sell government and peace, for both, as the Commission shows, are threatened by the frequently irresponsible and often false presentation of government activity and international relations. They are threatened even more by the usual absence of use-fill information on these vital areas.

The Commission might have made note of, but did not, those exceptional newspapers that operate on a very high level of responsibility to serve the reader with information essential to the citizen. But they are highly exceptional as every one knows who has tried counting them up and found lingers left over.

The Commission's recital of the increasing concentration of newspaper control and consequent, contraction in the number and diversity of outlets for information and ideas is a twice-told tale. Morris Ernst explored it in his *The First Freedom.* But it will bear emphasis. Even as this report was in the press, the sale was announced of the *Philadelphia Record* to the *Philadelphia Bulletin.* That leaves the third city of America at this writing with one morning and two evening newspaper ownerships.

It underscores the Commission's point that: Through concentration the variety of sources of news and opinion is limited. The insistence of the citizen's need has increased.

True, but some instances would have been in order. With $215,000 and a research stall and three years to work, the facts about the press handling of such stories as one destruction of the OPA and the wrecking of the housing program would have illuminated the report. It was possible to measure how much the public was told of the lobbies and pressures and industry sit-down strike, to end price control and to muscle out Wilson Wyatt's program, It would have been possible to show how little attention was paid to the profits made out of the removal of price limits when the headlines were crying over strikes for more wages. Fads are the most telling evidence. 1 lad the Commission been more journalistic in its own report, its conclusions would have more effect.

The report is a philosopher's summation of the state of the press. It would be more informative it contained more research into instances. The Commission cites "charges" of distortion and says "bias is claimed" against consumer cooperatives, food and drug regulations, and Federal Trade Commission orders on fraudulent advertising. "Many people believe," it says, "that the press is biased on national fiscal policy." The Commission had the means to run down these charges.

It is hard to believe that it did not. It heard fifty-eight witnesses from the press and its staff recorded interviews with 225 others. The report is derived from 176 separate documents developed in the study. Some of the cautious language of the report is quite evidently a device to appease the more conservative members in the interest of the unanimous agreement which they present.

Very usefully, the Commission shows that radio rates far below the newspaper as a responsible channel of information. Public affairs take from zero to 10 per cent of radio time. The Commission says bluntly that before it can be respectable radio must take control of its programs away from the advertisers: "Radio cannot become a responsible agency of communication as long as its programming is controlled by the advertisers. No newspaper would call itself respectable if its editorial columns were dominated by its advertisers and if it published advertising, information, and discussion so mixed together that the reader could not tell them apart."

It sums up radio programs with this: "The great consumer industries which in 1945 gave the networks three-quarters of their income determine what the American people shall hear on the air. A dozen and a half advertising agencies place contracts and prepare programs. The result is such a mixture of advertising with the rest of the program that one cannot be listened to without the other."

The devastating report on radio recalls the curious results of certain polls that have found more public confidence in news heard on the radio than read in the newspapers. There is no accounting for this except by the magic many people still feel in hearing a voice. Any newspaperman who at times performs on the radio has had the experience of receiving a charmed response from neighbors and acquaintances who never mention his familiar daily reports in his newspaper. Yet he knows, and so do they if they ever think about it, that he contributes far more to their information in the less restricted channels of the paper.

Alter reading its report on radio one can better understand the Commission's lack of enthusiasm for government regulation, though it doesn't oiler that as a reason. Radio has been under regulation from the start, and obviously regulation has failed to result in adequate radio service. To say that the FCC has been prevented by the power with Congress of advetiser-backed radio pressures from ever trying real regulation does not add much comfort or increase anticipation of benefits from press regulation.

This is not the reason the Commission seeks to avoid governmental action to require press responsibility, but it is a consideration not to be overlooked by those who disagree with them about it.

The Commission finds the quality of the press affected by the fact, that "wages and prestige of the working newspapermen are low and their tenure precarious." This is an understatement. The newspaper is a prep school for the fields of radio, magazines, movies, and public relations. The most talented of its staff are grabbed off by these competing enterprises often for an extra $20 or $30 a week and all the years of their development lost to press and public. This is one of the sorest points about American newspapering and one of its grievous ills.

Everybody else appreciates the value of a trained newspaperman except the newspaper publisher. So journalism is drained constantly of the men capable of operating at a level of public service.

It would have been easy to show this. Take the number of men in government agencies who left newspapers for a little more money, lake the whole personnel of radio and see how many were trained in newspapers. Take the salary levels of radio and compare with newspapers. Take the staff of a few representative papers of fifteen years ago and show where the featured reporters of that time are working now. This forfeiture of the press' own human resources has reached a point where even *Editor & Publisher,* the trade organ of the press, has been plaintively editorializing on it.

But a deeper disturbing note is the Commission's discovery of the "frustration" of reporters and editorial writers. "The Commission was disturbed by finding that many able reporters and editorial writers displayed frustration—the feeling that they were not allowed to do the kind of work which their professional ideals demanded. A continuation of this disturbing situation will prevent the press from assuming effective responsibility toward society."

As remedies, the Commission urges that the press "use any means that can be devised to increase the competence and independence of the staff."

That is all very well. And very true. Better reporters and better paid reporters are needed, but to say this and stop there misses the central issue.

Can the Commission imagine a journalist being "independent" and working for Hearst, Mc.Cormick, or the paper controlled by the First National Rank?

What is it that turns idealistic newspapermen into frustrated cynics? It is the context of the job itself. It is the very irresponsibility the report complains of. The Commission is going around in circles to say that the press is irresponsible, that it should be responsible, that it requires professional standards, and that the press should develop professional standards in its staff. The newest tyros in the city room have the standards desired until they are conditioned on the job to something else that defeats and frustrates the best of them.

It is a very insidious thing. The Commission has sensed it, explored it, been revolted by it, but never quite come to grips with it. The Commission realizes that a profession has been taken over and exploited. There is no parallel for that in other professions. It clearly baffles a Commission made up of members of the professions of law, education, religion, science, and philosophy. Any of their "frustrated" newspapermen could have told them more than they understand about the catch in the game. But their contribution is in describing the problem. That is a large contribution. They leave it is they must in the lap of the public:

> "We have the impression that the American people do not realize what has happened to them. They are not aware that the communications revolution has taken place. They do not appreciate the tremendous power which the new instruments and new organization of the press place in the hands of a few men. They have not yet understood how far the performance of the press falls short of the requirements of a free society in the world today. The principal object of our report is to make these points clear."

[*Courtesy:* Louis M. Lyons]

17

The Press Under Pressure

The newspaper press is so familial to us that we easily forget what an incongruous phenomenon it is in a highly controlled society like ours. Think of the tightly organised societies of the past. Rameses 11, Tiberius, Diocletian, Henry VIII, and Louis XIV could govern without being bothered by newspapers. Within only two centuries little news sheets issued by obscure printers have turned into enormous enterprises in each of which a handful of men can inform and influence millions of citizens. How they will go about it is often unpredictable. In 1019, for example, Hearst's love for the underdog led him to give opponents of sedition legislation space which most journals refused, whereas today he urges that every Communist be harried out of the land. The owner of the *Chicago Daily News* dies and the whole character of the paper changes. Comic strips, colored cartoons, boiler-plate editorials—we don't know what will happen next. Yet if the press is to be alive and vigorous, it must be unpredictable. The press is a sort of wild animal in our midst—restless, gigantic, always seeking new ways to use its strength.

Of course the press does not represent the only enterprises which since 1700 have grown from small beginnings to great power. The standard Oil Company, General Motors, the Bank of America, the New York Stock Exchange, the CIO, to name only a few, developed as fast as the Chicago *Tribune,* and the *New York Times.* Yet there is a striking contrast. Sooner or later the enormous power of these private bodies arouses public alarm, and they are put under some measure of governmental control to restrain possible abuses. They can no longer run loose. It is the first principle of our Bill of Rights that the government must let the press run loose. All of us, I fervently hope, believe this to be a wise taking of risks. The First Amendment presupposes, as Learned Hand says, "that right conclusions are more likely to be gathered out of a multitude of tongues, than through any kind of authoritative selection. To many this is, and always will be, folly; but we have staked upon it our all."

Nevertheless, we must face frankly the risks we have agreed to run. The press has become an "impcrium in imperio." No other powerful business organization in the United States now enjoys such almost complete independence from the federal government. Even among nonprofit organizations there is nothing to compare with the immunity of the press for abuses of power except the churches. A church's behavior can at least be predicted from its settled doctrines, and by its very nature its members are accountable to God. The sovereign press for the most part acknowledges accountability *to* no one except its owners and publishers.

Of course, there are notable exceptions to this attitude of self-sufficiency. We can all name some of them. The American Press Institute at Columbia and the Nieman Foundation at Harvard are in their different ways inculcating a different' conception. Sevellon Brown said in opening the Press Institute: "We are here because we recognize the tremendous social responsibilities which are ours, responsibilities of a scope and complexity scarcely dreamed of by newspapermen a short generation ago." The question remains, however, whether the leaders of newspapers and radio and motion pictures will of their own accord move fast enough toward giving the kind of service which American citizens need in order to govern themselves intelligently and encourage the President and Congress to make our country do what is necessary to maintain a durable peace. There is less time at our disposal than we used to think before Hiroshima.

In 1947 two wholly different efforts were made to create a greater responsibility in the American press.

The first was the publication in March of the general report of the Commission on Freedom of the Press. It was unfortunate, though quite natural, that most attention of reviewers was concentrated on the final chapter of recommendations. We had felt unable to urge any sensational remedies, and hence the book was often brushed aside. Much more important, I believe, are the opening chapters which analyze the problem of what sort of press the public needs in a free society. The following passage strikes the keynote:

> "Today our society needs, first, a truthful, comprehensive, and intelligent account of the day's events in a context which gives them meaning; second, a forum for the exchange of comment and criticism; third, a means of projecting the opinions and attitudes of the groups in the society to one another; fourth, a method of presenting and clarifying the goals and values of the society; and, fifth, a way of reaching every member of the society by the currents of information, thought, and feeling which the press supplies."

The book went on to examine the present performance of the press. It then stated that, despite some examples of "extraordinarily high quality of performance" in newspapers, radio, and motion pictures, "when we look at the press as a whole . . . we must conclude that it is not meeting the needs of our society. The Commission believes that this failure of the press is the greatest danger to its freedom." And so we appealed to the leaders of the press itself to recognize the gravity of the situation and "assume the responsibility of providing the variety, quantity and quality of information and discussion which the country needs . . . They must . . . themselves be hospitable to ideas and attitudes different from their own, and they must present them to the public as meriting its attention."

Some leaders of the industries reacted gratifyingly to this appeal, but most remained apathetic. A typical reaction was shown by the writer in *Editor & Publisher* who cited the total number of newspaper buyers in the United States as conclusive evidence that the public is satisfied with the press as it is. In 1910 there were millions . of passengers who rode on steam and electric railroads, and some apologists for the railroads might as well have cited that astronomical figure as proof of the complete public satisfaction with trains and trolleys. Yet that was on the eve of terrific legislative attacks on the railroads and the financial ruin of trolleys. Of course millions of citizens rend the newspapers they can now get, because they can't get anything better.

An incident at the one annual meeting of the Associated Press illustrates the newspaper leaders' lack of interest in their task—as the Commission described it—of providing information to enable the American people to make for themselves "fundamental decisions necessary to the direction of their government and their lives." After the election of officers for the ensuing year and other routine business, the publishers present from all our leading papers were asked whether they had any suggestions for a wider coverage of news by the Associated Press. There was a long silence, which was broken at last by one man. Did he ask whether the public could be told more of what goes on inside China beyond the birth of eight children at once? Did he regret the drastic reduction of Associated Press correspondents in Europe, or express the wish that we might learn more about the way American soldiers were governing our own zone in Germany? No—he complained because the Associated Press did not carry news of the Irish sweepstakes.

The second group of criticisms of our press in 1947 came from foreign representatives in the United Nations. The attack began mildly in the Sub-Commission on Freedom of Information in May, warmed up during the summer in the Economic and Social Council, and reached fever heat in the General Assembly. Newspapers at last awoke from the apathy with which they had received the report of the Hutchins Commission. Mr. Vishinsky in effect adopted the methods of King Rehoboam: "My predecessor hath chastened you with whips, but I will chasten you with scorpions."

Needless to say, I do not agree with Mr. Vishinsky. But this is not just a question of Mr. Vishinsky. As soon as I reached Lake Success, I became aware of a strong current of feeling in other nations that the sort of irresponsibility the press here and elsewhere has often displayed is a threat to peace which ought to be restrained, by moral suasion if not by law. Varying resolutions imposing responsibility have been constantly proposed in the U.N., not only by more moderate representatives of the U.S.S.R., but also by delegates from countries whose good will to us is unquestioned, like France, Norway, Chile, India, and Australia. At least three points in these proposals deserve examination in order to ascertain what lessons for us they convey.

First, the Soviets regard the press as an instrument of government policy and not as a neutral vehicle of information. My Soviet colleague. Mr. Lomakin, urged our Sub-Commission to list as one of the main tasks of the press: "To organize the struggle for democratic principles, for the unmasking of the remnants of Fascism and for the extirpation of Fascist ideology in all its forms.' The fact that this particular formula was decisively rejected should not blind us to the fact that there are plenty of adherents in America to the philosophy behind the formula. They want the communications industries to make specific political decisions and inculcate specific political ideals in citizens instead of providing citizens with the material for making their own decisions and ideals. The recent movie investigation in the Un-American Committee stands for just the same philosophy as my Soviet colleague—only the Committee's enforced aim is "free- enterprise" or "Americanism." There" is a much greater need for extirpating this philosophy in our country than for extirpating the remnants of Fascism—whatever that is now. By contrast we should insist, as my Norwegian colleague Mr. Christensen said, "That the basic task of the press and of other media of information is to tell the truth."

The first lesson, then, from the U.N. discussions is that no narrow political ideals of any sort should fetter the obligation of the American communications industries to ascertain the truth and furnish it to our citizens.

My next point is that Soviet writers and speakers use the phrase "freedom of the press" in a sense quite different from ours. To us it means that the law does not prevent anyone from saying what he wishes, within our sort of legal rights. Their constitution provides that "printing presses, stocks of paper . . . and other material requisites" shall he put at the disposal of working people and their organizations. Hence we feel that Soviet censorship by officials negates free presses in Russia, and they feel that our press is not free because owners and publishers can interfere with presentation of views unacceptable to them.

If the Commission on Freedom of the Press is right in asserting on the first page of its report that "the development of the press as an instrument of mass communication has greatly decreased the proportion of the people who can express their opinions and ideas through the press," then it is time something was done about it. I do not underrate the practical difficulties—newspapers cost money to produce and space cannot be "free" like free air. And I do not think the remedy lies in more laws. It is a matter for the conscience and professional skill of owners and publishers and everybody else engaged in the communications industries.

Although a newspaper cannot practicably open its pages to dissentient writers except in the column of Letters to the Editor, the journal is under a moral obligation to present fairly in its news and special articles the significant views of the various substantial groups in the community, and not merely the views of the particular group to which the owner and publisher belong. Both sides of a public, controversy should have a reasonable chance to reach the readers of newspapers of general circulation.

That is my second lesson from foreign criticisms of our press.

It is a specific application of one of the broad ideals of the press already stated—"To help maintain international peace and security through understanding and cooperation between peoples." It is very significant that when this aim of the press went from our U.N. Sub-Commission to the Economic and Social Council, the Council added, 'and to combat forces which incite war, by removing bellicose influences from the media of information."

Of course, American papers are not alone to blame, but the fact that others do wrong should not prevent us from doing right. This, again, is not a matter for law. Not law but the consciences of editors and other writers should lead them to weigh with unusual care proposed publications which will aggravate international ill-feeling. Especial attention should be given to the phrasing of headlines.

Is our press responsible? Yes, to some extent, but it should be more so. Is our press free? Yes, in our sense of freedom, but the different sense of "accessible to all significant views on public questions" is also important, and there we might do more. Finally, freedom from something is not enough It should also be freedom for something. The wide immunity from governmental control which the press claims will be empty if it be a mere negation. Freedom is not safety but opportunity Freedom ought to be a means to enable the press to serve the proper functions of communication in a free society.

[*Courtesy:* Zechariah Chaffe, Jr.]

18

The Full Dimensions of the News*

When an editor has decided to print as much news as his readers can digest, he has only begun the complex job of designing his newspaper. How much is enough? How much spate can be used for current news? How far must he go in printing non-news material in order to attract and hold circulation?

A few years ago a survey was made of the *Louisville Courier-Journal.* It showed the preferences of men and the preferences of women.

Out of every 100 men, 04 looked at the pictures on the picture-page (we no longer have enough newsprint to carry an entire page of pictures, but many American newspapers still do this); 69 of each 100 men read "Blondie," our most popular comic; 71 read the weather forecast; 60 looked at the editorial-page- cartoon; 44 at the radio schedules; 72 read a cartoon called "Private Lives," showing how easy it is to stimulate curiosity with a title; 36 read a sports column. Most of the other comics ranked close to "Blondie"—over half of our subscribers read them.

The front-page banner headline of that day (April 12, HMO) reported that 18 German ships had been sunk. Mr.

*Mr. Pope gave the talk from which this article was taken to a group of German editors attending seminars at the American Press Institute. He was then managing editor of the *Louisville Courier-Journal,* since relived. —*James S. Pope (January 1949)*

Churchill was quoted as saying "We're on the Road to Victory." He did not say how long that road was to be. With such news, the front page was well read. Seventy-eight of the same 100 men read the leading story. But after the front page was passed, readership of news dropped off sharply.

If you were designing a newspaper from that survey, and knew nothing else about your job, you would carry a front page of news and fill the remainder of your paper with comic strips, cartoons, and sporting features.

Such a product ought, to be perfect. But it would not be. It would be like a huge market -which displayed meat and bread in the windows, but offered for sale over the counters inside nothing but chocolate candy. Your customers would soon get the stomach-ache. They would look elsewhere for meat and bread.

We have never made news one half as appealing as it should be. News is the most interesting item we could offer. It is life. It has no other limitations. Its limits are merely those of human activity— mental, physical, spiritual. News is our very selves, multiplied and magnified to a world-wide stature.

News is the basic stuff from which is copied the little ersatz images, the comic drawing and the photographs. We have let the image-makers surpass us, though we have the blood and-bone original to offer. For this I think every American newspaperman should « feel shame.

News is endless in variety, but the comics and pictures are monotony itself. Comic characters go through familiar adventures day by day. They meet the same obstacles, triumph in the same old way. There is little novelty or surprise in them, and almost no real imagination.

And what of the pictures? Americans have looked at so

many of them so many times, it now takes a touch of magic from the photographer to get a photograph worth printing. For every dramatic news picture there are dozens that are simply tiresome.

Of course people look at pictures. It is a basic human instinct. But how many of them hold a fresh interest? The reader polls have not found a practical way to measure quality. That is our job, as editors.

Are we to admit that a cartoonist's stale "bag of tricks and an album of shopworn pictures can interest more readers than living news of living people, freshly gathered and told with humor, with drama, and with penetration?

We must always remember that these surveys have been made of newspapers as they are, not of newspapers as they should be. We have not begun to exploit the rich store of material that is ours. We have not trained reporters who can make a diplomatic conference —which may settle our fate for 100 years—as vital as the capture of a comic-strip crook by a witless detective.

What we need is a survey of our minds, of our imaginations, of our timidities and failures as editors. We need a survey to tell us why we have to push our priceless product with so many free confections.

When we begin to learn to reflect the true color that is a part of the news, we must be very careful not to pour false color into it.

I am sorry to say there is disagreement in this country about what we call objectivity in news reporting. That simply means that the reporter tries to keep himself out of his report. Me gives the reader full information, avoiding words that throw a favorable or an unfavorable light on the event. The reader thus can form his own opinion; the reporter's opinion is not pressed upon him.

Many newspaper and magazine editors openly question whether it is possible to be objective, and even whether it is desirable to be. There is a belief that what is objective is chill. Hut this is a part of the foolish myth that news is so pale it must have rouge smeared on its fate with blatant adjectives and adverbs. This is not true. It is seldom the news which is dull, but the manner in which it is told. Truth is not only stranger than fiction, it is much more exciting.

There is a great danger in writing "color," which usually means bias, into straight news. Every good newspaper has an editorial page. On this page the editor may express his opinion of the news. If he introduces those opinions into the columns where his readers expect to find only factual information, he is being dishonest, and in time his readers will find him out.

It is my argument, then, that news can be more interesting than any other material we choose to print, little news as well as big news; that it must not be accepted and printed in the form given to it by those with a selfish interest-/that it must be offered to the reader in its rich, natural color)

There is still another thing to consider in the proper handling of news. It must reflect vision and understanding on the part of the editor if it is to bring vision and understanding to the reader. No intelligent citizen of this world believes any longer that what happens; in his own town, or his own county, or in his own nation is all that matters to him, and all that he needs or wants to know.

What has happened in Germany in the last fifty years has had more influence in our lives in many ways than what happened here at home; and what happens in America and in Russia in the next ten years may easily determine the future of your children and grandchildren. Therefore, the editor who does not attempt to give his readers a clear account of foreign affairs is putting a blindfold over their eyes. They will be helpless pawns in the international game of chess.

On the *Courier-Journal* and the *Louisville Times* we have the world-wide news reports of the United Press and the Associated Press, and also the superb accounts of the foreign staff of the New *York Times.* In addition to this we buy the articles of the North American Newspaper Alliance, the *Chicago Daily News* Service, the Overseas News Agency, and the work of many independent writers. In recent months we have printed on some days as much as 15 or 20 columns of foreign news, out of the 45 or 50 columns of spot news in the paper. But we have not been content with that. We want the people who handle and comment upon the news to know something of the lands and the people whence it comes.

Within the past few years our editor, Barry Bingham, has been to Germany twice, studying the problems of reconstruction there and throughout Central Europe. Mark Ethridge, our publisher, has twice been to the Ralkans. We have been repaid for his total absence of some eight months on government missions by his grasp of the problems we face along the borders of the Soviet Union.

When it became clear to us in 1945 that India would not live in colonial bonds after the war ended, I flew to New Delhi and traveled over the country. I tried to learn something of the political and religious and economic background of India's struggle for independence.

These are merely examples. Other editors on other American newspapers have done likewise, and the frontiers of our understanding are steadily being pushed outward.

The world has a basic hunger for news. It is as deep as the hunger for food in many regions. This craving for information is being felt among millions who never had it before. And if we will satisfy it, we can remake our world into a vastly better place, a community in which peace can live without fighting daily for its life.

Appendices

APPENDIX—I

INFORMATION TECHNOLOGY ACTION PLAN

Preamble

In the history of civilisation, no work of science has so comprehensively impacted on the course of human development as Information Technology (IT). Undoubtedly, IT has been the greatest change agent of this century and promises to play this role even more dramatically in the coming decades. IT is changing every aspect of human life— communications, trade, manufacturing, services, culture, entertainment, education, research, national defence and global security.

IT is breaking old barriers and building new interconnections in the emerging Global Village. IT has also become the chief determinant of the progress of nations, communities and individuals.

For India, the rise of Information Technology is an opportunity to overcome historical disabilities and once again become the master of one's own national destiny. IT is a tool that will enable India to achieve the goal of becoming a strong, prosperous and self-confident nation. In doing so, IT promises to compress the time it would otherwise take for India to advance rapidly in the march of development and occupy a position of honor and pride in the comity of nations.

The Government of India has recognised the potential of Information Technology for rapid and all-round national development. The National Agenda for Governance, which is the Government's policy blueprint, has taken due note of the Information and Communication Revolution that is sweeping the globe. Accordingly, it has mandated the Government to take necessary policy and programmatic initiatives that would facilitate India's emergence as an Information Technology Superpower in the shortest possible time.

This commitment to Information and Communication Technology in the National Agenda for Governance has been forcefully articulated by Prime Minister Shri Atal Bihari Vajpayee on a number of occasions. In his first televised address to the Nation on March 25, the Prime Minister declared that promotion of Information Technology would be one of his Government's five top priorities. In his speech at the CII Annual Session on April 28, 1998, the Prime Minister said: "This is one area where India can quickly establish global dominance. India can be fully competitive in this area with tremendous pay-offs in terms of wealth creation and generation of high quality employment".

The Prime Minister announced at the CII Annual Session the Government's resolve to set up, within 30 days, a National Task Force on Information Technology, which would formulate the draft National Informatics Policy. Accordingly, the Office of the Prime Minister issued a Notification on 22nd May, 1998 constituting a National Task Force on Information Technology and Software Development. This Task Force is chaired by Shri Jaswant Singh, Deputy Chairman, Planning Commission and co-chaired by Shri N. Chandrababu Naidu, Chief Minister of Andhra Pradesh and Dr. M.G.K. Menon, former Minister of State for Science and Technology. Its members include eminent representatives from the Government, industry and academia.

The Prime Minister has given five main tasks and 15 terms of reference to the IT Task Force. The tasks include recommending, within one month, immediate steps that the Government needs to take to remove bottlenecks in the path of rapid development of IT in India and give a big boost to Indian IT and software industry.

The Task Force has completed its deliberations on this immediate task and is pleased to submit its first report to the Prime Minister. This report, called the Information Technology Action Plan, contains 108 recommendations covering both bottleneck areas and broad promotional measures that are crucial for boosting IT in India. These recommendations cover a wide spectrum of issues relating to telecommunications, finance, banking, revenue, commerce, electronics, human resource development, defence and rural development. They address critical national needs in the areas of information infrastructure, Internet access, software development and exports, hardware manufacture, electronic commerce, R&D in IT, manpower training and education.

Software exports has received much attention of the Task Force. Recognising India's competitive advantage in this area, the Action Plan has made many recommendations aimed at enabling Indian exporters to capture a large share of the global software market in a short time. A unique promotional campaign suggested in the report is *operation knowledge*, which aims at universalising IT and IT-based education at all levels of the education pyramid in India. A notable feature of these recommendations is the conscious effort of the Task Force to give Information Technology a pro-people and pro-development thrust.

These recommendations flow from a perspective that India can become a strong IT power only if information technology reaches out to the masses in rural areas and in small towns and if its use in Indian languages can also be given major encouragement. Taken together, the recommendations in the Information Technology Action Plan significantly broaden and deepen the process of economic reforms by encouraging competition, entrepreneurship and innovation — the three principles which are cardinal for India's progress in the emerging knowledge-driven global economy. The Task Force is confident that the implementation of these recommendations will send a strong signal to people within India and abroad that India can swiftly ride on the Information Superhighway.

Activities of the Task Force till date The Office of the Prime Minister issued a Notification on 22nd May 1998 constituting a National Task Force on Information Technology and Software Development. Dr. M.G.K. Menon, Co-Chairperson of the Task Force, Dr. N. Seshagiri, Member-Convener, and Shri Sudheendra Kulkarni of the PMO met Shri Jaswant Singh, Deputy Chairman, Planning Commission and Chairperson of the Task Force on 26th May 1998 for finalising the guidelines regarding the deliberations of the Task Force. The Task Force created a Web Site on the Internet, with a web-letter from the Chairman, inviting suggestions from IT professionals around the world. On the basis of a number of useful reports on the topic prepared earlier by various organisations like the Planning Commission, Ministry of Commerce, Department of Electronics, NIC, Government of Andhra Pradesh, as well as industry associations like NASSCOM, MAIT and ESC and the suggestions given by the various members of the Task Force, the Member-Convener prepared a Basic Background Report (BR-1) and hoisted the same on the Web. More than 3,000 suggestions have been received on the Web from IT professionals around the world. The Task Force held a number of preparatory meetings, and several formal and informal meetings with the Ministers concerned and their Secretaries and senior officials as per the following schedule: 26 May, 1998: Meeting with the

Deputy Chairman, Planning Commission & Chair-person of the Task Force 12, 13 & 15 June 1998: Preparatory meetings in New Delhi under the chairmanship of Professor M.G.K. Menon, Co-Chairperson of the Task Force 16 June 1998: Meeting in the Department of Telecommunication 18 June 1998: Meeting with the Chief Minister of Maharashtra, senior officials of the State Government and scientists and academicians and industry representatives in Mumbai 20 June 1998: Meeting with the Wireless Adviser, Government of India 22 & 23 June 1998: Meeting with the Minister for Communications 23 June 1998: Meeting with Chairman, Telecom Commission 24 June 1998: Meeting with Scientific Adviser to Raksha Mantri & Secretary, Defence (Research) 25 June 1998: Meeting with Finance Minister 25 June 1998: Meeting with Chief Minister of Andhra Pradesh & Co-Chairperson of the Task Force 26 June 1998: Meeting with Finance Secretary 27 June 1998: Meeting with Finance Secretary 29 June 1998: Meeting with Finance Secretary July 1, 1998: Meeting with Finance Minister July 1, 1998: Meeting with Wireless Adviser & Defence Ministry officials This is the first time in India that representatives of so many ministries, departments, industry associations, business houses, educational institutions and State Governments interacted so intensively and in such a short period of time to cover so many bottleneck and promotional areas in Information Technology. It is also the first time that agreement was reached and concurrence received on most of the points in the Action Plan. This, the Task Force believes, augurs well for its early and effective implementation. Future Activities After submission of the first report on bottleneck and immediate promotional issues, the Task Force will begin work on the more substantive work of formulating the draft National Informatics Policy. Towards this end, it will soon set up Working Groups on various specific subjects, on which representatives from Government, industry, academia and other sections of society from across the country will be represented. A few of the Working Groups have already started their work. The Task Force also plans to identify a large number of national missions which will be so designed as to make visible and catalytic impact on the use of IT in India. In order to broadbase its consultations, the Task Force has drawn up a plan to visit Bangalore, Hyderabad, Calcutta and Guwahati in the coming weeks. It has already held one such meeting in Mumbai on June 18, 1998. Within the next ten days, the Task Force will prepare a Vision Statement whose aim will be to excite and energise the people of India, creating the faith in them that Information Technology vitally aids personal growth and national growth. It will also embark on an awareness creation strategy for the effective articulation and dissemination of that Vision. The Information Technology Action Plan follows.

National Task Force on Information Technology and Software Development Information Technology Action Plan

The Government of India, recognising that the impressive growth the country has achieved since the mid-Eighties in Information Technology is still a small proportion of the potential to achieve, has resolved to make India a Global IT Superpower and a front-runner in the age of Information Revolution. The Government of India considers IT as an agent of transformation of every facet of human life which will bring about a knowledge based society in the twenty-first century. As a first step in that direction, the following revisions and additions are made to the existing Policy and Procedures for removing bottlenecks and achieving such a pre-eminent status for India. The revisions and additions are aimed at accomplishing the following basic objectives:

(i) *Info-Infrastructure Drive:* Accelerate the drive for setting up a World class Info Infrastructure with an extensive spread of Fibre Optic Networks, Satcom

Networks and Wireless Networks for seamlessly interconnecting the Local Informatics Infrastructure (LII), National Informatics Infrastructure (NII) and the Global Informatics Infrastructure (GII) to ensure a fast nation-wide onset of the INTERNET, EXTRANETs and INTRANETs.

(ii) *Target ITEX - 50:* With a potential 2 trillion dollar Global IT industry by the year 2008, policy ambiance will be created for the Indian IT industry to target for a $ 50 billion annual export of IT Software and IT Services (including IT-enabled services) by this year, over a commensurately large domestic IT market spread all over the country.

(iii) *IT for all by 2008:* Accelerate the rate of PC / set-top-box penetration in the country from the 1998 level of one per 500 to one per 50 people along with a universal access to Internet / Extranets/ Intranets by the year 2008, with a flood of IT applications encompassing every walk of economic and social life of the country. The existing over 600,000 Public Telephones / Public Call Offices (PCOs) will be transformed into public tele-info- centres offering a variety of multimedia Information services. Towards the goal of IT for all by 2008, policies are provided for setting the base for a rapid spread of IT awareness among the citizens, propagation of IT literacy, networked Government, IT-led economic development, rural penetration of IT applications, training citizens in the use of day-to-day IT services like tele-banking, tele-medicine, tele-education, tele-documents transfer, tele-library, tele-info-centres, electronic commerce, Public Call Centres, among others; and training, qualitatively and quantitatively, world class IT professionals.

(i) Info-Infrastructure Drive

With a target of 30 per cent of annual growth rate

from the 1998 level of Fibre Optic backbone of 75,000 route kilometers, VSATs of aggregate capacity of over 300 Megabit Per Second, Satellite Transponders of aggregate capacity of more than 3000 Megahertz and in the corresponding 'last mile' Wireless Communication as well as Data Communication based value added services, the Data and Multimedia Info-Infrastructure Policies are liberalised as under:

(1) INTERNET access nodes will be opened by DoT and authorised ISPs at all District Headquarters and local charging areas by 26th January 2000. As an interim measure, and till nodes are provided in all local charging areas, access to nearest INTERNET access nodes will be on local call rates with effect from 15th August 1998. ISPs will be responsible for ensuring that this facility is not misused for telephone traffic.

(2) Voice & Data Communication is permitted for IT Software Development and IT Services on dedicated or leased circuits, but no telephone traffic is permitted. Surcharge on 64 Kbps and higher capacity circuits for voice-cum-data applications is withdrawn with effect from 15th August 1998.

(3) Doubling of the lease rental charged by DOT for high speed data circuits leased by Closed User Group (CUG), Licensees of Basic Service, Cellular Service and other Value Added Services and users shall be reduced to single normal lease rental charge.

(4) Requests made by public sector Software Technology Park (STPs) or Private Sector STPs or IT promotional organisations approved by the Government for release of bandwidth shall be acted upon by the VSNL by intimating INTELSAT within two weeks of receipt.

(5) Setting up of Central call centres by IT Service Providers shall be permitted for which DOT and other

Basic telecom Service Providers will make available bandwidth.

(6) Intelligent Network (IN) Services including free phone and premium Service (e.g. 1-800 and 1-900) Services shall be introduced by DoT by 31 December 1998 in several cities over an Intelligent Network (IN) Platform.

(7) For setting up ISP Operations by companies, there shall be no license fee for first five years and after five years a nominal license fee of one rupee will be charged.

(8) The monopoly of the VSNL on International Gateway for INTERNET shall be withdrawn and authorised public/ government organisations will be allowed to provide INTERNET Gateway access directly without going through VSNL Gateways. Private ISPs are allowed to provide such Gateways after obtaining Defence clearance. Suitable monitoring mechanisms will be put in place to take care of security considerations.

(9) The Railways, Defence, State Electricity Boards, National Power Grid Corporation as well as organisations like ONGC, GAIL and SAIL who have rights of way shall be allowed to host fibre optic backbone. These organisations shall be allowed to provide service to the public based on this backbone by having an interface with the existing or new public networks, but without necessarily having to go through DOT network.

(10) Networks such as NICNET, STPs, as well as private networks shall be allowed inter-connectivity without necessarily having to go through the DoT's INET network.

(11) Providing access to INTERNET through authorised Cable TV shall be permitted to any service provider without additional licensing.

(12) The 'last mile' linkages shall be freely permitted either by fibre optic or radio communication for IT application

enterprises, IT promotional organisations and ISPs. In case of radio linkages, coordination by the Wireless Adviser will be observed to avoid frequency interference.

(13) The radio frequency band in the range of 2.4 - 2.483 GHz shall be open as 'public wireless' for any Government organisation or PSU or Private Sector Company to set up Spread Spectrum based non-interference type Wireless data/multimedia communication equipment subject to a maximum of 4 Watt EIRP; WPC will periodically issue a district-wise directory of two or three selected subbands of 10 MHz each for each of the districts on the criteria of least congestion and reserve these subbands maximally for the exclusive use of Spread Spectrum Communication as above. The use of the band will be on the basis of non-interference, non-protection and non-exclusiveness. Private sector, Public sector and Government operators shall bilaterally obtain Defence Clearance for location, the area covered and the frequency sub-band: The Private Sector Units will be required to obtain MHA clearance directly; The security agencies shall convey their decision within 30 days of application failing which the application would be deemed to have been cleared from the security angle; If cleared, the Private and Public Sector operators shall be required to obtain a registration and automatic license directly from WPC by producing the copies of security clearances; the Government operators will directly register with WPC; WPC will be empowered to monitor the violation of the above conditions and impose penalties on defaulters in three stages: Written warning, monetary penalty and debarring for two years. A Public Wireless Technical Audit Unit comprising a representative each from the Defence, DOT, NIC and from NASSCOM for the limited purpose of representing private user interests, shall monitor the implementation of the above policy.

(14) Data communication requirements for Electronic Commerce (EC/EDI) shall be met by DoT in a liberal

framework by assigning the highest priority under their priority classification if the EC/EDI requirement is certified by authorities in Government authorised by the Ministry of Commerce.

(15) Public TeleInfo Centres (PTIC) having multimedia capability specially ISDN Services, Remote Database Access, Government and Community Information systems, Market Information, Desk Top Videoconferencing, TeleInfo and INTERNET/Web Access Services shall be permitted and encouraged by the Government. DoT and other Basic Service Providers, Value Added Service Providers and authorised IT promotional organisations shall be permitted to promote these services on non-exclusive basis. No license fee will be charged for operating these services and the usual tariff, where applicable, will be payable by the PTIC Service providers/franchisees. Efforts will be made by DoT and other Service Providers to upgrade STD/ISD PCOs to convert them into these powerful PTICs for which ISDN or other digital facilities shall be provided on priority without necessarily having to make additional investment on this account.

(16) DOT shall take suitable action to delicense Multimedia services, including FAX, provided by PCOs.

(17) To enhance the pace of PC and INTERNET penetration in remote and far flung areas in the country, the Defence Services shall enable provisions of connectivity for civilian applications to their communication backbone.

(18) Existing Software Centres by themselves may not be able to fulfill the high targets now set for the IT industry by the year 2008. International experience has shown that hi-tech industries flourish essentially in the rural hinterland adjacent to cities with modern telecom and communication infrastructure and top class hi-tech educational/research institutions. India will promote such 'Hi-tech Habitats' in the rural hinterland adjacent to suitable cities. For this

purpose suitable autonomous structures will be designed and progressive regulations will be framed to facilitate infrastructurally self-contained self-financed Hi-Tech Habitats of high quality. Initially, five such Hi-Tech Habitats shall be planned and implemented in the rural hinterland of the cities: Bangalore, Hyderabad, Pune, Delhi and Bhubaneswar. It is estimated that progressively 50 such Hi-Tech Habitats can be viably set up by empowering the State Governments to autonomously nucleate them within a technologically progressive and administratively liberal set of guidelines to be prepared by a special Working Group on Hi-Tech IT Habitats to be set up by the Task Force.

(ii) Target ITEX - 50

For creating a congenial ambiance for exporters of IT Software and IT Services (including IT enabled services) to reach the export target of US $ 50 billion by the year 2008, the following incentives shall be provided:

(19) (a) Definition: "IT Software" means any representation of instructions, data, sound or image, including source code and object code, recorded in a machine readable form, and capable of being manipulated or providing interactivity to a user, by means of an automatic data processing machine falling under heading 'IT Products', but does not include 'non-IT products'. 'IT service' is defined as any service which results from the use of any IT software over a system of IT products for realising value addition. The term 'IT Industry' shall cover development, production and services related to IT Products. The term 'IT Software' shall be substituted in place of 'Computer Software' in all notifications.

(b) Finance Ministry (CBEC) shall introduce a new classification called, 'Information Technology (IT) Products' including Computer, Digital/Data communication and Digital/Data Broadcasting products, by recognising the progressive technological convergence of these three categories and in line with the classification list in Attachment A (Section I and Section II) of the WTO (ITA) Agreement and, additionally, Data Communication equipment.

(c) IT Software shall be entitled for zero customs duty and zero excise duty.

(20) A revised Notification giving the following new schedule for the Government of India acceding to the WTO-ITA Ministerial Declaration of 13 December 1996 at Singapore shall be issued by the Ministry of Finance: In Attachment A, Section I and II of WTO-ITA:

(a) Duty shall be brought down to zero by 1 January 1999 on the following items: Parts & components excluding populated PCBs in HSN 8473.30, all storage devices in HSN 8471.70, ICs above Rs. 1000 in HSN 8542, Stepper Motors in HSN 8501.10, Colour Graphic Display Tube in HSN 8540.40 and Deflective components for Colour monitor in HSN 8504.

(b) Out of the 217 items listed in ITA-I, 94 items which were proposed earlier for zero duty by 1st January 2000 shall now be advanced to 1st January 1999.

(c) The remaining items earlier proposed for zero duty by the 1st January 2003/2004/2005 shall now be advanced to 1 January 2002. Concomitantly, the following schedule will be adopted: (d) Duty on Capital Goods for the manufacture of items in (c), wherever applicable, becomes zero by 1 January 2000.

- Inputs/raw materials for the manufacture of the items in (c), wherever applicable, becomes zero by 1 January 2001
- Dual purpose items will be taken care of, wherever applicable, by allowing duty drawback benefits or

by treating the supplies to the IT industry as deemed export.

- Zero excise duty is concomitant with zero Customs duty with in-phase reduction. Additionally, other suitable supportive measures shall be taken to encourage Indian hardware industry to become globally competitive in the light of the revised WTO-ITA schedule.

(21) Customs duty on import of CD-ROMs or Optical Disc Media or Magnetic Media containing text, data or multimedia as content shall be charged only on the media and not on the contents.

(22) Imported IT Products shall be permitted to be taken out of bonded offices or out of Electronics/IT Units under EOU/EPZ/STP/EHTP Schemes after a period of 2 years from the date of import if these are donated to recognised educational institutions, Government organisations and registered charitable hospitals, etc., as defined in the Clause 9.19 of the Handbook of Procedures (Volume I) of the EXIM Policy through a customs notification.

(23) IT Software and IT Services companies, being constituents of the knowledge industry, shall be exempted from inspection by Inspectors like those for Factory, Boiler, Excise, Labour, Pollution/Environment etc.

(24) With technological advancements in Wide Area Computer-Communication networks, which have brought about 'Virtual Technology Parks' in which IT Software and IT services are developed through online integration of software and services subsystems from widely separated locations in the country, the concept of physical bonding has become obsolete. Accordingly, Software developers/ exporters are exempted from Customs bonding at various export promotion schemes including STP/EOU/EPZ, etc. The export obligation shall be the same value as given

under the EPCG Scheme. Existing bonded units under the various Software Export Promotion schemes will also be considered under the above scheme.

(25) A clarification shall be issued by CBEC that Service Tax is not applicable on computer software development industry.

(26) The Ministry of Civil Aviation shall issue the following notifications/ amendments in the regulations:

- Export shipment time for air cargo will be reduced to less than 24 hours.
- "Known Shipper" will be introduced to avoid delays on account of cooling off period.
- Cargo companies and other associated agencies to allow consolidation of export air cargo.

(27) Section 80 HHE of the Income Tax Act provides for income tax exemption to profits derived from software and services exports. This section shall be amended as follows:

- The existing formula will be so changed that tax on profits shall not have any relation to domestic turnover.
- The definition of software and export turnover will be changed so as to include IT services exports.
- The benefits of this Section for income tax exemption to profits from exports will be extended to supporting IT Software & IT Services developers.

(28) IT software and IT services shall be deemed as manufacturing activity for the limited purpose of applicability of Section 10 (15) (iv) of the Income Tax Act.

(29) IT Software and IT Services shall be exempted from withholding tax through amendments in the 'explanation' of Section 9 of the Income Tax Act.

(30) For individuals buying IT products including computer, the expenditure shall be deductible under Section 88 of the Income Tax Act.

(31) No gift tax shall be charged for the giver or Income Tax for the receiver on PCs upto Rs. 30,000 of the original purchase price.

(32) For any investment made in IT products and IT software 100 % depreciation shall be allowed in two years for which Ministry of Finance shall take suitable action.

(33) As the traditional method of asset-based funding of working capital would not meet the adequate and timely requirements of fund of the software sector, a differential and flexible approach shall be adopted by giving special dispensation towards working capital requirements of this sector in view of the unique nature of the industry. Accordingly, RBI shall issue, by 15th August 1998, new guidelines with regard to working capital requirements for the IT software and services sector which would be based on simple criteria such as turnover. Banks shall be advised to give 25 per cent of the contract value for 18 months, with the first six months as term loan (without collaterals) and from the 7th month onwards annualised Cash Flow Statements shall be accepted instead of collaterals.

(34) IT software and services industry shall be treated as a Priority Sector by banks for the next five years. This would help to meet the requirements of IT software and services exports, and also the IT industry and applications within the country. Major banks will be advised to create specialised IT financing cells in important branches, where IT Software and Services units are sufficiently large in number. Performance in this dimension will be monitored by the Ministry of Finance.

(35) Against the present estimate of Rs. 400 crores of working capital for the industry, the amount shall be

increased to around Rs. 1200 crores by the year 2000 subject to the broad criteria of pro-rata increase for the prospective requirements 24 months ahead as compared to the actuals of the current requirements at any given time. As quantitative targeting is not appropriate, a system will be put in place which would enable substantial increase in working capital provided by the banks.

(36) Bank lending to IT Software and Services exporters shall be made eligible for RBI refinancing with sufficiently low interest rates.

(37) The banks shall be allowed to invest in the form of equity in dedicated venture capital funds meant for IT industry as part of the 5 per cent of increment in deposits currently allowed for shares.

(38) Banks/FIs like ICICI, IDBI, UTI and SBI shall set up joint ventures with Indian or foreign companies for setting up of at least four different venture capital dedicated funds of a corpus of not less than Rs. 50 crores each to cater to the credit need of the industry. Such venture capitalists may be allowed to set off losses in one invested company and profit in another invested company during the block of years for the purpose of income tax.

(39) The Company's Act shall be amended to facilitate issuance of Sweat Equity to employees. A new definition No. (66) will be added after definition No. (65) in Clause 2 as under: "(66) Sweat Equity means equity allotted to promoters, Directors or employees for providing any intellectual property or value addition to the Company".

(40) Ministry of Finance shall include IT software and IT service sector while issuing general guidelines for dual listing of companies, as well as while considering two-way fungability for ADRs/GDRs.

(41) Dollar Linked Stock Options to employees of

Indian Software companies were announced in the 1998 Budget and detailed guidelines on this have been issued by DEA, Ministry of Finance. This shall be modified in accordance with the definition of IT Software and IT Services given under (19)(a) and (b) above.

Employee Stock option schemes for stock listed in India would also be encouraged. Also, clarification shall be issued that income tax is applicable only at the time of sale and not at the time of excise of option.

(42) Recognising the high velocity of business, high degree of competition and fast technological obsolescence faced by the IT software and IT service exporters, RBI shall be maximally accommodate the following:

(a) A blanket approval for overseas investment for acquisition of software/IT companies across the board for software exporters with previous three years cumulative actual export realisation in excess of US $ 25 million to be given up to 50 % or US $ 25 million, whichever is lower, out of the cumulative actual export earning of the previous three years. This is subject to submission of a certificate of software industry by appropriate authorities.

(b) For FERA approvals beyond this limit, RBI would set up a mechanism for expeditious processing of applications from this sector. This shall be announced by 15 August 1998.

(c) For overseas ventures, a dispensation shall be given for allowing the capitalisation of both goods and services; RBI shall accordingly notify this in consultation with Commerce Ministry by 15 August 1998.

(d) As the present allowable limit of 70% of the contract amount for expenditure abroad does not provide flexibility for utilisation for the purpose of general corporate objectives or for business growth purposes, RBI shall permit IT exporters to freely spend upto 5% of the export proceeds abroad (out of the total 70%) for miscellaneous/sundry purposes to give full flexibility. Also, a new list of allowable expenses under the 70% limit would be worked out by RBI in consultation with NASSCOM.

(e) RBI shall issue revised EEFC guidelines to eliminate restrictions on staggered remittance, second and higher generation subsidiaries and also to allow 20% of the EEFC balances for the use on the following:

i) Advance remittances for downloading software (upto US $ 1 lakh per transaction).

ii) Purchase of equipment and related expenditure.

iii) Miscellaneous expenses not detailed in EEFC guidelines (upto 5%) of EEFC balances. Such EEFC accounts shall be permitted for making payments from offshore branches of Indian banks directly.

(f) Use of International Credit Cards (ICC) abroad for a variety of purposes required by the IT Software and IT Services sector shall be permitted, the detailing of which will be carried out by RBI and notified by 15 August 1998, in particular:

i) All payments currently made under Exchange Earnings Foreign Currency (EEFC) Account shall also be allowed to made through International Credit Cards (ICC). Advance payment for IT software and IT services shall be permitted to be done through ICC for which RBI will issue a notification. Notification shall be issued that ICC may also be used for paying for IT Software and IT services purchased over INTERNET or EXTRANET and also for registering domain names.

ii) RBI shall issue a modified and simplified SOFTEX form required for IT Software and IT Services export by 15 August 1998.

(43) In the EPCG scheme a system of self-declaration shall be introduced with 100% post-checking subject to punitive penalty for default.

(44) The value limit for import of IT Products including personal computers shall be reduced from Rs. 1.50 lakhs (c.i.f) to Rs. 70,000 (c.i.f).

(45) Private and public organisations providing IT infrastructure shall be included for duty exemption for importing capital goods. Such service providers, in view of such capital goods imported, shall undertake the export obligations as provided for import of capital goods in the EPCG Scheme.

(46) The India Brand Equity Fund Scheme operated by the Ministry of Commerce shall be made available for Software companies with lower interest and longer interval.

(47) On-site IT Services should be made easier by combating Visa regulations of the recipient countries through a planned diplomatic strategy by the Ministry of External Affairs and the Indian Missions abroad for which MEA will create a suitable dedicated structure. This will also include signing of totalisation agreements, wherever necessary so as to maintain the competitive advantage of Indian companies.

(48) Returns from package software development shall be increased by enabling Indian Marketing companies to set up wholesale companies abroad. They shall also be given maximum flexibility in organising the marketing of package software from India through INTERNET.

(49) For benchmarking our country with our emerging competitors, a study shall be conducted at Government

cost once in two years by internationally reputed consultancy companies.

(50) Restrictions on the location of IT software and IT Services (including IT training) companies in residential areas shall be removed.

(51) To enable organisations and companies to identify, explore and plan strategies for Large Niche Markets like Y2K and Euro, nationally and corporate wise, all applicable provisions shall be made applicable on higher priority basis. Through MOC and DOE funds 'India Pavilions' shall be set up in several major IT exhibitions around the world through the initiative and coordination of ESC and NASSCOM.

(52) Recognising the catastrophic effect of the Y2K problem for solving which a few hundred billion dollars are being spent around the world, an immediate investment of Rs. 700 crore as corpus funds shall be mobilised to control the crisis in critical Government, Public and Private organisations and services; efforts to sensitise such organisations in the country facing the crisis shall be taken up by the Government immediately including issuance of Government orders for strict compliance in a time bound manner; a High level empowered Task Force with respresentatives from the Government, Industry Associations, Banks and Financial Institutions, Defence Services, Utility and other Public Service organisations, Railways, among others, shall be constituted by the Government of India.

- 'Mega Web sites' shall be created on INTERNET for promoting marketing and encouraging Indian Software products and packages under multiple initiatives.
- Creation and hosting of websites on servers located in India will be encouraged.

(54) Under DEPB Rupee trade arrangement, IT Software, IT Services and IT product export to Russia shall be permitted with promotional support given by the Electronics and Software Export Promotion Council (ESC), STP, etc.

(55) All promotional and liberalisation policy instruments available to IT Software and IT Services shall be made available to IT enabled services including the Information Content Industry by classifying IT enabled Services as tantamount to IT Software and IT Services.

(56) For promoting Indian Software Packages (system as well as application software) users shall be given fiscal incentives for buying Indian packages. A special screening mechanism will be worked out for identifying the more promising packages developed in India and giving consistent support by the Government as well as the industry for ensuring acceptance in international markets.

(57) Private STPs shall be encouraged to be set up by combining the provisions under (4), (7), (8), (12), (13), (24), (43), (45), (54) and (55), among others. III. IT FOR ALL BY 2008 For enabling a proactive drive for 'IT for all by 2008', the following new policy instruments shall be devised and activated. 'Operation Knowledge' Recognising Information Technology to be a frontier area of knowledge, and also a critical enabling tool for assimilating, processing and productivising all other spheres of knowledge, the Government shall launch 'OPERATION KNOWLEDGE'. The aim of this national campaign will be to universalise computer literacy and also to spread the use of computers and IT in education. 'OPERATION KNOWLEDGE' shall be developed into a comprehensive policy within the next three months. However, the following initiatives shall be taken for the immediate implementation of some of its key objectives.

(58) The Government shall soon launch three schemes — Vidyarthi Computer Scheme, Shikshak Computer Scheme and School Computer Scheme — to enable every student, teacher or school respectively desirous of buying computers to do so under attractive financial packages. These schemes will be supported by a suite of initiatives such as lowering the cost of PCs, easy-instalment bank loans, computer donations by IT companies and other business houses, bulk donations of computers by NRI organisations, large-volume bargain price imports, multi-lateral funding, etc.

(59) Computers and Internet shall be made available in every school, polytechnic, college, university and public hospital in the country by the year 2003.

(60) All universities, engineering colleges, medical colleges and other institutions of higher learning in the country as well as Research and Development Organisations shall be networked for a supplementary programme of distance education for improving the quality of education before year 2000.

(61) The seven national level institutions (IITs, IISc.) shall be encouraged to triple their output of students in IT by suitably restructuring the programme.

(62) A National Council of IT Education comprising experts from both the industry and the academicia, shall be set up for defining courses and their content in the light of rapid developments taking place in Information Technology. The Council will also initiate a 'Teach the Teachers' (3T) programme for upgrading on a regular basis the IT knowledge and skills of teachers.

(63) An IT Course Module shall be made a compulsory component of all Degree Courses within a short period.

(64) The setting up of Indian Institutes of Information Technology (IIIT) shall be implemented with urgency to

make up for the lost time. Hi-tech institutions like the Indian Institute of Information Technology (IIIT) will be given the Deemed University status without insisting upon the mandatory three-year stipulation.

(65) The Government shall promote the pairing of our Universities with centres of excellence in IT in developed countries.

(66) Specific courses shall be launched in association with the Software Industry and IIMs to provide Project Management skills and develop specialised courses on Software Marketing.

(67) The concept of SMART Schools where the emphasis is not only on Information Technology in Schools, but also on the use of skills and values that will be important in the next millennium, shall be started on a pilot demonstrative basis in each State.

(68) An Institute for Computer Professionals of India shall be set up on the pattern of the Institute of Chartered Accountants of India; the Institute will be nucleated by NASSCOM with initial financial support from the industry and the Government. The Institute will be given the responsibility as an Accreditation Body for IT Education and Training Programmes with full Government recognition in addition to the DOEACC Programme of the Department of Electronics.

(69) To enhance the knowledge base of IT related education at all levels the Government shall establish Information Technology, System Engineering and IT Security Institutes from within existing manpower of the Armed Forces. The Centres of Excellence in IT Software and System Engineering in the Defence Services will be utilised to the national advantage.

(70) Virtual Institutes in different parts of the country shall be set up to achieve excellence in distance education.

(71) The talent and expertise of IT-trained ex-servicemen shall be utilised for IT penetration in rural India and Government will fully support this offer of the Armed Forces. A Plan will be prepared and implemented for utilising the services of the large number of IT literate defence personnel retiring every year for propagating the IT culture at sub-district levels.

(72) A 'National Qualification Framework' shall be established for computerised online objective system of knowledge acquisition; An 'Educational Credit Bank' shall be implemented for giving flexibility to integrate credits earned in different institutions/systems towards the eligibility for diplomas and degrees.

(73) A specialised sub-committee of this Task Force shall coordinate the setting up of National and State level Digital Libraries Projects.

(74) A pilot project under the aegis of the National Task Force on Information Technology shall be launched in some lead districts which have already attained universal literacy, with the aim of achieving universal computer literacy in all the secondary schools in these districts. Alongside, the network of educational institutions in these districts will be assisted to maximise the induction of IT in order to create world-class talent at the top-end of the education pyramid. These pilot projects will be joint initiatives of the local educational institutions, respective State Governments and the Centre. In the first instance, such a pilot project will be launched in Dakshin Kannada and Udupi Districts in Karnataka on a substantive self-financing basis. Within a short time, the same will be extended to suitable districts in other States.

(75) In view of the lower-than-national-average levels of technical and IT education facilities in Uttar Pradesh, Bihar, Madhya Pradesh and Rajasthan, several educational

centres will be identified with a view to making them models for IT-based education and training at all levels. The aim of this initiative will be to promote IT education and awareness in Hindi-speaking States and thereby revitalise the Hindi heartland in all the fields of knowledge and knowledge-based enterprises. Allahabad shall be developed as the first such model IT-based education-cum-business centre. Within a short time, this initiative will be extended to other States which are underdeveloped in IT. IT Penetration & IT Awareness

(76) Government shall encourage the setting up of value-added network services including ATMs, Electronic Kiosks, Telephones, Smart Cards, etc., for providing a 'One-Stop Non-Stop' service to the public.

(77) To make IT a mass movement, an awareness creation strategy shall be worked out within two months and the structures for implementing the same shall be put in place.

(78) A major promotional campaign shall soon be launched to boost IT in Indian languages. This campaign will be based on a multi-pronged approach, involving fiscal and other incentives for R&D, production, marketing and popularisation of IT products in Indian languages. This recommendation addresses the reality that India can become a major IT power only if IT penetration in the country deepens and widens-which in turn, is dependent on large-scale use of IT in Indian languages.

(79) The Government shall take all the necessary steps to boost IT for agricultural and integrated rural development. Towards this end, a number of demonstration projects will be devised in each State taking into account the specific strengths and needs at the local level. A unique 'WIRED VILLAGES' pilot project has been launched under the aegis of the National Information Technology Task Force

on Information Technology at the Warananagar Cooperative Complex in Kolhapur District in Maharashtra. Efforts will be made to quickly replicate such projects in other states.

(80) The Government shall take necessary measures to develop, productivise and use, in domestic and global markets, indigenous technologies in wireless telecommunication such as CorDECT, remote access switch, etc., to achieve the national objective of rapid, low-cost expansion of telephone and Internet connectivity in rural and remote areas. Similarly, promotional measures shall be taken to encourage technologies that bring IT and Internet to the masses through the vast network of Cable TV houses.

(81) For promoting electronic commerce in a time-bound manner, a strict directive shall be given to Sea Ports, Airports Authority of India, DGFT, Banks, Container Services, Customs and Indian Railways in accordance with the programme approved in the tenth Export Promotion Board meeting.

(82) Bar Coding of every item sold in the country shall be made compulsory within a five-year period.

(83) The Armed Forces shall integrate far-flung and remote areas (Ladakh, North-East, Andaman & Nicobar Islands, Kutch, Lakshadweep and Minicoy Islands, border areas of Himachal and Rajasthan) with mainstream India, through IT penetration as part of their Civic Action Programme. The funds for this initiative shall be provided through the Government/Venture/Seed Capital. Citizen IT Interface.

(84) The Cabinet has approved NIC's proposal to make government Information, other than that having a bearing on security, available to the public. This decision shall be implemented by suitably empowering NIC to do so. This

recommendation addresses the felt need for easy availability and extensive transparency of government information.

(85) District Information System (DISNIC) Plan Programme shall be made widespread and databases updated online, shall be made available to the public and Panchayats, among others. Courts Information System (COURTIS), Parliament Information System (PARLIS), Computerised Rural Information System Programme (CRISP) and other such databases shall be updated online over NICNET and access to public facilitated.

(86) A Citizens Charter for effective and responsive administration in terms of time-bound service to the public shall be framed and implemented under the coordination of the Department of Administrative Reforms & Public Grievances and hoisted on the official INTERNET Web Site 'India Image' of the Government of India. IT in Government.

(87) Each Department/Agency in the Central Government and State Governments shall be required to prepare a Five Year IT Plan.

(88) 1-3% of the budget of every Ministry/Department shall be earmarked for applying IT in the Department/ sector; this investment will include not only the purchase of IT products, IT Software, but also for training and IT services; Reappropriation of the Department's budget for the IT sub-budget head shall be within the delegated powers of the Head of the Department.

(89) NIC, at the national level, and technology service organisations at the State level, shall establish 'Framework Contracts' with reputed suppliers to provide a wide range of IT consultancy, specialist services and IT products to Government agencies to reach the benefit of lower costs through bulk purchases.

(90) India shall participate in international projects like 'Government Online' Project of G-8 countries so as to not only learn from the experience of others but also to contribute to the global experience in planning and implementing projects to promote IT in Government.

(91) Tele-commuting is recognised as a new modality of doing work in an office and labour laws accommodating the same shall be enacted. An option shall be given to employees, where feasible and efficient, to accomplish part of their work through telecommuting in the framework of 'Management by Objectives' (MBO).

(92) The Government of India shall set up a central repository of data elements in Government with the NIC and make it accessible through NICNET.

(93) The recommendations of the TG-MAP Committee for Map and GIS Data Policy approved by the Committee of Secretaries under the Cabinet Secretary, shall be notified by the Ministry of Defence expeditiously.

(94) A computerised National Inventory of Training pertaining to different areas shall be maintained.

(95) A computerised Inventory of Government best practices for electronic access shall be maintained.

(96) Government shall stipulate IT literacy as an essential requirement for all future Government and public sector employment; in the Annual Confidential Reports of government employees, a column shall be introduced regarding contribution to IT utilisation in the department/ organisation.

(97) A National Institute of Smart Government shall be set up to focus on all issues concerning IT-supported governance.

(98) State Institutes of Public Administrations shall be re-engineered to help bring about IT-responsive State Governments.

(99) Suitable floor space in Government buildings, which are not utilised during non-office hours, could be given to private educational institutions for IT training purposes in return for a proportionate number of free nominations of Government employees for IT training. Data Security Systems and Cyber Laws.

(100) A National Computerised Records Security Document shall be prepared within three months for enforcing security requirements by consulting similar documents prepared by SAG, JCB, WESEE, etc.

(101) An Information Security Agency shall be set up at the National level to play the role of Cyber Cop.

(102) A National Policy on Information Security, Privacy and Data Protection Act for handling of computerised data shall be framed by the Government within six months.

(103) Cyber infractions shall be addressed within the legal framework by the Ministry of Law, Justice and Company Affairs.

(104) The cryptology and Cyber Security knowledge and experience developed by the Defence establishments shall be suitably transferred to the civilian information security agencies for wider dissemination in the country to increase information security, network security and bring about a greater degree of secure use of EFT, Digital Signature, etc.

(105) The procedure of keeping records in paper form in public and private STPs shall be restricted to a maximum duration of two months after which the records shall be kept only in the Electronic/Magnetic/Optical media.

(106) The Indian Telegraph Act of 1885, the Indian Post Office Act of 1888 and the Indian Wireless Telegraphy Act of 1993 shall be suitably modified in the light of the growing predominance of IT in day-to-day life. Suitable changes will also be made in other Laws/Acts, wherever necessary.

(107) The draft set of Cyber Laws prepared by the Cyber Law Committee set up by the Committee of Secretaries, shall be approved by the Government with suitable modifications and implemented, as a first step, within six months.

(108) All necessary instructions, notifications and amendments to procedures/Law shall be issued by the respective Ministries/Departments within three months.

APPENDIX—II

THE PRESS COUNCIL ACT, 1978

This act establishes a press council for the purpose of preserving the freedom of the press and of maintaining the standards of newspapers and news agencies in India. Be it enacted by parliament in the 29th year of the Republic of India as follows.

Chapter I: Preliminary

1. Short title and extent

(1) This act may be called the Press Council Act, 1978.

(2) It extends to the whole of India.

2. Definitions

In this act, unless the context otherwise requires,-

(a) 'Chairman' means the chairman of the council;

(b) 'Council' means the Press Council of India established under section 4; (c) 'Member' means a member of the council and includes its chairman ;

(d) 'Prescribed' means prescribed by rules made under this act;

(e) The expressions 'editor' and 'newspaper' have the meaning respectively assigned to them in the Press and Registration of Books Act, 1867 (25 of 1867) and the expression 'working journalist' has the meaning assigned to it in the working Journalists and other Newspaper Employees (Conditions of Service) and Miscellaneous Provision Act, 1955 (45 of 1955).

3. *Rule of construction respecting enactments not extending to the state of Jammu and Kashmir or Sikkim*

Any reference in this act to a law which is not in force

in the state of Jammu and Kashmir or Sikkim shall, in relation to that state, be constructed as a reference to the corresponding law, if any inverse in that state.

Chapter II: Establishment of the Press Council

4. Incorporation of the council

(1) with effect from such date as the central government may, by notification in the official gazette, appoint, there shall be established a council by the name of the press council of India.

(2) the said council shall be a body corporate having perceptual succession and a common seal and shall by the said name sue and bemused.

5. Composition of the council

(1) The council shall consist of a chairman and 28 other members.

(2) The chairman shall be a person nominated by a committee consisting of the chairman of the council of states (Rajya Sabha), the speaker of the house of the people (Lok Sabha) and a person elected by the members of the council under sub-section (6) and the nomination so made shall take effect from the date on which it is notified by the central government in the official gazette.

(3) Of the other members - (a) Thirteen shall be nominated in accordance with such procedure as may be prescribed from among the working journalists, of whom six shall be editors of newspapers and the remaining seven shall be working journalists other than editors; so, however that the number of such editors and working journalists other than editors in relation newspapers published in Indian languages shall be not less than three and four respectively;

(b) Six shall be nominated in accordance with such

procedure as may be prescribed from among persons who own or carry on the business of management of newspapers, so, newspapers, so, however, that there shall be two representatives from each of the categories of big newspapers, medium newspapers.and small newspapers;

(c) One shall nominated in accordance with such procedure as may be prescribed from among persons who manage news agencies;

(d) Three shall be persons having special knowledge or practical experience in respect of education and science, law and literature and culture of whom respectively one shall be nominated by the University Grants Commission one by the Bar Council of India and one by the Sahitya Academy;

(e) Five shall be members of Parliament of whom three shall be nominated by the speaker from among the members of the House of the People (Lok Sabha) and two shall be nominated by the chairman of the council of States (Rajya Sabha) from among its members: Provided that no working journalist who owns, or carries on the business of management of any newspaper shall eligible for nomination under clause (a): Provided further that the nominations under clause (a) and clause (b) shall be so made that among the persons nominated there is not more than one person interested in any newspaper or group of newspaper under the same control or management.

Explanation - for the purposes of clause (b), a 'newspaper' shall be deemed to be -

(i) 'Big newspaper' if the total circulation of all its editions exceeds 50,000 copies for each issue;

(ii) 'Medium newspaper' of the total circulation of all its editions exceeds 15,000 copies but does not exceed 50,000 copies for each issue;

(iii) 'Small newspaper' of the total circulation of all its editions does not exceed 15,000 copies for each issue.

(4) Before making any nomination under clause (a) clause (b) or clause (c) sub-section (3) the central government in the case of the first council and the retiring chairman of the previous council in the case of any subsequent council shall, in the prescribed manner, invite panels of names comprising twice the number to be nominated from such associations of persons of the categories referred to in the said clause (a) clause (b) or clause (c) as may be notified in this behalf by the central government in the case of the first council and by the council itself in the case of subsequent councils: Provided that where there is no association of persons of the category referred to in the said clause (c) the panels of names shall be invited from such news agencies as may be notified as aforesaid.

(5) The central government shall notify the names of persons nominated as members under sub-section (3) in the official gazette and every such nomination shall take effect from the date on which it is notify.

(6) The members of the council notified under sub-section (5) shall elect from among themselves in accordance with such procedure as may be prescribed, a person to be a member of the committee referred to in sub-section (2) and a meeting of the members of the council for the purpose of such election shall be prescribed over by a person chosen from among themselves.

6. Term of office and retirement of members

(1) Save as otherwise provided in this section, the chairman and other members shall hold office for a period of three years: Provided that the chairman shall continue to hold such office until the council is reconstituted in accordance with the provisions of section five for a period of six months whichever is earlier.

(2) Where a person nominated as a member under clause (a) clause (b) or clause (c) of sub-section (3) of section 5 if censured under the provisions of sub-section (1) of section 14, he shall cease to be a member of the council.

(3) The term of office of a member nominated under clause (e) of sub-section (3) of section 5 shall come to an end as soon as he ceases to be a member of the House from which he was nominated.

(4) A member shall be deemed to have vacated his seat if he is absent without excuse, sufficient in the opinion of the council, from three consecutive meetings of the council.

(5) The chairman may resign his office by giving notice in writing to the central government and any other member may resign his office by giving notice in writing to the chairman and upon such resignation being accepted by the central government, or as the case may be, the chairman, the chairman or the member shall be deemed to have vacated his office.

(6) Any vacancy arising under sub-section (2) sub-section (3) sub-section (4) or sub-section (5) or otherwise shall be filled, as soon as may be, nomination in the same manner in which the member vacating office was nominated and the member no nominated so nominated shall hold office for the remaining period in which the member in whose place he is nominated would have held office.

(7) A retiring member shall be eligible for re-nomination for not more than one term.

7. Conditions of service of members

(1) The chairman shall be a whole-time officer and shall be paid such salary as the central government may think fit, and the other members shall receive such allowances of fees for attending the meetings of the council

as may be prescribed.

(2) Subject to the provisions of sub-section (1) the condition of service of members shall be such as may prescribed.

(3) It is hereby declared that the office of a member of the council shall not disqualify its holder for being chooses, as or for being a member of either House of Parliament.

48. Committees of the council

(1) For the purpose of performing its function under this act, the council may constitute from among its members such committees for general or special purposes as it may deem necessary and every committee so constituted shall perform such func-tions as are assigned to it by the council.

(2) The council shall have the power to co-opt as members of any committee con-stitute under sub-section (1) such other number of persons, not being members of the council, as it thinks fit.

(3) Any such member shall have the right to attend any meeting of the committee on which he is so co-opted and to take part in the dis-cussions thereat, but shall not have the right to vote and shall not be a member for any other purpose.

9. Meetings of the council and committees

The council or any committee thereof shall meet at such times and places and shall observe such trolls of procedure in regard to the transaction of business at its meetings as may be provided by regulations made under this act.

10. Vacancies among members or defect in the constitution not to invalidate acts and proceedings of the council -

No act or proceeding of the council shall be deemed to

be invalid by reason merely of the existence of any vacancy in, or any defect in the constitution of, the council.

11. Staff of the council

(1) subject to such rules as may be made by the central government in this behalf, the council may appoint a secretary and such other employees as it may think necessary for the efficient performance of its function under this act.

(2) the terms and conditions of service of the employees shall be such as may be determined by regulations.

12. Authentication of orders and other instruments of the council

All orders and decisions of the council shall be authenticated by the signature of the chairman or any other member authorised by the council in this behalf and other instruments issued by the council shall be authenticated by the signature of the secretary or any other officer of the council authorised in manner in this behalf.

Chapter III: Powers and functions of the council

13. Objects and functions of the council

(1) the objects of the Cancun shall be to preserve the freedom of the press and to maintain and improve the standards of newspapers and news agencies in India.

(2) The council may, in furtherance of its objects, perform the following functions, namely -

(a) to help newspapers and news agencies to maintain their independence;

(b) to build up a code of conduct for newspapers news agencies and journalists in accordance with high professional standards;

(c) to ensure on the part of newspapers news agencies

and journalists, the maintenance of high standards of public taste and foster a due sense of both the rights and responsibilities of citizenship;

(d) to encourage the growth of a sense of responsibility and public service aiming all those engaged in the profession of journalism;

(e) to keep under review any development likely to restrict the supply and dissemination of news of public interest and importance;

(f) to keep under review cases of assistance received by any newspaper or news agency in India from any foreign source including such cases as are referred to it by the central government or are brought to its notice by any individual, association of persons or any other organisation: Provided that nothing in this clause shall preclude the central government from dealing with any case of assistance received by a newspaper or news agency in India from any foreign source in any other manner it thinks fit;

(g) to undertake studies of foreign newspapers, including those brought out by any embassy or other representatives in India of a foreign state, their circulation and impact.

Explanation - For the purpose of this clause, the expression 'foreign state' has the meaning assigned to it in section 87A of the code of civil procedure, 1908 (5 of 1908);

(h) to promote a proper functional relationship among sell classes of persons engaged in the production or publication of newspapers or in news agencies: Provided that nothing in this Calais shall be deemed to confer on the council any functions in regard to dis-putes to which the Industrial Disputes Act, 1947 (14 of 1947) applies;

(i) to concern itself developments such as concentration of or other aspects of ownership of newspapers and news agencies which may affect the independence of the press;

(j) to indurate such studies as may be entrusted to the council and to espousers its opinion in regard to any matter referred to it by the central government;

(k) to do such other acts as may be incidental or conductive to the discharge of the above functions.

14. Power to censure

(1) where on receipt of a complaint made to it or otherwise, the council has reason believe that a newspaper or news agency has offended against the standards or journalist ethics or public taste or that an editor or a working journalist has committed any professional; misconduct, the council may, after giving the newspaper, or news agency, the editor or journalist concerned an opportunity of being heard, hold an inquiry in such annett as may be provided by regulations made under this act and, if it is satisfied that it is necessary so to do, it may, for reasons to be recorded in writing, warn, admonish or censure the newspaper, the news agency, the editor or the journalist or disapprove the conduct of the editor or the journalist, as the case may be: Provided that the council may not take cognisance of a complaint if in the opinion of the chairman there is no sufficient ground for holding an inquiry.

(2) If the council is of the opinion that it is necessary or expedient in the public interest so to do, it may require any newspapers to publish therein in such manner as the council thinks, fir any particulars relating to any inquiry under this section against a newspaper or news agency, an editor or a journalist working therein, including the name of such newspaper, news agency, editor or journalist.

(3) Nothing in sub-section (1) shall be deemed to empower the council to hold an inquiry into any matter in respect of which any proceeding is pending in a court of law.

(4) The decision of the council under sub-section (1) or sub-section (2) as the case may be shall be final and shall not be questioned in any court of law.

15. General powers of the council

(1) For the purpose of performing its functions or holding any inquiry under this act, the council shall have the same powers throughout Indies are vested in a civil court while trying a suit under the code of civil procedure 1908 (5 of 1908) in respect of the following matters, namely:

(a) summoning and enforcing the atten-dance of persons and examining them on oath;
(b) requiring the discovery and inspection of documents;
(c) receiving evidence on affidavits;
(d) requisitioning any public record or copies thereof from any court or office;
(e) issuing commissions for the examination of witness or documents; and (f) any other matter which may be prescribed.

(2) Nothing in sub-section (1) shall be deemed to compel any newspaper news agency editor or journalist to disclose the source of any news ore in-formation published by that newspaper or received or reported be that news agency editor or journalist.

(3) Every inquiry held by the council shall be deemed to be a judicial proceeding within the meaning of sections 193 and 228 of the Indian Penal Code (45 of 1860).

(4) The council may, it if considers Ir.necessary for the purpose of carrying out its objects or for the performance of any of its function under this act, make such observation

as it may think, fir, in any of its decisions or reports, respecting the conduct of any authority, including government.

16. Levy of fees

(1) The council may, for the purpose performing its functions under this act, levy such fees, at such rates and in such manner as my be prescribed from registered newspapers and news agencies and different rates may be prescribed for different newspapers banging regard to their circulation and other matters.

(2) Any fees payable to the council under sub-section (21) may be recovered as an areas of land revenue.

17. Payments to the council

The central government may after due appropriation made by Parliament by law in this behalf, pay to the council by way of grants such sums of money as the central government may consider necessary for the performance of the functions of the council under this act.

18. Fund of the council

(1) The council shall have its own fund; and the fees collected by it all such sums as may from time to time be paid to it by the central government and all grants and advances made to it by any other authority or person shall be credited to the fund and all payments by the council shall be made therefrom.

(2) All moneys belonging to the fund shall be deposited in such banks or invested in such manner as may subject to the approval of the central government, be decided by the council.

(3) The council may spend such sums as it thinks fit or for performing its functions under this act, and such sums shall be treated as expenditure payable out of the fund of the council.

19. Budget

The council shall prepare, in such form and at such time each year as may be prescribed a budget in respect of the financial year next ensuing showing the stimulated receipts and expenditure and copies thereof shall be forwarded to the central government.

20. Annual report

The council shall prepare once every year, in such form and at such time as may be prescribed an annual report giving summary of its activities during the previous year, and giving an account of the standards of newspapers and news agencies and factors affecting them, and copies thereof, together with the statement of accountants audited in the manner prescribed under section 22 shall be forwarded to the central government and the government shall cause the same to be laid before both houses of Parliament.

21. Interim reports

Without prejudice to the provisions of Section 20, of the council may prepare at any time during the course or a year a report giving a summary of such of its activities during the year as it considers to be of public impor-tance and copies thereof shall be forwarded to the central government and the government shall cause to be laid before both Houses of Parliament.

22. Accounts and audit

The accounts of the council shall be maintained and audited in such as may in consultation with the comptroller and auditor of India be prescribed.

Chapter IV: Miscellaneous

23. Protection of action taken in good faith

(1) No suit or other legal proceeding shall lie against the council or any member thereof or any person acting under the direction of the council in respect of anything

which is in good faith done intended to be done under this act.

(2) No suit or other legal proceeding shall lie against any newspaper in respect of the publication of any matter therein under the authority of the council.

24. Members, etc., to be public servants

Every member of the council and every officer or other employee appointed by the council shall be deemed to be a public servant within the meaning of section 21 of the Indian Penal code (45 of 1860).

25. Power to make rules

(1) The central government may, be notification in the official gazette, make rules to carry out the purposes of this ct. Provided that when the council has been established no such rules shall be made without consulting the council.

(2) In particular and without prejudice to the generality of the foregoing power such rules may provide for all or any of the following matters, namely:

(a) the procedure for nomination of members of the council under clauses (a) (b) and (c) of sub-section 5;

(b) the manner in which panels of names may be invited under sub-section (4) of section 5;

(c) the procedure for election of a number of the committee referred to in sub-section (2) of section 5 under sub-section (6) of that section;

(d) the allowances of fees to be paid to the members of the council for attending the meetings of the council, and other conditions of service of such members under sub-section 91) and (2) of section 7;

(e) the appointment of the secretary and other employees of the council under section 11;

(f) the matters referred to in clause(f) of sub-section (1) of section 15;

(g) the rates at which fees may be levied by the council under section 16 and the manner in which such fees any be levied;

(h) the form in which and the time within which the budget and annual report are to be prepared by the council under section 19 and 20 respectively;

(i) the manner in which the accounts of the council are to be maintained and audited under sections (3) every rule made under this section shall be laid as soon as may be after it is made, before each house of parliament while it is in session for a total period of 30 days which may be comprised in one session or into or more successive sessions, and if before the expiry of the session immediately following the session or the successive sessions aforesaid, both houses agree in making any modification in the rule or both houses agree that the rule should not be made the rule shall thereafter have effect only in such modified form or be of no effect, as the case may be; so however that any such modification or annulment shall be without prejudice to the validity of anything done under that rule.

26. Power to make regulations

The council may make regulations not inconsistent with this act and the rules made thereunder for -

(a) regulating the meeting of the council or any committee thereof and the procedure for conducting the business thereat under section 9;

(b) specifying the terms and conditions of service of the employees, appointed by the council under sub-section (2) of section 11;

(c) regulating the manner of holding any inquiry under this act;

(d) delegating to the chairman or the secretary of the council, subject to such conditions as it may think fit to impose, any of its powers under sub-section (3) of section 18;

(e) any other matter for which provision any be made by regulations under this act; Provided that the regulations made under clause (b) shall be made only with the price approval of the central government.

27. Amendment of Act 25 of 1867

In sub-section (1) of section 8C of the Press and Registration of Books Act, 1867, for the words 'consisting of a chairman and another member to be appointed by the central government', the words and figures 'consisting of a chairman and another member to be nominated by the Press Council of India, established under section 4 of the Press Council Act 1978, from among its members' shall be substituted.

*(Section 27 of the Press Council Act, 1978 repealed vide the Repealing and Amending Act, 1988, Section 2, Sch.I: upon amendment of Sec. 8 (c) of Press and Registration Act, 1867 to incorporate the above men-tioned words and figures).

Published in the Gazette of India
Part III Section 4
Gazette Extraordinary
Press Council of India

Notification

New Delhi dated November 14, 1979

In exercise of powers conferred by clause (c) of section 26 of the Press Council Act, 1978 (37 of 1978), and all other powers 'hereunto enabling, the Press Council of India hereby makes the following regulations, namely:

1. Short title and commencement

(1) These regulations, may be called the Press Council (Procedure for Inquiry) Regulations, 1979

(2) They shall come into force on the date of their publication in the official gazette.

2. Definitions

(a) 'Act' means the Press Council Act, 1978 (37 of 1978).

(b) 'Committee' means the inquiry committee constituted by the council under Section 8 (1) of the act for the purpose of inquiry into complaints under Sections 13 (2) and 14 (1) of the act

(c) 'Council' means the Press Council of India constituted under the act;

(d) 'Complainant' means a person or authority making a complaint to the council regarding a newspaper, news agency, editor or other working journalist, in the case of complaints under section 14 (1) of the act, and with regard to complaints relating to other matters, means a person making a complaint to the council in respect of any matter which the council has jurisdiction to entertain, examine and pronounce its views upon, and

(e) 'Matter' means an article, news-item, news-report, or any other matter 'which is published by a newspaper or transmitted by a news agency by any means whatsoever and includes a cartoon, picture, photograph strip or advertisement which is published in a newspaper:

3. Contents of complaint in respect of a newspaper, news agency, editor or other working journalist under section 14 (1) of the act:

(1) where a person makes a complaint to the council in respect of the publication or non-publication of any matter

in any newspaper or news agency, under section 14 (1) of the act he shall -

(a) furnish the name and address of the newspaper, news agency, editor or other working journalist against which or whom the complaint is preferred and in cases where the complaint relates to the publication of matter in a newspaper or to the transmission by a news agency, forward along with the complaint a cutting of the matter complained of in original and such other particulars as are relevant to the subject-matter of the complaint; and where the complaint is in respect of non-publication of matter, the original or a copy of the matter, non-publication of which is complained of;

(b) state in what manner the publication or non-publication of the matter complained of is objectionable within the meaning of section 14 (1) of the act;

(c) before filing the complaint before the council, draw the attention of the newspaper, news agency, editor or other working journalist concerned, to the matter appearing in the newspaper etc. or to the non-publication there of which, in the opinion of the complainant, is objectionable and he shall also furnish to the newspaper, news agency, editor or the working journalist, as the case may be, the grounds for holding such opinion. The complainant shall, along with the complaint, enclose a copy of the letter written by him to the newspaper, news agency, editor or other working journalist together with a copy of the reply, if any received by him, provided that the chairman may in his discretion waive this condition;

(d) in case where the complaint is that an editor or a working journalist has committed any professional misconduct, other than the way of the publication or non-publication of any matter in a newspaper, the complainant shall set out clearly in detail the facts which according to him justify the complaint and the provisions of clause (c) above shall also apply to such complaints.

(e) In every case place all other relevant facts before the council; and

(f) (i) In the case of a complaint relating to the publication or non-publication of any matter in respect of newspaper or news agency the same shall be lodged with the council within the following periods of its publication or non-publication: (a) Dailies, news agencies and weeklies... within two months, (b) In all other cases... within four months.

Provided that a relevant publication of an earlier date may be referred to in the complaint.

(ii) In the case of a complaint against an editor or working journalist under clause (d) above the same shall be lodged within four months of the misconduct complained of:

Provided that the council may, if satisfied that the complainant has acted promptly, but that the delay in filing the complaint within the period prescribed under subclause (i) or sub-clause (ii) of regulation (3)1(f) has been caused by reason of the time taken to comply with the condition laid down in sub clause (c) supra or on account of other sufficient cause condone the delay and entertain the complaint. The power of condonation shall be exercised by the chairman, subject to the approval of the council.

(2) The complainant while presenting the complaint shall at the foot thereof make and subscribe to a declaration to the effect:

(i) that to the best of his knowledge and belief he has placed all the relevant facts before the council and that no proceedings are pending in any court of law in respect of any matter alleged in the complaint.

(ii) that he shall inform the council forthwith if during the pendency of the inquiry before the council any matter alleged in the complaint becomes the subject-matter of any proceeding in a court of law.

4. Return of complaint

(1) Where a complainant does not comply with the requirements of regulation 3, the chairman may return the complaint asking the complainant to bring it in conformity with such requirements and represent it within such time as he may fit in that behalf.

(2) The complainant shall be informed of the reasons for the return of the complaint.

5. Issue of notice

(I) As soon as possible, and in any case not later than 15 days from the date of receipt of a complaint, under the direction of the chairman, a copy thereof shall be sent to the newspaper, news agency, editor or other working journalist against which or whom the complaint has been made, under regulation three along with a notice requiring the newspaper, news agency, editor or other working journalist, as the case may be, to show cause why action should not be taken under section 14 of the act.

Provided that in appropriate cases the chairman shall have the discretion to extend time for the issuance of the notice.

Provided further that the chairman may decide not to issue a notice to show cause to the newspaper, news agency, editor or working journalist where, in his opinion, there is no sufficient ground for holding an inquiry. The council at its next meeting shall be apprised by the chairman of the reasons for his decision not to issue a 'showcause' notice and it may pass such orders as it deems fit.

(2) The notice issued under sub-regulation (I) above shall be sent to the newspaper, news agency, editor or other working journalist concerned by registered post, acknowledgement due, at the address furnished in the complaint.

6. Filing of written statement:

(1) The newspaper, news agency, editor or other working journalist against which or whom the complaint is made may, within 14 days from the date of service of the copy of the complaint and notice under regulation 5 or within such further time as may be granted by the chairman in this behalf, submit a written statement in reply to the complaint.

(2) A copy of the written statement when received shall be forwarded to the complainant for his information.

(3) After receipt of the complaint or written statement, the chairman may, if he considers necessary, call for any further information either from the complainant or the respondent newspaper, news agency, editor or working journalist, as the case may be, in order to clarify matters appearing in the complaint or written statement and in doing so, may call for such documents or further statements as he might consider necessary. All the document and statements called for by him shall form part of the record and shall be placed before the committee at the time of the inquiry.

7. Power to call for additional particulars etc.

The committee may after considering the complaint and the written statement, call for such additional particulars or documents or relevant to the subject-matter of the case as it may consider necessary from both the parties or either of them.

8. Rejection of complaint of the same nature previously inquired into

(I) Where at any time in the course of the inquiry into the complaint it appears to the committee that the subject-matter of the complaint is substantially the same as, or has been covered by any former complaint dealt with by the council under these regulations, the committee shall hear the complainant, if he desires to be heard and also if the committee considers it necessary, the newspaper, news agency, editor or other working journalist, as the case may be, and make its recommendation to the council which may pass such order as may be considered necessary and the same shall be duly communicated to the parties.

9. Inquiry by the committee

Notice of the time, date and place of hearing shall be served on the complainant as well as on the newspaper, news agency, editor and working journalist, as the case may be, and shall be sent by registered post, acknowledgement due. In the inquiry before the committee, the parties shall be entitled to adduce relevant evidence, oral or documentary, and make submissions in support of their contentions.

(2) At the close of the inquiry, the committee shall make a report of its findings on the allegations contained in the complaint together with its reasons and submit the record of the case to the council.

10. Decision by the council

(1) The council shall after perusing the record of the case, pass orders giving its decision or it may remit the case to the committee for such further inquiry as the council may deem necessary and after receipt of its report dispose of the case.

(2) Every case shall be determined by a majority of votes of the members of the council present and voting, and in the event of the votes being equal, the chairman shall have a casting vote and shall exercise the same.

(3) The order of the council shall be communicated in writing to the parties to the case.

11. Appearance of parties etc.

In any inquiry under these regulations, the editor, news agency or other working journalist, or any authority including government, or the newspaper through its editor, against which or whom a complaint has been made may appear in person, or with the permission of the committee or council as the case may be, by a counsellor or a duly authorised representative.

12. Restrictions on power of members to discuss and vote in certain cases.

No members of the committee shall vote or take part in the discussion of, and no member of the council shall vote or take part in the discussion of any complaint coming up for consideration at a meeting of the committee or the council if the case is one in which he is personally involved or has any direct or indirect interest by himself or his partner, or in which he is interested professionally on behalf of a client or as an agent or representative for any newspaper, news agency, editor or other working journalist as the case may be.

13. Power to take suo motu action: The chairman may suo motu issue notice or, as the case may be, take action in respect of any matter which falls within the mischief of section 14 (1) of the act or in respect of or relating to any matter falling under section 13 (2) thereof and thereupon the procedure prescribed by these regulations from regulation five onwards shall be followed as if it were a complaint under regulation three.

14. Procedure in respect of complaints etc. under section 13: The procedure prescribed by these regulations in respect of complaints under section 14 (1) of the act shall apply, as far as may be, to complaints or representations received by the council with regard to any subject falling within the provisions of section 13.

15. Procedure in matters not provided for in these regulations:

The council as also the committee shall have the power to regulate their own procedure in respect of any matter for which no provision or inadequate provision is made in these regulations and shall also have the power in appropriate cases to hold inquiries in camera.

Select Bibliography

Alves, Rosental Calmon. "Many Newspaper Sites Still Cling to Once-A-Day Publish Cycle." USC Annenberg Online Journalism Review, July 21, 2004. Web site: http://209.200.80.136/ojr/workplace/1090395903.php

American Society of Newspaper Editors and Newspaper Association of America joint meeting April 2004. Transcript provided to Rick Edmonds by ASNE.

American Society of Newspaper Editors. "Keeping cash in circulation." Published August 11, 2003., "Newsroom Employment Survey," Ginocchio, Paul et al. http://www.asne.org/index.cfm?id=5147 (Data as of the end of 2003).

American Society of Newspaper Editors, "Newsroom Employment Survey," Web site: http://www.naa.org/info/facts04/diversity.html.

Anderson, Nick. "Silence of the wolves, and their ilk, in swing states," Los Angeles Times, November 2, 2004.

Andrew, Paul. "Bloggers clog up news at convention." Seattletimes.com, August 16, 2004.

Angwin, Julia. "The right price: for Fox News, ad-sales market isn't fair, balanced," The Wall Street Journal, May 20, 2004.

Arbitron/Edison Media Research (New York, New York). "Internet 9: The Media and Entertainment World of Online Consumers." Published 2002. Web site: http://www.arbitron.com/downloads/I9summary.pdf.

Asaravala, Amit. "Nielsen 'people meters' draw fire," Wired, April 16, 2004. Online: http://www.wired.com/news/business/0,1367,63080,00.html

Associated Press Wire, "Dallas Morning News to close Cuba news bureau." October 29, 2004.

Associated Press Wire, "McClatchy snaps up Merced paper for $40.5 million." December 5, 2003.

Associated Press Wire, "Newspapers cut hundreds of jobs." October 28, 2004.

Associated Press Wire, "USA Today to raise its cover price to 75 cents," USAToday.com, June 22, 2004. Web site: http://www.usatoday.com/money/media/2004-06-22-usa-today-price_x.htm.

Associated Press. "Clear Channel chooses Fox for news deal." December 6, 2004. Web site: http://www.forbes.com/associatedpress/feeds/ap/2004/12/06/ap1694545.html.

Association of Alternative Newsweeklies. Unpublished.

Audit Bureau of Circulations News bulletin. "400th Reader Profile Report Released: The Philadelphia Daily News." August 2004. Web site: http://www.accessabc.com/newsbulletin/news0804a.htm.

Berkowitz, Harry. "Murdoch plans summer launch of new financial channel," Newsday, November 17, 2004.

Bernstein Research. "Media: TV Equilibrium Ahead as Distribution Burst Ends, 25-Year Broadcast Net Slide Nearly Over." August 20, 2004.

Bigelow, Bruce V. "Backlash hits Sinclair on disputed 'news event.'" San Diego Union-Tribune, October 20, 2004.

Blanton, Dana. "Voters Still Evenly Divided." Foxnews.com, March 25, 2004.

Blogads. "Reader Survey for blog advertising." Henry Copeland. May 21, 2004. Web site: http://www.blogads.com/survey/blog_reader_survey.html.

Bloomberg Television fact sheet. Web site: http://about.bloomberg.com/pressctr/factsheets/television.pdf.

Broadcasting & Cable, "The shape of things to come." January 5, 2004.

Broadcasting & Cable. "Powell's agenda for '04." January 26, 2004.

Brokamp, Robert. "General Electric and its army," The Motley Fool, January 20, 2000. Web site: http://www.fool.com/news/2000/ge000120.htm.

Burt, Tim. "A New Media Model?" The Financial Times. November 30, 2004.

Carter, Bill. "Anti-Kerry film reaps storm for broadcaster," The New York Times, October 19, 2004.

Carter, Bill. "Courage, CBS News." The New York Times. November 24, 2004.

CBSNews.com. "Dan Rather Statement on Memos."

Chunovic, Louis. "A 'fierce warrior' learns the ropes," Broadcasting & Cable, October 25, 2004.

CNN.com, June 30, 2004.

Coates, James. "Speedy reader delivers news from many sites." Chicago Tribune, August 28, 2004.

Collins, Bob. Minnesota Public Radio website, "Public radio listeners asking, 'What about Bob?,'" April 1, 2004.

Columbia Journalism Review editors, "American's Best Newspapers." Columbia Journalism Review, November/December 1999. Web site: http://archives.cjr.org/year/99/6/best.asp.

Corzen, Inc. "Web-only Recruitment Advertising Option Continues to Rise Among Newspapers." Press release, February 16, 2004.

Cotts, Cynthia, "California, Ho!," The Village Voice, March 24 - 30, 2004.

Crawford, Krysten. "Howard Stern Jumps to Satellite," CNN Money, Oct. 6, 2004

Cuprisin, Tim. "Inside Radio & TV," Milwaukee Journal Sentinel, July 21, 2004.

Currie, Jon. Interview, August 25, 2004.

Cyberjournalist.net. "Top news sites for December [2004]." January 12, 2005. Web site: http://www.cyberjournalist.net/news/001831.php.

Dawidziak, Mark. Cleveland Plain Dealer, "CBS network's shining stars hit milestones," November 14, 2004.

de Moraes, Lisa. "Other Networks' Election Loss Is Fox News's Gain," Washington Post, November 4, 2004.

de Moraes, Lisa. "Sweeps Week: The Vote Count," Washington Post, November 15, 2000.

Deutsche Bank Securities (New York, New York). "Wal-Mart takes a bite out of local." Paul Ginocchio et al. Published September 20, 2004.

Diaz, Kevin. "Satellite Radio: Ad-free for a fee; 'What it's about is control,' subscribers say," Star Tribune (Minneapolis, MN), October 8, 2004.

Downey, Kevin. "Boston stink bomb over people meter," Media Life Magazine, February 7, 2002. Web site: http://www.medialifemagazine.com/news2002/feb02/feb04/4_thurs/news2thursday.html

Economic Policy Insitute. "Income Picture." August 26, 2004. Web site: http://www epinet.org/content.cfm/webfeatures_econindicators_income20040826.

Editor &Publisher Staff, "LA Times Cuts 160 Jobs, Shuts 2 Papers, in Round of Cutbacks." EditorandPublisher.com, June 21, 2004.

Editor and Publisher Yearbook, 2004. Online data, 1940-2003. Web site: www.editorandpublisher.com.

Editor and Publisher. "Alternative Newspapers Turn in Strong '03." January 14, 2004.

Edmonds, Rick. "Public Companies No Worse than Private." Poynteronline, December 5, 2002. Web site: http://www.poynter.org/content/content_view.asp?id=12122

Edmonds, Rick. "Readers vs. Subscribers." Poynteronline, October 21, 2002.

Edmonds, Rick. "What Top Executives Are Talking About." Poynteronline, June 25, 2004. Web site: http://www.poynter.org/content/content_view.asp?id=67538.

Elber, Lynn. "Smiley's brave new face," AP, printed in the Milwaukee Journal Sentinel, January 10, 2005.

Elkin, Tobi. "Just An Online Minute...Broadband Penetration Slows." MediaPost.com, August 18, 2004.

Elkin, Tobi. "The Art of the Cross-Media Deal." Mediapost.com, August 23, 2004.

Fadner, Ross. "Survey: Consumers Want More Personalized Online Ads, But Don't Want Identities Known," Media Post.com, September 10, 2004.

FAIR Extra! "Goliath vs. Goliath." Update, December 1996. Web site: http://www.fair.org/extra/9612/goliaths.html.

FCC Guidelines. Web site: http://www.fcc.gov/eb/broadcast/opi.html.

FD Wire, "Q2 2004: The News Corporation Limited Earnings Conference Call," February 11, 2004.

Fitzgerald, Mark. "Diversity Analysis Says Only 13% of Daily Newsrooms Reflect Populations of Their Communities." Editor&Publisher.com, May 12, 2004.

Fitzgerald, Toni. "Nielsen breaks Boston revolt," Media Life Magazine, January 10, 2003. On line: http://www.medialifemagazine.com/news2003/jan03/jan06/5fri/news1friday.html

Fleeson, Lucinda. "Bureau of Missing Bureaus.," American Journalism Review, October/November 2003. Online: http://www.ajr.org/Article.asp?id=3409.

Flint, Joe. "NBC, Microsoft declare support for MSNBC unit," The Wall Street Journal, August 27, 2004.

Freedom du Lac, J. "Viacom move puts local TV folks on edge," Sacramento Bee, December 7, 2004.

Frew, Wendy. "Murdoch packs his kitbag and heads off," Sydney Morning Herald, November 3, 2004.

Frontline. "The Jesus Factor." April 29, 2004.

Gannett press release, "Gannett to acquire Home Town Communications Network." November 19, 2004. Web site: http://www.gannett.com/go/press/pr111904.htm.

Geewax, Marilyn. The Atlanta Journal-Constitution, "CBS tab for Super blunder: $550,000," September 23, 2004.

Geraci, Charles. "Nevada Newspaper Responds to Wildfire With Blog." Editor&Publisher.com, July 28, 2004.

Gershberg, Michele. "Clear Channel cuts commercials to gain ad dollars," Reuters, July 19, 2004.

Gillespie, Elizabeth M. for the Associated Press. "Seattle Times rejects Hearst's Offers in JOA Discussions." July 2, 2004.

Gillmor, Dan. "We the media." (Sebastopol, CA: O'Reilly Media, 2004).

Glaser, Mark. "Best Coverage of the U.S. Elections." OJR.org, December 11, 2003.

Glaser, Mark. "Business Side if Convergence Has Myths, Some Real Benefits." OJR.org, May 19, 2004.

Glaser, Mark. "Hold the Froth: MarketWatch, Slate Sales Signal Online Rebound." OJR.org, November 9, 2004.

Glaser, Mark. "Outsourcing News Sites May Prove Short-Sighted for Local TV Stations." OJR.org, March 26, 2004.

Glaser, Mark. "Papers' Online Units Allow Editorial Boards to Lift Veil with Video, Blogs." OJR.com, March 9, 2004.

Goodman, Ellen. "Morning Edition's Wake-up Call," Working for Change Web site, April 2, 2004.

Gough, Paul J. "Nielsen succumbs to political pressure, delays New York meters," MediaPost's Media Daily News, April 7, 2004. On line: http://www.mediapost.com/PrintFriend.cfm?articleId=245611

Grossman, Andrew. "Fox, Univision sights on ad mart," Hollywood Reporter, March 4, 2004.

Grossman, Lawrence K. Triangle Institute for Security Studies. The American Media and Wartime Challenges. March 22, 2002

Hart and Teeter Research Companies. Survey by Council for Excellence in Government. February 5-February 8, 2004.

Hart, Jon and Ken Salomon, "Proposed FCC rule on indecency could hinge on election outcome," The Wall Street Journal, November 1, 2004.

Higgins, John M. "A mixed bag," Broadcasting & Cable, August 16, 2004.

Higgins, John M. "Still Strutting After All These Years." Broadcasting and Cable. December 13, 2004.

Ho, David. "For CNN in New York, bigger is better," Atlanta Journal-Constitution, May 15, 2004.

Holloway, Diane. "TV losing its convention focus," Austin American-Statesman, July 25, 2004.

Hooker, Cliff, "Hard News: Black newspapers fighting against the worst climate in decades," Black Enterprise, December 2002.

Hu, Jim. "AOL beings testing new site revamp." CNET News.com, September 13, 2004.

Interactive Advertising Bureau. "Annual Industry Revenues Grow Nearly 21% as Year Totals Nearly $7.3 Billion." Press release, April 21, 2004.

Interactive Advertising Bureau. "$2.37 Billion Internet Ad Revenue for Q2 2004-Up 42.7 Percent from the Second Quarter 2003." IAB.com. Press release, September 20, 2004.

International Digital Media & Arts Association Journal. "Middletown Media Studies." Vol. 1, no. 1 (Spring 2004).

Internetweek.com. "Online Advertising Market: $9.1 Billion in 2004." August 13, 2004.

Jensen, Elizabeth. "Conservative TV group to air anti-Kerry film," Los Angeles Times, October 9, 2004.

Johnson, Dean. "Left for Debt: Liberal yakker seeing red," Boston Herald, April 14, 2004.

Johnson, Peter. "CBS Fires 4 over Bush Guard Story," USA Today, January 26, 2005.

Johnson, Peter. "Easy Like 'Sunday Morning,' " USA Today, January 21, 2004.

Johnson, Steve. Chicago Tribune, October 19, 2004.

Journal Register Company. "Journal Register Company to Acquire 21st Century Newspapers." Press release, July 6, 2004. Web site: http://www.journalregister.com/press/07062004.html

Journalism and Mass Communication Quarterly. "Non-Metropolitan Daily Newspaper Markets." Summer 2004.

Kagan Research. "100 Leading Media Companies." AdAge.com. August 2004. Web site: http://www.adage.com/page.cms?pageId=1084.

Kaplan, Jonathan E. "Howard Stern says he can deliver swing voters to Kerry," The Hill. June 15, 2004.

Kerschbaumer, Ken. "CNN heats up with Pathfire," Broadcasting & Cable, February 3, 2003.

KeyNote. "KeyNote Research: News Video Quality Survey," May 2004. Web site: www.keynote.com.

Kirk, Jim. "For sale sign off Sun-times." Chicago Tribune Online, May 28, 2004.

Kropf, Schuyler. "Tenenbaum, DeMint raised $12M for race," Charleston Post and Courier, October 16, 2004.

Kuhnhenn, James. "Press feels partisan pressure to perform," Contra Costa Times, July 5, 2004.

Kumler, Emily. "Activism Goes Digital." PCWorld.about.com, April 23, 2004.

Kurtz, Howard. "Osama Who? When No News Is 'Bad

News,' " The Washington Post, January 24, 2005.

Kurtz, Howard. "Rick Kaplan, Putting more NBC in MSNBC," The Washington Post, January 31, 2005.

Lafayette, Jon. "CNN touting greater out-of-home viewers," Television Week, March 22, 2004.

Larson, Megan. "Klein named president, CNN/U.S.," Mediaweek, November 22, 2004.

Lazaroff, Leon. "Green Bay paper's battle ends; owner sells to Gannett." Chicago Tribune Online, July 24, 2004.

Leeds, Jeff. "Clear Channel ready to push Spanish radio." New York Times News Service. September 17, 2004. Web site: www.signonsandiego.com/uniontrib/20040917/news_1b17radio.html.

Levere, Jane L. "The Fox News Channel tops CNN's audience, and casts its eyes toward its advertising rates," The New York Times, January 30, 2002.

Levy, Harlan. "Courant parent could face antitrust lawsuit," The Journal-Inquirer (Manchester, Conn.), May 7, 2003.

Life Magazine website. http://www.life.com/Life/lifeabout.html.

Linnett, Richard. "Fox claims win over CNN in cable upfront," Advertising Age, July 14, 2003.

Lorek, L.S. "Clear Channel Communications downplays Write-Off," San Antonio Express-News," March 1, 2005.

Loviglio, Joann. The Associated Press. "Newspapers riding out complaints over online registration," June 13, 2004.

Mack, Ann M. "Rick Media Usage Grows in First Quarter." Adweek.com, May 11, 2004.

Malcolm, Vince general manager, KTLA-Los Angeles, in Pat Maio, "New ratings meter could alter TV news:

without sweeps, the need for over-the-top newscasts might go away for good." Los Angeles Business Journal, July 19, 2004.

Malone, Julie. "Unrestricted Internet Opens Way for Political Humor." Cox News Service, May 18, 2004.

Mandese, Joe. "Broadband Breaks 50% of Mass, Marks a Critical Pass." Mediapost.com, August 19, 2004.

Mandese, Joe. "Marketers Plan Slower Ad Expansion in '05." Mediapost.com, September 15, 2004.

Mandese, Joe. "Papers, local TV seen as more credible than network news; consumers, trade split on bias," MediaPost.com, November 1, 2004.

Marshall, Joshua Micah. "Feel the Buzz." Talkingpointsmemo.com. September 7, 2004.

McClellan, Steve. "Attack mode," Broadcasting & Cable, April 5, 2004.

McClellan, Steve. "Changing the Guard; As McLaughlin's stock sinks, Matthews rises." Broadcasting and Cable, June 28, 2004.

McClellan, Steve. "Meters take big bite out of Big Apple," Broadcasting & Cable, June 13, 2004.

McClellan, Steve. "War of Addition," Broadcasting & Cable, May 17, 2004.

McConnell, Bill. "Playing for keeps," Broadcasting & Cable, August 9, 2004.

McGinty, Tom et al., "Anatomy of a Circulation Fabrication." Newsday, September 12, 2004.

Media Matters for America, "FOX aired 48 minutes more (20 percent) of RNC speeches than of DNC speeches," September 3, 2004.

Mediaweek, Advertisement. November 22, 2004.

MediaMark Research, Inc. (New York, New York). "Newspaper Section Readership 2004." Published Spring 2003.

Mediamark Research. “Magazine Audience Estimates” 1995 - 2004. Web site: www.mediamark.com.

MediaPost, TV Watch, September 24, 2004, Wayne Friedman, “Let’s Talk About Sex, FCC.”

Mellman, Jeremy. “Tribune frets over Bush media move,” Chicago Business, January 27, 2005.

Merrill Lynch (New York, New York). “Newspaper Industry Primer (8th Edition).” Lauren Rich Fine. August 26, 2004.

Merrill Lynch (New York, New York). “The Newspaper Industry.” Lauren Rich Fine. Published June 21, 2004.

Merrill Lynch (New York, New York).”Newspaper Industry Primer (8th Edition).” Lauren Rich Fine. August 26, 2004.

Metz, Rachel. “We Don’t Need no Stinkin’ Login.” Wired.com, July 20, 2004.

Meyer, Philip. “The Vanishing Newspaper: Saving Journalism in the Information Age.” (Columbia, MO: University of Missouri Press, 2004).

MORI Research. “Power User 2004: Reaching Influentials & Influencing Purchases Via Newspaper Websites,” January 2004. Web site: http://www.moriresearch.com

Morlino, Robert. “Sinclair flap proves exception,” Center for Public Integrity, October 28, 2004.

MSNBC.com. “MSNBC.com reports quarterly profit.” July 22, 2004.

New California Media. “Public Opinion Survey of California Ethnic Groups About Criminal Justice Issues.”

Newspaper Association of America presentation (Washington, D.C.). “Why the Current Business Model Needs to Change.” April 21, 2004. Web site: http://www.naa.org.

Newsweek. Staff box, July 26, 2004.

Nielsen Media Research. “VNU’s Nielsen Media Research

and Viacom's television operations sign multi-year agreements for expanded TV measurement." Press release, July 29, 2003. Online: http://www.vnunet.de/testticker/ueber_vnu/Pressemitteilung_29juli2003.asp

Nielsen Monitor Plus, "John Kerry Local Political Ad Spending On The Rise - George Bush Scaling Back," press release, June 17, 2004.

Nielsen Monitor-Plus and the University of Wisconsin Advertising Project, "High Volume of Presidential Campaign TV Advertising in Battleground States, Yet 60 % of Americans Live in Areas Where No Ads Have Aired," July 18, 2004, p. 6.

Nielsen NetRatings, "Top 20 Online Current Events & Global News Destinations," October 2004.

O'Malley, Gavin. "Blog Readership Up in '04; Advertisers not Sold." Mediapost.com, January 4, 2005.

Online Publishers Association, "Convenience and Accessibility Key Factors in Media Use of 18-34 Year-Olds, According to New Online Publishers Association Report." Press release, April 20, 2004. Web site: http://www.online-publishers.org/?pg=press&dt=042004.

Online Publishers Association. "Online Paid Content U.S. Market Spending Report." November 2004. Web site: http://www.online-publishers.org/pdf/opa_paid_content_report_nov_04.pdf.

Oser, Kris. "Online Ad Spending Up 27%; Growth Twice as Fast as Cable." AdAge.com, July 29, 2004.

Oxfeld, Jesse. "Watching the Newspaper on the Web." Editor&Publisher.com, December 16, 2004.

Papper, Bob. "Salaries soar," RTNDA Communicator, June 2004.

Papper, Bob. "Survey shows solid growth in TV news and staffing," RTNDA Communicator, September 2004.

Papper, Robert A., Michael E. Holmes, PhD., Mark N. Polovich, PhD. "Middletown Media Studies," The

International Digital Media & Arts Association Journal, Spring 2004.

Papper, Robert. "Middletown Media Studies," presentation, July 22, 2004.

Papper, Robert. Ball State University, communication, November 28, 2004.

Parker, Pamela. "AOL's Ads Surge, Subscriptions Drop." Click Z.com, November 3, 2004.

Pelofsky, Jeremy. "FCC's Powell sees long road ahead for media rules," Reuters, December 2, 2004.

Pew Internet & American Life Project. "The State of blogging." January 2005.

Pew Research Center for the People and the Press, "Strong opposition to media cross-ownership emerges," July 13, 2003. Web site:: http://people-press.org/reports/display.php3?ReportID=188.

Pew Research Center for the People and the Press, "Voters impressed with campaign but news coverage gets lukewarm ratings," questionnaire, question 1a. Released October 24, 2004. Online: http://people-press.org/reports/print.php3?PageID=902.

Pew Research Center for the People and the Press. "Polls Face Growing Resistance, But Still Representative." April 20, 2004.

Pew Research Center, "News audiences increasingly polarized," June 8, 2004.

Pew Research Center. "Cable and Internet Loom Large in Fragmented Political News Universe." Survey, January 11, 2004. http://people-press.org/reports/display.php3?ReportID=200.

Porter, Tim. "Dismantling the Language Barrier." American Journalism Review. October/November 2003. Web site: www.ajr.org/Article.asp?id=%203415.

Postman, David. "As campaign struggles, backers say Dean's value lies online." The Seattle Times, A1, February 14, 2004.

Potter, Deborah and Walter Gantz, "Bringing viewers back to local TV: What could reverse the ratings slide?" NewsLab.org. Online: http://www.newslab.org/research/bringback.htm.

PR Newswire Association, Inc. "Tacoda Launches Online Industry's First Audience-Centric Ad Network; Will Provide National Reach for Behavioral-Targeted Ads," November 15, 2004.

Project for Excellence in Journalism research and Borell Associates, "What Local Web Sites Earn." May, 2004.

Project for Excellence in Journalism. "ePolitics 2004." February 2004. Web site: http://www.journalism.org/resources/research/reports/campaign2004/epolitics/epolitics.pdf.

Project for the Excellence in Journalism, "The Debate Effect", October 27, 2004. Web site: http://www.journalism.org/resources/research/reports/debateeffect/default.asp.

Pruitt, Scarlett. IDG News Service. "Microsoft guns for Google on news search." Infoworld.com, July 27, 2004.

Pulley, Brett. "Commander of the airwaves," Forbes, April 29, 2002.

Ranii, David and Michael Biesecker, "Herald-Sun fires executives, others." Newsobserver.com, January 4, 2005. Web site: http://www.newsobserver.com/business/story/1983511p-8364366c.html.

Ranii, David. "Local weekly newspapers to be sold to Florida group." The News & Observer, April 8, 2004, page D3.

Readership Institute at Northwestern University. Various studies. Web site: www.readership.org.

Redmond, Tim. "Bay Guardian sues New Times chain for predatory pricing," San Francisco Bay Guardian, Oct. 20 - Oct. 26 2004.

Richman, Dan. "Justices to hear Seattle newspapers' dispute." Seattle Post-Intelligencer, December 1, 2004.

Rogalinski, Paul. "Fox News updates N.Y. facility," Broadcast Engineering, August 1, 2004.

Romano, Allison. "Behind the cameras," Broadcasting & Cable, July 12, 2004.

Rosen, Jody. "Peril in the Air for Bush: Howard Stern," Los Angeles Times, April 28, 2004.

Rosenstiel, Tom and Marion Just, "Five ways to build viewership," Columbia Journalism Review, November/December 2002.

Rottenberg, Josh. "Conventional power," Entertainment Weekly, September 24, 2004.

Russell, Ron. "Looking inside INdTV," SF Weekly, July 28, 2004.

San Jose Mercury News. Web site: jobs.sjmercury.com/about.html

Scanlon, Mavis. "A day in the life: CNN ad sales' Greg D'Alba," CableWorld, September 20, 2004.

Scott Woolley, "Broadcast Bullies," Forbes, September 6, 2004.

Senia, Al. "The Powell play," America's Network, September 1, 2004. Web site: http://www.americasnetwork.com/americasnetwork/article/articleDetail.jsp?id=117973

Shields, Michael. "Ethnic Print Media Group to Audit Community Newspapers." Media Daily News. Web site: www.mediapost.com/dtls_dsp_news.cfm?newsID=275347.

Sloan, Harold S. and Arnold J. Zurcher. Dictionary of Economics. (New York: Barnes &Noble Books, 1970).

Smith Barney Citigroup Report. June 17, 2004.

Sorkin, Andrew Ross. "Dow Jones Agrees to Buy MarketWatch." New York Times, November 15, 2004.

Span, Paula. "Radio Waves," Washington Post, September 12, 2004.

Stanford Center for the Quantitative Study of Society. "Ten Years After the Birth of the Internet, How Do Americans Use the Internet in Their Daily Lives?" December 2004.

Steinberg, Jacques. "Fox News, media elite," The New York Times, November 8, 2004.

Streisand, Betsy. "The tracker behind the tube," U.S. News & World Report, November 8, 2004.

Strupp, Joe. "Blessing or Curse? Editors Examine Blogs' Role in '60 Minutes' Uproar." Editor&Publisher.com, September 15, 2004.

Subervi, Federico. "NAHJ Survey of News Professionals Working at Spanish-Language Media Companies in the U.S." August 2004.

Suhler, Veronis. Stevenson Communications Industry Forecast & Report / Consumer Magazine Publishing.

Sullivan, Andrew. "The Blogging Revolution." Wired.com, May 2002.

Suro, Roberto. "Changing Channels and Crisscrossing Cultures: A Survey of Latinos on the News Media." April 2004.

Teitelman, Bram. "Radio Reacts To Indecency Flak," Billboard, March 13, 2004.

Telecommunications Association, Cable Programming Guidebook, June 2004. Web site: http://www.ncta.com/Docs/PageContent.cfm?pageID=240.

Thomas, Mike. "NPR host Smiley: Network lacked commitment; Why he's quitting public radio's most successful African-American show," Chicago Sun-Times, December 12, 2004.

Thompson, Kevin D. "MSNBC and the cable news war," Palm Beach Post, October 27, 2004.

Turner, Ted. "My beef with big media," Washington Monthly, July/August 2004.

"Testimony of Paul Taylor, Executive Director, Alliance for Better Campaigns before the House Committee on Energy and Commerce, Subcommittee on Telecommunications and the Internet on Campaign Finance Reform: Proposals Impacting Broadcasters, Cable Operators and Satellite Providers." June 20, 2001. Web site: http://www.bettercampaigns.org/reports/display.php?PageID=4.

U.S. Bureau of Census. "U.S. Population Projections by Race and Hispanic Origin: 2000-2050."

U.S. Department of Commerce news release, "Foreign-Born Population Surpasses 32 Million, Census Bureau Estimates," March 10, 2003.

University of Miami, School of Communication (Coral Gables, Florida). "The Credibility of Newspapers, Television News, and Online News." Rasha A. Abdulla et al. Presented to the Mass Communication and Society Division, Association for Education in Journalism and Mass Communication, annual convention, Miami Beach, Florida, August 9, 2002. Web site: http://com.miami.edu/car/miamibeach1.htm.

Univision. "Univision Primetime Novela Audience Soars 23% over Course of Third Quarter." Press release, October 7, 2004.

USC Annenberg Institute for Justice and Journalism, Pew Hispanic Center, New California Media, "The 2003 Multilingual Survey of California Voters," September 25, 2003.

USC Annenberg School Center for the Digital Future. "Digital Future Report." September 2004. Web site: http://www.digitalcenter.org

Van Klaveren, Adrian. "Newsgathering," BBC News, November 4, 2004. Web site: http://news.bbc.co.uk/

newswatch/ifs/hi/newsid_3960000/newsid_3964600/3964687.stm.

Vanishing Voter Project. "Election Interest is Up Sharply but Convention Interest is Not," July 21, 2004. Web site: www.vanishingvoter.org/Releases/release072104_charts.shtml.

Washington Post. "Tom Brokaw's 'Nightly News' Retirement Date: Dec. 1," Reuters, April 20, 2004.

Weiss, Joanna. "Left-Leaning Northampton, Stern, On the Same Wavelength," Boston Globe, July 21, 2004.

Whisler, Kirk. "Hispanic Publications in 2003." Latino Print Network, (Carlsbad. CA).

Whitney, Daisy. "NBC-owned stations attract Olympics effect in late news," TV Week, September 6, 2004.

Whitney, Daisy. "Study identifies hot political markets," TV Week, October 18, 2004.

Wildermuth, John. "Cash shortfall may undo Jones' plan for TV ads," San Francisco Chronicle, October 16, 2004.

Glossary of Terms

A/D Converter: A circuit which converts a signal from analogue to digital form; the opposite of a D/A converter.

Adobe: A software manuafacturer based in San Jose, California, and traded on the Nasdaq National Market under the symbol ADBE. Adobe is a leading provider of media productivity software.

Advertisement: The promotion of a product or service

Advertising manager: The person who oversees the sales representatives who sell space to advertisers, and ensures that ads are in the appropriate section

Advertorial: An advertisement section in a magazine that looks like an article or a feature

Advocacy: A style of journalism in which a reporter takes sides in controversial issues and develops a point of view: a style of journalism which is opposite of mainstream journalism, in which reporters are expected to be objective

AGC: Automatic Gain Control. A circuit which automatically adjusts the input gain of a device, in order to provide a safe and consistent signal level. AGCs can be handy features, but professional applications often require manual gain control for optimum results.

AM: Amplitude Modulation. A method of radio transmission which sends information as variations of the amplitude of a carrier wave.

Amperage: The amount of electrical current transferred from one component to another.

Amplifier: A device which increases signal amplitude.

Amplify: To increase amplitude.

Amplitude: The strength or power of a wave signal. The "height" of a wave when viewed as a standard *x vs y* graph.

Analogue: Information stored or transmitted as a continuously variable signal (as opposed to digital, in which the analogue signal is represented as a series of discreet values). Analogue is often technically the more accurate representation of the original signal, but digital systems have numerous advantages which have tended to make them more popular (a classic example is vinyl records versus CDs).

Anamorphic Lens: A special type of wide-angle lens which stretches the width of the image but not the height, creating a widescreen aspect ratio.

Angle: Particular emphasis of a media presentation, sometimes called a *slant*

Antenna: A device which radiates and/or receives electromagnetic waves.

Aperture: Literally means "opening". The camera iris; the opening which lets light through the lens. By adjusting the size of the aperture, the amount of incoming light is controlled. The aperture size is measured in f-stops.

ASF: Windows Media file format ending with the extension *.asf*. Used for delivering streaming video.

Aspect Ratio: The ratio of width to height of an image. Can be expressed as a number, or a relationship between two numbers. For example, the standard television screen ratio is 4:3 (4 units wide by 3 units high) or 1.33 (the width is 1.33 times the height). The new "wide screen" television ratio is 16:9 (1.78), and many new video cameras have the option to record using this format. Theatrical film aspect ratios vary, but the most common is 18.5:10 (1.85).

ASX: Windows Media file format ending with the extension *.asx.* This is a metafile which works in conjunction with ASF files for delivering streaming video.

Attribution: Credit given to who said what or the source of facts

Audio Dub: The process of adding audio to a video recording without disturbing the pictures. The original audio may be replaced, or kept and combined with the new audio.

Audio Insert: A feature of some video equipment which allows audio dubbing.

Audio: Sound. Specifically, the range of frequencies which are perceptable by the human ear.

Automatic functions: Functions which are performed by equipment with little or no input from the operator. Auto-functions can be very useful, but tend to have serious limitations. As a general rule, it is desirable to be able to operate audio-visual equipment manually.

Auxiliary Channel: On audio mixers, a bus which has an independent feed from each individual channel. Each channel has a pot to adjust the level being sent to the auxiliary master output, which in turn has a pot to adjust the overall level at the output bus. The auxiliary channel may be a simple output (to feed a device such as a tape machine or monitor), or it may be a "loop". An auxiliary loop sends a signal from the auxiliary output bus to a signal processing device such as a reverb generator, then brings the output of that device into an "auxiliary return" bus (thus creating a loop from the desk to the device, back to the desk). This return bus will have a level control pot, which is used to mix the incoming signal into the mixer's master output bus.

AVI: "Audio Video Interleaved". A common digital video format, in which the audio is interleaved as "packets", into the video frames.

Back Focus: The focus between the lens and the camera. Adjusted by a ring at the rear of the lens (the closest ring to the camera body). If the camera appears focused when zoomed in, but becomes out of focus when zoomed wide, the back focus needs adjusting.

Background: Information that is not intended for publication

Backlight Correction (BLC): A feature of some cameras which increases the apparent brightness of the subject when lit from the rear.

Backlight: A light which is positioned behind the subject. It's primary purpose is to make the subject stand out from the background by highlighting the subject's outline.

Balanced Audio: An audio signal which consists of two "hot" signals plus the shield. The hot signals are inverted relative to each other as they travel along the balanced cable. They are re-inverted when entering an audio device — this has the effect of inverting any unwanted interference, thus eliminating it.

Bandpass Filter: A circuit which filters out all but a certain range of frequencies, ie. it allows a certain band of frequencies to pass.

Bandwidth: A range of frequencies.

Barn Doors: Metal projections attached to the front of a light, which can be positioned in various ways to control the dispersal of the light.

Batch Capture: The process of capturing multiple video clips automatically. A batch command is set up from the capture software which includes in and out points for each clip.

Baud: Unit of signal speed — the number of signal "bits" per second.

Best Boy: On a film set, the assistant to the Gaffer and Key Grip.

Beta (1): A group of video formats developed by Sony Corporation. Beta, Beta SP, Digital Beta and other variations are all professional television formats. Betamax is a failed consumer version, losing to VHS in the 1980's. **(2):** A pre-release version of computer software. Often distributed widely without charge, in order to obtain feedback, identify bugs, and attract customers.

Bias: A position that is partial or slanted

Bit: Binary digit. One piece of binary (digital) information. A description of one of two possible states, eg 0 or 1; off or on.

Bitmap: A series of digital image formats, which record colour information for each individual pixel. As a result, the quality is very high, as is the size of the file.

Black balance: A camera function which gives a reference to true black. When auto-black balance is activated (by a switch, positioned with the white balance switch), the iris is automatically shut, and the camera adjusts itself to absolute black.

BlackBurst: A composite video signal with no luminance information, but containing everything else present in a normal composite video signal.

Bluetooth: A wireless data transfer system which allows devices to communicate with each other over short distances, e.g. phones, laptops, etc.

Bridge: Another term for A/D converter.

Broadband: A general term to describe an internet connection faster than 56K. Broadband usually means 512K or greater.

Broadcast feature: longer than usual broadcast news story that gives reporters 5-25 minutes (compared to usual 30-60 seconds) to develop a deeper look at a news event, trend, or individual: the broadcast equivalent of a newspaper feature story; also known as "television magazine piece" or radio feature

B-roll: Video images shot specifically to be used over a reporter's words to illustrate the news event or story, to cover up audio edits of quotes (to avoid the jerking head effect), or to cover up bad shots (out of focus, poorly lighted, etc.)

Bucket: A solid coloured horizontal bar across the bottom of a colour bar test pattern. The most commonly used bucket colour in PAL patterns is red, referred to as a "bucket of blood".

Burn: The process of recording information to an optical disk (CD or DVD).

Bus: Pathway which a signal passes along. For example, the main output of an audio mixer is referred to as the master bus.

By-line: The name of the reporter

Byte: A group of eight binary (digital) bits.

Cable Television: A system of television progam delivery via cable networks.

Camcorder: A single unit consisting of a video camera and recording unit.

Canadian press: National news agency set up by the daily newspapers of Canada to exchange news among themselves and with international news agencies

Candlepower: A measurement of light, generally that which is output from an electric lamp.

Cans: Headphones.

Caption: Copy which accompanies a photograph or graphic

Capture Card: A type of computer card with video and/or audio inputs which allows the computer to import an analogue signal and convert it to a digital file.

CCD: Charged Coupled Device.

CCU : Camera Control Unit.

Channel (1) : On audio mixers, the pathway along which each individual input travels before being mixed into the next stage (usually a sub-group or the master bus). Each channel will typically have an input socket where the source is physically plugged in, followed by a sequence of amplifiers / attenuators, equalisers, auxiliary channels, monitoring and other controls, and finally a slider to adjust the output level of the channel.

Charged Coupled Device: The image sensing device of video and television cameras — the component which converts light from the lens into an electrical signal. Made up of pixels - the more pixels, the higher the resolution. CCDs are commonly referred to simply as "chips". They replaced previous tube technology in the 1980's. Larger CCDs can naturally accommodate more pixels, and therefore have higher resolutions. Common sizes are 1/3" (pro-sumer level), 1/2" and 2/3" (professional level). Consumer cameras generally have a single CCD which interprets all colours, whereas professional cameras have three CCDs — one for each primary colour.

Chroma Key: The process of replacing a particular colour in an image with a different image. The most common types of chroma keys are bluescreen and greenscreen.

Chrominance: Chroma, or colour. In composite video signals, the chrominance component is separated from the luminance component, and is carried on a sub-carrier wave.

Cinematographer: AKA *Director of Photography*, the person on a film production responsible for photography.

Cinematography: The art and science of movie photography, including both shooting technique and film development.

Classified ads: Categories of products or services: short, direct text ads which clearly indicate WHAT is being advertised, the PRICE, WHERE, and HOW the advertiser can be contacted

Clear Scan: A video camera function which allows the camera to alter it's scan rate to match that of a computer monitor. This reduces or eliminates the flicker effect of recording computer monitors.

Codec: Short for compressor/decompressor. A tool which is used to reduce the size of a digital file. Can be software, hardware or a combination of both.

Colour Bars: A television test pattern, displaying vertical coloured stripes (bars). Used to calibrate vision equipment. There are numerous variations for different applications.

Column: An article in which a writer or columnist gives an opinion on a topic

Commercial: An advertisement that is presented on television, radio, or film

Common Mode Signal: A signal which appears equally on both wires of a two wire line, usually unwanted noise. Common mode signals are eliminated with balanced audio cable.

Component Video: A type of high-quality video signal which consists of separate signal components. Usually refers to Y/Pb/Pr, which includes one channel for luminance information and two for colour.

Composite Video: A type of video signal in which all components are recorded or transmitted as one signal.

Compression (1): A method of reducing the size of a digital file, whilst retaining acceptable quality. This may be desirable in order to save memory space or to speed up access time. In the case of digital video, large files must be processed very quickly, and compression is still essential for playback on consumer-level computers. Professional digital systems can work with uncompressed video. There are many compression techniques in common use, and digital video often uses various combinations of techniques. Compression can be divided into two types: "lossless" and "lossy". As the names imply, lossless techniques retain all of the original information in a more efficient form, whereas lossy techniques discard or approximate some information. With lossy compression, there is an art to finding a compromise between acceptable quality loss, and file size reduction. **(2):** Audio compression is a method of "evening out" the dynamic range of a signal. Compression is very useful when a signal is prone to occasional peaks, such as a vocalist who lets out the odd unexpected scream. The compressor will not affect the dynamic range until a certain user-definable level is reached (the "threshold") - at which point the level will be reduced according to a pre-determined ratio. For example, you could set the compressor to a threshold of 0db, and a compression ratio of 3:1. In this case, all signals below 0db will be unaffected, and all signals above 0db will be reduced by 3db to 1 (i.e. for every 1db input over 0db, 1/3db will be output). Other controls include the attack and decay time, as well as input and output levels.

Conflict of interest: The conflict that is created when a writer allows personal interests (friendship, family, business connections, etc.) to influence the outcome of the story

Copy: The words of an article, news story, or book: any broadcast writing, including commercials: any written material intended for publication, including advertising

Copyreader: The person who "proofreads" copy as it comes in, checking for spelling, punctuation, accuracy of style, and clarity

CPU: Central Processing Unit., the "brain" of a computer.

Credibility: Believability of a writer or publication

Crossover: An electrical network which divides an incoming audio signal into discreet ranges of frequencies, and outputs these ranges separately.

CRT: Cathode Ray Tube.

Cut (1): An instantaneous transition from one shot to the next. **(2):** A location director's instruction, calling for the camera and audio operators to cease recording and all action to halt

D Series Tape Formats: A series of broadcast digital formats, designated D1, D2, etc. Dx is basically a replacement for 1-inch formats. D2 and D3 combine chrominance and luminance information, whereas D1 and D5 store them separately (and are therefore higher quality).

DAT: Digital Audio Tape.

Data Rate: The amount of data which is transferred per second. In a video file, this means the amount of data the file must transfer to be viewed at normal speed. In relation to optical disks, this means the amount of data which can be read or written per second.

Date line: the place the story was filed

DC: Direct Current. The electrical current output by batteries, etc.

Decibel (dB): Logarithmic measurement of signal strength. 1/10 of a Bel.

Deck: A smaller headline which comes between the headline and the story

Depth of Field: The zone between the nearest and furthest points at which the camera can obtain a sharp focus.

Device Control: A tool which allows you to control another device. For example, a window within a video editing package from which you can control a video camera.

Differential Amplification: Method of amplifying a signal, in which the output signal is a function of the difference between two input signals.

Digital S : Professional digital tape format, introduced by JVC in the mid-1990s.

Digital Video Editing: Editing using digital video formats and computer software. Also known as *non linear editing*.

Digital: A signal which consists of a series of discreet values, as opposed to an analogue signal, which is made up of a continuous information stream.

Display ads: Ads that include a visual image to advertise a product or service

Dissolve : A transition in which one shot dissloves (fades) into the next.

Docutainment: From the words *documentary* and *entertainment*. A television programme which includes both news and entertainment content, or a blending of both.

Dolly : Any apparatus upon which a camera can be mounted, which can be moved aound smoothly.

Downstage: Toward the camera.

Driver: A piece of software which enables a piece of hardware to work with a computer. Usually supplied with the hardware, but can often be downloaded from the vendor's website.

Dropout: Loss of part of a recorded video or audio signal, showing up as glitches on playback. Can be caused by damaged record heads, dirty tapes or heads, etc.

Dry Run: Rehearsal, without recording or transmitting etc.

DVD Authoring: The process of taking video footage, adding chapter stops, menus, and encoding the footage into MPEG files ready to be burned

DVD Burning: Taking the authored DVD files and physically writing them to a disk.

DVD: (Digital Video Disc or Digital Versatile Disc). An optical disc format which provides sufficient storage space and access speeds to playback entire movies.

Dynamic Loudspeaker: Loudspeaker which uses conventional cone and dome drive elements.

Dynamic Microphone : A moving coil microphone, which doesn't require power.

Earth Hum: An unwanted noise which has been induced into a video or audio signal by faulty earthing.

Edit Decision List (EDL): A list of all in points and out points for an editing task. Can be stored on a removeable disc (eg. floppy disc). This enables an edit to be constructed in one edit suite, then taken to another (better) suite to make the final version.

Edit: The proccess of assembling video clips, audio tracks, graphics and other source marerial into a presentable package.

Editor: the person who "edits" a story by revising and polishing: the person whose job is to approve copy when it comes in and to make decisions about what is published in a newspaper or magazine

Editorial: An article expressing a newspaper or magazine owner's or editor's position on an issue

ENG : Electronic News Gathering. This term was introduced with the evolution of video cameras for shooting news in the field (as opposed to film cameras). It is still widely used to describe mobile news crews.

Equalisation: The proccess of adjusting selected ranges of audio frequencies in order to correct or enhance the characteristics of a signal.

Exposure : The amount of light which is passed through the iris, and which the CCD or film is exposed to.

Facts sheet: A page of significant information prepared by Public Relations people to help news media in covering a special event

Fade: A transition to or from "nothing". In audio, to or from silence. In video, usually to or from a colour such as black.

Feature article: The main article on the front page of a newspaper, or the cover story in a magazine

Field: In interlaced video, half a video frame. A field comprises every second horizontal line of the frame, making a total of 312.5 lines in PAL and SECAM, 262.5 lines in NTSC.

Filter: A transparent or translucent optical element which alters the properties of light passing through a lens.

Five Ws and H: the primary questions a news story answers —Who? What? When? Where? Why? How?

Flying Erase Head: In video recorders, an erase head which is mounted on the drum assembly. The erase head wipes any previous recordings as new ones are made. "Normal" erase heads are stationary, and mounted to the side of the head drum. Because of their close proximity to the record heads, flying erase heads provide cleaner edits. Related info: How to clean video heads

Focal Length: The distance from the centre of the lens to the camera CCD.

Frame (1): The edges of a television / video / film image. **(2):** To compose a camera shot. **(3):** One complete video, television or film picture. In video and television, each frame is divided into two interlaced fields. PAL and SECAM systems deliver 25 frames per second, with 625 horizontal scan lines. NTSC delivers 30 fps with 525 lines.

Frame Rate: The number of video or film frames displayed each second (frames per second; fps). PAL frame rate is 25 fps, NTSC is 30 fps, film is 24 fps.

Frequency Response: The sensitivity of a microphone (or other component) to various frequencies, i.e. the amount each frequency is boosted or attenuated.

F-stop: Measurement of aperture. The higher the f-stop number, the smaller the aperture.

F-type : A family of cable connectors, in which the centre (hot) pin is the centre wire of the cable itself.

Gaffer (1): Chief electrician on a film set. **(2):** Industrial-strength sticky tape, AKA duct tape.

Gain: The volume/amplification level of an audio or video signal.

Gatekeepers: People who determine what will be printed, broadcast, produced, or consumed in the mass media

Geosynchronous: A satellite orbit in which the satellite remains in a fixed position above the Earth.

Gobbledygook: Language that is unnecessarily complicated, unclear, wordy, or includes jargon

Gray Card: A gray-coloured card which reflects a known, uniform amount of the light which falls upon it. Used as a reference to calibrate light meters and set exposure.

Grip: Person who is responsible for constructiong and dismantling film sets, as well as laying down dolly tracks.

Gutter: Narrow margin of white space in the center area in a magazine, newspaper, or book, where two pages meet

Halogen: Any of the four non-metallic elements flourine, chlorine, bromine and iodine.

Hard news stories: Factual accounts of important events, usually appearing first in a newspaper

Head (1): The component which records an electrical signal onto magnetic tape, or reads a signal from tape into an electrical signal. Related info: Cleaning video heads. **(2):** The part which the camera is mounted on, atop a tripod, pedestal or other mounting. Allows the camera to pan and tilt.

Headline: The "title" of a newspaper or magazine story

Headroom: The amount of space between the top of the subject's head and the top of the picture frame.

Hertz: Unit of frequency. One cycle per second.

Hot : An image or part of an image which is excessively bright, ie. overexposed.

Human interest story: a story that focuses on the human side of news and often appeals to the readers' emotion

Hz: Hertz. Cycles per second.

Impedance: A term in electronics which measures the amount of opposition a device has to an AC current (such as an audio signal). Technically speaking, it is the combined effect of capacitance, inductance, and resistance on a signal.

Indeo: A digital video compression format.

Infotainment: Television programming which blends *info*rmation and enter*tainment*.

Infra-red: Frequencies beyond the red end of the visible spectrum, i.e. frequencies with longer wavelengths than red light. Perceived by humans as heat. Commonly used for remote-control devices.

In-point: The beginning point of an edit.

Interface: The point of contact between a tool and it's operator. A human/computer interface could be a keyboard or a mouse.

Interlace: The method of dividing a video frame into two fields; one made up of the odd-numbered horizontal lines, the other made up of even-numbered lines.

Internet: If you don't know what the Internet is, you're in trouble. Related info: Internet tutorials

Intranet: A "closed-circuit internet". A local network of computers linked in much the same way as the wider internet.

Inverted pyramid: The structure of a news story which places the important facts at the beginning and less important facts and details at the end, enabling the editor to cut bottom portion of the story if space is required

Investigative journalism: A story that requires a great amount of research and hard work to come up with facts that might be hidden, buried, or obscured by people who have a vested interest in keeping those facts from being published

Iris: The circular opening (aperture) which controls the amount of light passing through to the camera's sensing element or film.

Jackfield: AKA Patch-panel. A board which accomodates connections between multiple sources.

Jargon: Any overly obscure, technical, or bureaucratic words that would not be used in everyday language

Jib: A revolvable camera mounting arm, which can be attached to a dolly or crane.

Journalese: a type of jargon used by newspaper writers: language used by journalists that would never be used in everyday speech

JPEG: Joint Photographic Experts Group. A standard for still-image compression.

Jump line: Line of type at the bottom of a column which directs the reader to somewhere else in the paper where the story is completed, allowing more space for stories to begin on the front page

Kelvin: A unit of temperature measurement. Colour is measured in degrees Kelvin.

Key Frame: In some forms of digital compression, uncompressed frames (key frames) are placed at regular intervals (eg. every 6th frame is uncompressed). Each subsequent frame exists as variations on the keyframe, until a new keyframe is introduced. The further apart the keyframes, the worse the overall picture quality.

Key Grip: Person in sharge of constructing and dismantling film sets and dolly tracks. Related info: Jobs in Film

Kicker: An ending that finishes a story with a climax, surprise, or punch line

LAN : Local Area Network. A network of computers connected via cables or a wireless system.

LANC: A connection developed by Sony, used to link remote-control units, edit decks, etc.

Layout editor: The person who begins the layout plan, considering things like placement and amount of space allotted to news and advertising copy, graphics, photos, and symbols

Lead: The first sentence or first few sentences of a story

Lens: A structure made of transparent glass or other material, with at least one curved surface, which causes the light rays passing through it to converge or diverge in a controlled fashion.

Letterbox Format: In video and television, the practice of placing black bars at the top and bottom of the frame, in order to simulate a wide-screen format (as if the viewer were looking through the slot in a letterbox).

Libel: Publishing in print (or other media) false information that identifies and deframes an individual

Light: That section of the electromagnetic spectrum which is visible, ie. perceptable to the human eye. Specifically, white light contains the wavelengths from 400nm (nanometres) to 700nm. Light travels through a vacuum at approximately 300,000 km (186,000 miles) per second.

M, MII: Professional tape formats from Panasonic. The M format was based on VHS technology, and was introduced at about the same time as Beta (in the mid-1980's). The MII format was introduced a few years later to compete with Beta SP. MII uses a different sized cassette.

Managing editor: The person who co-ordinates all news departments by collecting all copy and ensuring that all instructions for printer or typist are clear and consistent: the person who meets and consults with the staff to make a plan

Masthead: The "banner" across the front page which identifies the newspaper and the date of publication: the publication information on the editorial page

Media relations: A function of public relations that involves dealing with the communications media in seeking publicity for, or responding to media interest in, an organization

MIDI: Musical Instrument Digital Interface. A standard of communication between musical instuments, controllers and computers.

Mid-Shot: A camera framing term, half-way between a wide-shot and a close-up. A mid-shot of a person will show them from about the waist or chest up.

Mixer: A device which accepts multiple signal inputs (video or audio), proccesses them, and provides one or more outputs. The outputs are "mixes" of the input sources.

Modulate: To "change". A signal can be transmitted via a carrier wave, by modulating the wave to represent the signal.

Monitor: A device used to view a video, graphic or text source, or to listen to an audio source. Video monitors use CRTs (cathode ray tubes), LCDs (liquid crystal displays), and other technologies. Audio monitors generally use cone drivers and horn divers, mounted in speaker cabinets.

Monopod: Camera stand, like a tripod with one leg. Has the advantage of being light and easily portable.

Morgue: Newsroom library

Morph: Computer-assisted proccess in which an image (or video) is gradually transformed (morphosed) into another.

Motion-JPEG: A digital video compression format based on the still image JPEG compression standard.

MPEG: Moving Picture Coding Experts Group. A digital video compression standard.

ND (Neutral Density) Filter: A filter which reduces the amount of light coming through the camera lens, without affecting it's colour temperature. Related Info: Colour Temperature

News angle: The aspect, twist, or detail of a feature story that pegs it to a news event or gives it news value for the reader

Newspaper styles: styles of various newspapers including dailies, tabloids, and weeklies

Newsspeak: Language that distorts, confuses, or hides reality

Noddies: Shots of the presenter / interviewer nodding, smiling, frowning etc. These can be shot after the interview and inserted during post-production.

Non-Linear: Any method of video editing which doesn't require all shots to be assembled in a linear fashion.

NTSC: National Television Standards Commission. Video/ broadcast standard used in the USA, Canada, Japan, Mexico, and other countries. Delivers 525 horizontal lines of resolution at 30 fps (frames per second).

Off the record: Something a source does not want repeated in a news story

Off-Line Edit: A "draft" edit, usually prepared in an off-line edit suite (at a lower cost), then taken to an on-line facility to make the final cut. Related info: Video Editing

Off-Line: Out of action, not currently useable.

On-Line (1): Operational. **(2):** In multi-camera or multi-tape set-ups, the camera or videotape machine which is currently selected by the director. For example, in an outside broadcast, the on-line camera is the camera which is currently live.

On-Line Edit: The final version of an edit, prepared in a professional edit facility.

Op-ed page: A page in a newspaper that is opposite the editorial page, and contains columns, articles, letters for readers, and other items expressing opinions

Optical Image Stabiliser (OIS): A system of stabilizing a camera image by constantly adjusting the optics.

Optical: Of light/optics.

Optics: Dealing with properties of light. Camera optics: The components which deal with light rays, before they are converted into electrical signals (i.e. the lens, etc).

Oscilloscope: Device which accepts an electrical input, and represents the variations of the input as a display on a CRT screen.

Out-point: The end point of an edit.

Outside Broadcast: A radio or television program which is broadcast from location, rather than from a studio.

Package: A completed television news story on tape, which is edited before a news show goes on air and contains reporter's stand-ups, narration over images, and an out-cue for the anchor to start speaking at the end of the tape

PAL: Phase Alternate Line. Video/broadcast standard developed in Germany, and used primarily in Europe and Australasia. Delivers 625 lines at 25 fps (frames per second).

Pan (1): Horizontal camera movement. **(2):** The amount which a signal is divided between two pathways. For example, on an audio mixer, an input source can be panned across two stereo channels. Related info: Stereo

Pan Pot: Pan Potentiometer. A component which pans a signal across two pathways. Typically a knob or slider. The knob on a domestic stereo which pans between left and right speakers is a pan pot.

Paraphrase: an indirect quote or summary of the words the news maker said

Patch Panel: AKA *jackfield*, a panel containing a series of connection points for electronic equipment. This allows equipment to be inter-connected in various configurations.

Photos: Still images which communicate the photojournalist's angle or perceived reality

Pix: Short for pictures

Plagiarism: Using the work of another person (both written words and intellectual property) and calling that work your own

Public affairs: Various activities and communications that organizations undertake to monitor, evaluate, influence, and adjust to the attitudes, opinions, and behaviours of groups or individuals who constitute their publics

Quicktime: A digital media format originally developed for the Apple Computer range, but is now also available for other platforms.

RAM: Random Access Memory. A system of computer memory in which data can be retrieved in any order with equal speed.

Real Time: Anything which occurs without delay. A real-time effects proccessor will add effects instantly, without having to wait to render.

Reflector Board: A specially-designed reflective surface which is used as a light source.

Reporters: The people who gather facts for the stories they are assigned to write

Resolution: The amount of detail in an image or signal. On a computer screen, the resolution is the number of pixels. In an analogue video signal, the resolution is the number of horizontal lines. In digital audio, the resolution is the number of samples per second. "Colour resolution" refers to the colour depth of an image, ie. how many colours are present.

Reverberation: The amount of time it takes an emmitted sound to cease bouncing of objects such as walls. In audio work, adding a reverberation effect gives the sound more body and can make it sound as if it was recorded in a large room, hall, etc.

RGB: Red, Green and Blue. The primary colours of video.

Rule of Thirds: A technique in camera framing where the frame is divided into imaginary sections to create reference points.

Rules: Lines used to separate one story from another on a newspaper page

Sample: A near-instantaneous recording of a signal, measured in thousandths of a second. Digital signals are constructed by sampling analogue signals thousands of times per second. Each of these individual samples are strung together to make a close approximation of the original signal.

Saturation: The level of colour in a vision signal or still image. A highly-saturated signal has very strong colours.

Scene: In film, television or stage, all the action/shots which take place at a certain time and location and comprise a segment of the program.

Scissor Platform: AKA *scissor lift*, a mechanical work platform which can be raised and lowered. Sometimes used to elevate a camera position.

Screens: Shaded areas of copy in a newspaper

SECAM: Systeme Electronique Couleur Avec Memoire. Video standard used primarily by France and various Eastern Bloc countries. Provides 625 horizontal lines at 25 frames per second.

SEG: Special Effects Generator. A device used to create special video effects.

Servo: Remote control of camera functions such as zoom and focus, by means of a motor. Servo controls can be mounted an the lens housing, on the tripod/pedestal handles, or on a remote-control unit.

Setup: The black level of a video signal.

Shot: A continuous piece of video or film footage. Everything you get between pressing "record" and "stop". Related info: Camera shots

Sidebar: a column of copy and/or graphics which appears on the page of a magazine or newspaper to communicate information about the story or contents of the paper

Signal Processing Device: Any device which takes a signal input, then modifies the signal before outputting it.

Slander: Similar to libel, but spoken instead of published

SMPTE: (Pronounced "simptee") Society of Motion Picture and Television Engineers. A group which has set various video standards.

Snow: Random patterns of black and white dots on a TV screen or vision monitor. Snow can be caused by an improperly tuned television (or very poor reception), an unrecorded video tape, or dirty VCR heads.

Soft news: stories that are interesting but less important than hard news, focusing on people as well as facts and information and including interviews, reviews, articles, and editorials

Solder: An alloy of tin and lead that melts at a relatively low temperature. Used for securing electrical connections between components and wires.

Sound bite: The videotaped quote in television news

Source: A person who talks to a reporter on the record, for attribution in a news story

Spin: Hidden slant of a press source, which usually casts the client in a positive light

Stand-up: A reporter's appearance in a TV news story: usually a head and shoulders shot which features the reporter talking into a microphone at the scene of the news event, often used as a transition, or at the beginning or ending

Stereo (1): Audio which is split into two channels. **(2):** Duplicate images of the same scene, taken to simulate 3-D human vision.

Style: Conformity of language use by all writers in a publication (e.g., AP style is conformity to the rules of language according to the Associated Press)

Summary lead: The traditional journalism tool used to start off most hard news stories: the first few sentences of a news story which usually summarizes the event and answers the questions: Who? What? When? Where? Why? How?

Super: A video effect that allows the television station to print and superimpose the name of a news source over his or her image when the source is shown talking in a news story

Suspension of disbelief: The semi-conscious act of allowing yourself to believe a fictitious premise for the sake of enjoying a story.

Tabloid: Technically, a publication half the size of a standard newspaper page; but commonly, any newspaper that is splashy and heavily illustrated: a "supermarket" tabloid that stresses dramatic stories, often about sensational subjects

Tally Light: A small light on a video camera which turns on when recording is in progress. In multi-camera situations; a light on a camera, or in it's viewfinder, which turns on when the camera is switched on-line or live.

Target audience: A specific group of people that media producers or advertisers want to reach

Telecast: Material broadcast by television.

Telecine: The process (or equipment used in the process) of transferring film to video and/or television.

Telephoto: Telephotographic.

Telephotographic Lens: Magnifying lens, or combination of lenses. Related info: Video camera zoom

Teleprompter: Device which scrolls text on a screen, to provide cues for a television/video presenter.

Televise: To transmit by television.

Television: Literally, vision at a distance. The transmission, reception, and reproduction of moving pictures and audio. Refers to both the process in general, and the receiving appliance.

Tele-zoom: Longer zoom, producing greater magnification.

Test Pattern: Pattern of colours, lines and/or shapes designed to assist equipment calibration.

Tilt: Vertical camera movement, i.e. adjusting the framing up and down.

Time Base Corrector : A device which adjusts, improves and corrects defects in a video signal. Can be used to synchronise different vision sources before being mixed together, to avoid picture disturbances when cutting from one source to another. Related info: Timing video sources

Tone: An audio test signal. Used to set signal levels, test signal quality, identify signal pathways, etc.

Transducer: A device which coverts energy from one form into another. For example, a microphone is a transducer which converts acoustical energy into electrical energy. Related info: Microphones

Transistor: A device used for switching or amplifying.

Transition: A rhetorical device used in writing to move the story smoothly from one set of ideas to the next by finding a way to connect the ideas logically

Transmitter: A device which converts video, audio and/or data signals into modulated radio frequency signals, and transmits them as radio waves.

Trend story: a feature story that focuses on the current fads, directions, tendencies, and inclinations of society

Tripod: A three-legged stand for mounting equipment such as a camera, etc.

UHF: Ultra High Frequency radio waves.

Ultrasonic: Audio frequencies above the upper limit of human hearing (approx 20,000 kHz).

Unbalanced Audio: An audio signal which consists of one "hot" signal plus the shield. This is common in home entertainment systems, as well as other systems with short audio cables. Unbalanced audio cables are prone to external interference, and are not prefered in professional situations. Related info: Balanced audio

UV Filter: A filter which blocks out a certain percentage of ultra-violet light.

UV: Ultra-violet light.

Vacuum Tube: A multi-electrode valve which controls the flow of electrons in a vacuum from electrode to electrode.

VCR: Video Cassette Recorder.

Vector Image: A graphics image which exists as a series of geometric shapes, rather than as a series of values for each pixel. Has the advantage of being resizable without loss of quality.

Vectorscope: A device which graphically displays information about the chroma (colour) part of a vision signal. Used in conjunction with a waveform monitor (in fact, many devices are switchable between waveform and vectorscope modes). Related info: Calibrating video sources

VHF: Very High Frequency. This is a popular television broadcast band. It is lower than UHF (Ultra-High Frequency), and generally has a higher broadcast range.

Video press release: a press release for television, prepared on tape, complete with images and sound which can be used by the news media without additional permission or editing

Voice: a writer's development of distinctive characteristics and idiosyncrasies of language use that make his or her writing as easily recognizable as the inflections, tone, and pronunciation of speech that make a person's vocalized speech pat terns distinctive

Watt: Unit of power; equivalent to one joule per second. 1 watt (W) = 1 volt (V) x 1 amp (A)

Wattage: Amount of electrical power, in watts.

Wave: An oscillation which is propogated from place to place. Related info: Sound waves

Waveform Monitor: An oscilloscope specifically designed to display the waveforms of video signals. Used to monitor signal strength, sync timing, etc.

Waveform: The shape (form) of a wave, or a representation of this form.

Wavelength: The distance between any point on a wave and the equivalent point on the next phase.

Whizz-Pan: A very fast camera pan, usually such that individual frames are severely blurred.

Wide Screen: Generally refers to any video aspect ratio greater than 4:3.

Wide Shot (WS): A framing term, meaning a camera shot which shows the whole of the subject.

Wipe: A transition in which parts of one shot are successively replaced by equivalent parts of the next shot.

Wire services: services that provide news from around the world to publications that subscribe for a fee (e.g., Associated Press, Canadian Press, Reuters, and United Press International): co-operatives that share news stories among members (e.g., Canadian Press)

WMA: Windows Media Audio file, a file format used for delivering digital audio.

WMVHD: Windows Media Video file which features high-definition resolution.

World Wide Web: large directory of information on the Internet

Wow: Wavering of audio reproduction due to speed fluctuations.

XLR: A lockable connector, available with various numbers of pins (the most common being the 3-pin XLR). Often referred to as a "Canon", after the popular manufacturer of XLR connectors.

Y/C: Luminance/chrominance. A video signal which consists of two signals: The luminance (brightness) and chrominance (colour). S-video connections use a Y/C signal.

Y-Lead: AKA "Split lead". A lead with one connector at one end, and two at the other. For example, a mono audio output could be split (using a y-lead) into two signals, to be plugged into the left and right inputs of another device.

YUV: A type of component video consisting of one luminance signal (Y) and two chrominance signals (U and V).

Zebra Stripes: A feature of professional cameras, which

places diagonal lines across any over-exposed parts of the picture in the viewfinder. These stripes will not show on the output/recorded picture, they are only there as a guide for the camera operator. Related info: The video camera viewfinder

Zone System: A photographic system which divides light into ten tonal steps, from Zone 0 (absolute black) to Zone IX (absolute white). Zone V is medium gray, the same value found on an 18% gray card.

Zoom Lens: A lens with a moveable element, which is able to "zoom" between various focal lengths. This has the effect of making the subject appear closer to, or further away from the camera.

Zoom Microphone: A microphone on a video camera which adjusts it's pickup pattern to match the zoom lens, i.e. the mic becomes more directional as the lens zooms in.

Zoom: Framing movement, in which the focal length of the zoom lens is altered to make the subject appear closer to, or further away from the camera. Note that this effect is similar, but not the same as moving the camera itself closer to or further away from the subject.

Index

S

T

U

V

●●●